Adrian Renner

Does carbon-conscious behavior drive firm performance?

GABLER RESEARCH

Adrian Renner

Does carbon-conscious behavior drive firm performance?

An event study on the Global 500 companies

With a foreword by Prof. Dr. Kai-Ingo Voigt

GABLER

RESEARCH

Bibliographic information published by the Deutsche Nationalbibliothek
The Deutsche Nationalbibliothek lists this publication in the Deutsche Nationalbibliografie; detailed bibliographic data are available in the Internet at http://dnb.d-nb.de.

Dissertation University Erlangen-Nuremberg, 2011

1st Edition 2011

Editorial Office: Ute Wrasmann | Jutta Hinrichsen

Gabler Verlag ist eine Marke von Springer Fachmedien.
Springer Fachmedien ist Teil der Fachverlagsgruppe Springer Science+Business Media.
www.gabler.de

Cover design: KünkelLopka Medienentwicklung, Heidelberg
Printed on acid-free paper
Printed in Germany

ISBN 978-3-8349-2964-8

This is dedicated to my loving mother, Hannelore Renner, and girlfriend, Carolin Ulrich, whose constant support and words of encouragement have been a cornerstone for the success of this journey.

Foreword

Scientific research is still at the beginning to understand the relationship between disclosure of carbon information, carbon performance and stock price reaction. For almost any listed company the investors' pressure to disclose climate-relevant information has increased significantly over the last years. Additionally, businesses are ranked by independent parties (such as the Carbon Disclosure Project) in regards to their ability to cope with the challenges posed by climate change. Consequently corporate leaders need to decide whether their company shall take part in these kind of projects, possibly facing negative evaluations or rejecting the investors request, which might also have adverse implications. Knowing how equity holders, which ultimately determine the corporate leaders' fate, will react is crucial for their decision making.

To address these identified gaps in research and practice, Mr. Renner provides interesting insights into how investors react if businesses are moving towards a green future. The strength of this thesis is that research is grounded in appropriate and relevant theory and that sound and mature quantitative research method (event study approach) is pursued. Simultaneously, it addresses a highly relevant topic for practitioners, who are analyzing the capital markets response to carbon-conscious behavior depending on various factors e.g. region, sector, share of institutional investors, carbon intensity, etc.

Since this research project was trying to answer questions on a global scale, Mr. Renner used the Carbon Disclosure Project report on the Global 500 companies, which allowed him to synthesis results from 387 companies from 28 countries.

In conclusion, this book offers new and outstanding insights and can, thus, be highly recommended for researchers and practitioners who are engaged in this field of research.

Prof. Dr. Kai-Ingo Voigt

Acknowledgements

Although I understood from the beginning that writing a thesis would be a long and lonely journey full of pain and self-doubt, I was always able to count on a terrific group of people who helped me through even the darkest hours and helped to shape this dissertation. Indisputably, I would not have been able to master this challenge without them and will remain deeply indebted and grateful to each and every one of them.

First, I would like to thank my advisor, Prof. Dr. Kai-Ingo Voigt, for his support. His input during our discussions has been of significant importance and brought this document to an even higher level. Second, I would like to express my gratitude towards Prof. Dr. Peter Klaus for his questions, comments and advice, which greatly enhanced this thesis.

Third, I wish to thank my best friends, Dr. Gerhard Trautmann, Dr. Christian Funke, Fabian Frank, Holger Gürich, Thorsten Schrenk and Christopher Krauss, who gave up their weekends and came from all over Germany to criticize, comment on, but finally improve this document. Without you, I would have never been able to accomplish this project, and I will remain deeply indebted and grateful.

Fourth, I thank several McKinsey partners (Dr. Andreas Tschiesner, Dr. Andreas Cornet, Dr. Wolgang Pointner and Dr. Nicolai Müller) for taking the time to give their highly valuable input on my work. Their ideas were outstanding and their support another reason why this company is so great.

Last but not least, I'm especially grateful to Carolin, whose patience was a never-ending source of encouragement. Her affection, loyalty and patience gave me the strength necessary to finish this dissertation.

Dipl.-Kfm. Adrian Renner

TABLE OF CONTENTS

List of abbreviations

APT	Arbitrage Pricing Theory
AR	Abnormal return
B2B	Business-to-Business
B2C	Business-to-Consumer
BAU	Business as usual
BRIC	Brazil, Russia, India and China
CAC 40	Cotation Assistée en Continu 40
CAPM	Capital Asset Pricing Model
CDP	Carbon Disclosure Project
CDLI	Carbon Disclosure Leadership Index
CEO	Chief Executive Officer
CEP	Center on Economic Priorities
CO_2	Carbon dioxide
COGS	Cost of goods sold
CH_4	Methane
CSR	Corporate Social Responsibility
DAX	Deutscher Aktien Index
EBIT	Earnings before interest and taxes

EMS	Environmental Management System
EPA	Environmental Protection Agency
ET	Eastern Time
ETF	Exchange Traded Fund
EU	European Union
EUR	Euro
FRDG	Franklin Research and Development Group
GAAP	Generally Accepted Accounting Principles
GDP	Gross Domestic Product
GHGs	Greenhouse gases
GICS	Global Industry Classification Standard
GM	General Motors
GSCM	Green Supply Chain Management
IFRS	International Financial Reporting Standards
IPCC	Intergovernmental Panel on Climate Change
IRRC	Investor Responsibility Research Center
ISO	International Standardization Organization
IT	Information Technology
JV	Joint Venture
M&A	Mergers and Acquisitions
MBA	Master of Business Administration
MSCI	Morgan Stanley Capital International

NO_2	Nitrous dioxide
NGO	Non-governmental organizations
OEM	Original Equipment Manufacturer
OLS	Ordinary Least Squares
PPM	Parts per million
PR	Public relations
PWC	PriceWaterhouseCoopers
RoA	Return on Assets
RoI	Return on Investment
RoS	Return on Sales
S&P 500	Standard and Poor's 500
SRES	Special Report on Emission Scenarios
SUV	Sport Utility Vehicle
TCTF	Total Company Target Fulfillment
UK	United Kingdom
US	United States
USD	United States Dollars
UV	Ultraviolet
W	Watt

Table of symbols

$\sum$	Summation

Index of figures

Index of tables

1 Introduction

"There is an increasing consensus among scientists of various fields that society is currently on a long-term unsustainable course."[1]

Since 2007, when Al Gore received an Oscar for his documentary, "An Inconvenient Truth", the public has become more focused than ever on the issue of climate change.[2]

Since then, magazines and newspapers constantly monitor and report on recent publications regarding current developments in the field of global warming research, thereby alarming the public even further.[3] Recent articles have described threats of climate change that exceeds expectations and their implications for the global nutrition supply, vector-borne diseases and extreme weather events.[4] This interest from the public and the media supports the thesis that climate change is the biggest global health threat in the 21st century.[5]

1.1 PROBLEM DEFINITION

1.1.1 Description of environmental challenges posed by climate change

Environmental issues did not just become major concerns for most global citizens following Hurricane Katrina in 2005, which devastated New Orleans entirely. During the decades prior to this extreme weather event, the environmental consequences of industrial activities were conspicuous to the public eye.[6] Apparent developments like "ozone depletion, loss of bio diversity, acid rain, toxic wastes, and industrial accidents"[7] have created serious environmental problems.[8]

In recent years, though all of these developments have been highly visible, attitudes towards environmental degradation have changed tremendously, gaining more and more importance. This

1 Ny, 2006, p. 1
2 Nagourney, 2007
3 Spiegel Online, 2009b, p. 1
4 Spiegel Online, 2009a, p. 1
5 Costello et al., 2009, p. 1693
6 Rao, 2004, p. 289 and Stafford, Stafford, & Chowdhury, 1996, p. 68
7 Shrivastava, 1995, p. 183
8 Shrivastava, 1995, p. 183

increased interest can be explained by the fact that the worrying consequences of mankind's behavior will not happen in a distant future, but within our lifetime.[9]

The following sections shall elaborate on the recent environmental challenge of climate change, describing the cause and effect relationship between human behavior and the changing global climate and its implications for mankind. Afterwards consumers' and policymakers' reaction on this development will be illustrated, followed by the consequences for investors and corporate leaders.

1.1.1.1 Relationship between human behavior and increased CO_2

For several decades, scientists have observed that CO_2 levels in the atmosphere are increasing significantly, but in recent years this trend appears to have accelerated, starting from a level of approximately 280 parts per million (ppm) of CO_2 at the beginning of the Industrial Revolution and quickly increasing to 387 ppm in 2008. This increase corresponds to a surge of almost 40% within a few centuries,[10] as indicated in Figure 1 below.

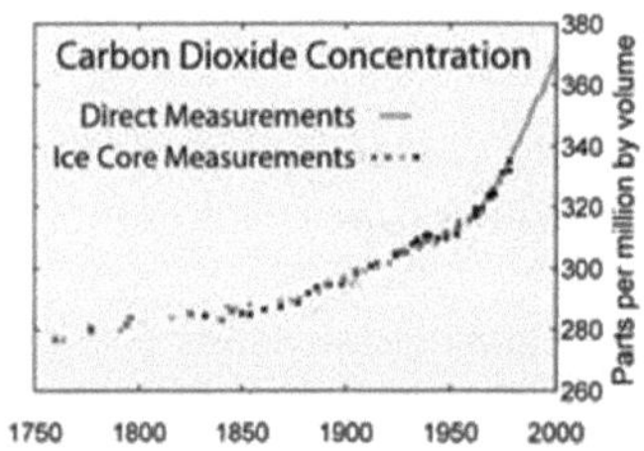

[11]

Figure 1: Development of carbon dioxide concentration over the last 250 years

Critics say that high CO_2 concentrations existed at other times in earth's history and that they have nothing to do with human activity. Although there are no direct data (such as ice cores), showing CO_2 levels prior to the most recent 800,000 years, different models suggest quite extensive variations in CO_2 levels. For example, 500 million years ago, CO_2 concentrations were likely to be 10 times higher than they are today.[12]

9 Lev & Adenso-Díaz, 2004, p. 324, and Klassen, 2000, p. 127
10 Le Treut & Somerville, 2007, p. 100, and Adam, 2008, p. 1
11 Depiction created by Globalwarmingart.com. Data based on Keeling et al., 2009, Etheridge et al., 1998, Neftel et al., 1994, Monnin et al., 2004, and Marland, Boden, & Andres, 2008
12 Rothmann, 2001, p. 4167

Changes to CO_2 levels have been caused by a variety of factors, e.g., changes in solar radiation or volcanism.[13]

However, never in earth's history did an increase in CO_2 levels happen as quickly and to such a magnitude as observed at present. Normally, a change of 80 ppm CO_2 took several thousand years. Now it is happening in less than 100 years.[14]

To exemplify this, carbon dioxide concentrations and their development over the last 50 years are plotted below.

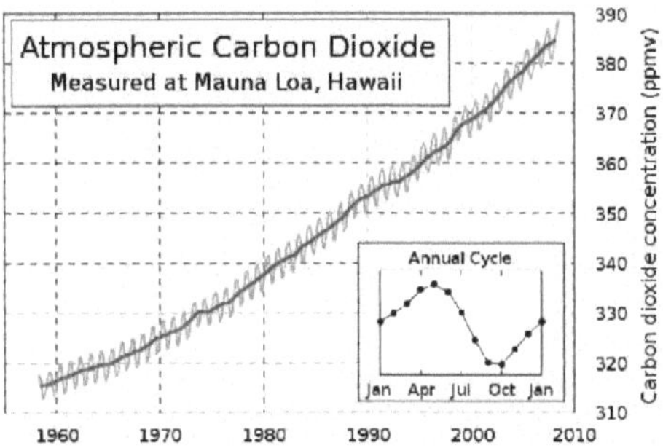

[15]

Figure 2: Development of carbon dioxide concentration over the last 50 years

The depiction above shows the development of atmospheric CO_2 concentrations. The data come from direct measurements taken at Mauna Loa, Hawaii. These data are among the major pieces of evidence supporting anthropogenic global warming (i.e., caused by humans). Data from Mauna Loa are frequently used because it has one of the longest histories of taking such measurements. One might note that there are fluctuations within the years; these fluctuations occur because of seasonal effects. During summer, plants take up large amounts of CO_2, and thereby, atmospheric CO_2 levels fall. Because more forests are located in the northern hemisphere than in the southern, the southern hemisphere summer cannot offset the carbon-releasing effect of northern-hemisphere plants during the winter.[16]

13 Sagan & Mullen, 7, p. 52, National Research Council., 1994, p. 36, Dunbar, 2008, p. 1 and Oppenheimer, 2003, p. 230
14 Costello et al., 2009, p. 1698
15 Depiction created by Globalwarmingart.com. Data based on Keeling et al., 2009
16 Keeling et al., 2009

For several decades, there has been a scientific discussion about the extent to which human activity can be held accountable for this development. From year to year it seemed to become increasingly likely that this change was anthropogenic, and in 2007 the IPCC (Intergovernmental Panel on Climate Change) stated that the evidence is unequivocal and demonstrates that the recent increase in CO_2 has resulted from human activity. This point of view is shared by many governments, scientists and various organizations, including the Royal Society and the American Association for the Advancement of Science.[17]

IPCC also states that environmental elements like solar radiation and volcanism had a cooling effect in the first half of the 20th century that will eventually diminish.[18]

In the search for the reasons for this anthropogenic effect, it seems obvious that the Industrial Revolution was involved. In fact, since the beginning of industrial activity, humans have emitted approximately 900 billion tons of CO_2, and roughly 50% of it has stayed in the atmosphere. Costello et al. (2009) argued that "About 80% of CO_2 is caused by industrialization and the rest by land use such as deforestation."

If one considers more carefully the human activities releasing significant amounts of CO_2, it can been seen that this effect stems mainly from the burning of fossil fuels, in particular petroleum, coal and natural gas. It must be noted that CO_2 is not the only emission causing global warming. All gases having the same effect belong to the group of greenhouse gases (GHGs). The greenhouse effect will be explained in more detail in the next chapter.[19]

Nevertheless, CO_2 is the major contributor to global warming (77% of total GHGs). Other gases, like methane (14% of total GHGs) and nitrous oxide (8% of total GHGs), are also significant contributors to climate change but originate from completely different sources than CO_2 does. Whereas CO_2 is mainly emitted through industrialization-related processes like power generation (25.9%), industrial processes (19.4%) and transportation (13.1%), methane and nitrous oxide are released primarily during agricultural activities.[20] For a summary, see Figure 3 and 4.

17 Intergovernmental Panel on Climate Change, 2007b, p. 2
18 Hegerl et al., 2007, p. 690
19 Intergovernmental Panel on Climate Change, 2007a, p. 28
20 Intergovernmental Panel on Climate Change, 2007a, p. 28 and Volkswagen Aktiengesellschaft, p. 12

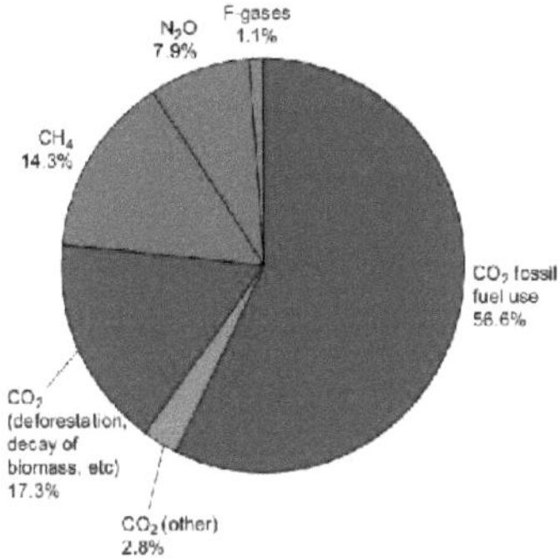

[21]

Figure 3: Composition of greenhouse gases by type (e.g., CO_2, CH_4)

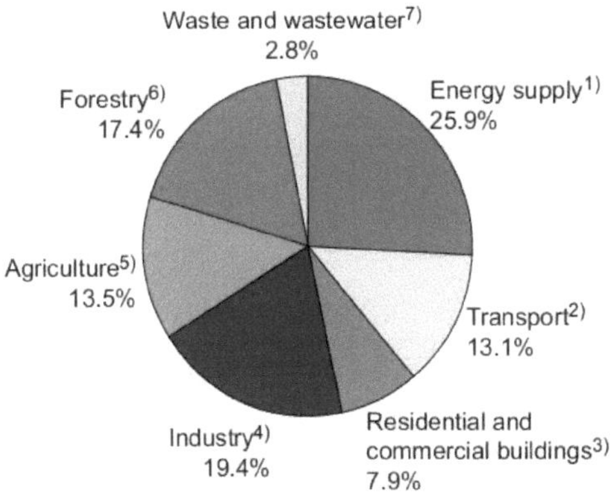

[22]

Figure 4: Greenhouse gas emissions by sector in 2004

21 Intergovernmental Panel on Climate Change, 2007a, p. 28
22 Intergovernmental Panel on Climate Change, 2007a, p. 29

1.1.1.2 Relationship between CO_2 increase and temperature rise

The previous chapter described how the concentrations of GHGs like CO_2, CH_4 and N_2O have increased over the last few centuries. What are the consequences of this development and why is this a problem?

In order to answer these questions, it is necessary to understand what makes gases GHGs. In general, GHGs are defined as gases that are able to absorb and emit radiation within the thermal infrared range.[23] This effect was discovered by Joseph Fourier in 1824 and investigated in quantitative terms by Svante Arrhenius in 1896.[24] Without this effect, Earth would be a very hostile place to live, with an average temperature of -18°C, more than 30°C cooler than today.[25]

Knowing that this basic physical effect allows humans to exist on this planet makes it worthwhile to take a deeper look at this mechanism. (See Figure 5)

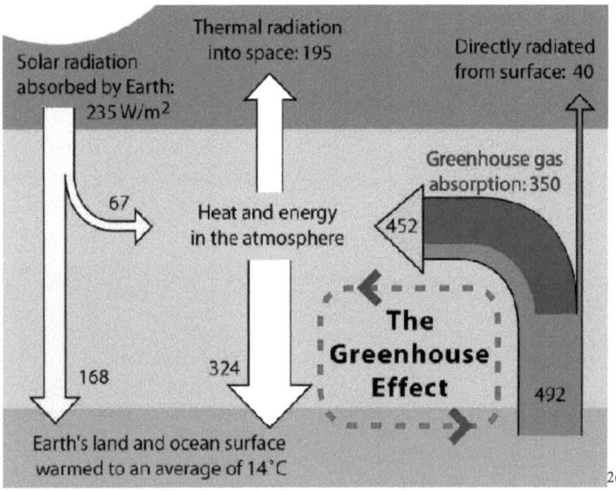

[26]

Figure 5: Greenhouse effect

The above picture shows a schematic representation of the energy flow between the sun, Earth's surface and its atmosphere.

23 IPCC AR4 SYR, pp. 81–82
24 Weart, 2008, pp. 5-7
25 Anschober & Ramsauer, 2007, pp. 122–124
26 Adapted from Kiehl & Trenberth, 1997 p. 206

Energy is expressed in Watts per square meter (W/m^2).

The sun emits all energy that reaches the earth's surface. However, just 17% (235 W/m^2) of all sunlight reaching Earth's atmosphere is absorbed. The remaining 83% (1,131 W/m^2) is lost through geometric and reflective effects.[27]

Of the 235 W/m^2 passing through the atmosphere, just 168 W/m^2 hits the surface of the Earth. The rest, 67 W/m^2, remains in the atmosphere. Then, the GHG molecules recycle the energy reflected by the soil and deliver an additional 324 W/m^2 back to the surface. However, 195 W/m^2 is radiated into space. This process of recycling energy is called the greenhouse effect and is an essential contributor to earth's climate.[28]

In short, GHG molecules allow short-wave radiation (such as UV and visible light) to pass but capture and re-emit long-wave radiation (such as infrared) back to the Earth's surface. Because mankind has increased the burning of fossil fuels, an action that is ultimately burning stored CO_2 from dead plants that were buried under sediments millions of years ago, this CO_2 is now being released back into the atmosphere, increasing its concentration and thereby the atmospheric temperature.[29]

Furthermore, scientific data (from measurements of ice cores) show that there is a strong correlation between CO_2 level and temperature.[30]

With an understanding of the process of global warming through the GHG effect, it further becomes interesting to ask what temperature increases have been observed so far and will most likely be seen in the future.

The graph below depicting the development of average global temperature over the last 120 years clearly demonstrates that temperatures have increased.

27 Kiehl & Trenberth, 1997, pp. 197 - 208
28 Kiehl & Trenberth, 1997, pp. 197 - 208
29 Costello et al., 2009, pp. 1697–1698
30 Petit et al., 1999, p. 429, Caillon et al., 2003, p. 1728 and Weaver et al., 1998, pp. 847-853

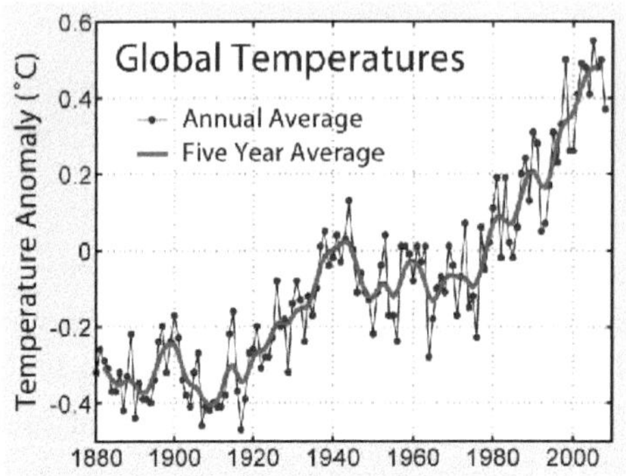

31

Figure 6: Development of global temperatures since 1880

Figure 6 demonstrates that between 1900 and 2005, the five-year average increased by more than 0.7°C.[32]

Additionally, Figure 6 demonstrates that the pace of the temperature increase has accelerated in the last 30 years to 0.13°C per decade. This led to the warmest year on record in 2005.[33]

However, the increase in temperature has not been evenly distributed around the globe; land temperatures have increased twice as quickly as ocean temperatures (0.25°C vs. 0.13°C). This divergence has occurred mainly because oceans have a far larger effective heat capacity than land does and because oceans lose some of the warming effect as a result of evaporation. Consequently, the northern hemisphere warms faster than the southern hemisphere because it has more land, not because it emits more GHGs (which is nevertheless true), but GHGs stay in the atmosphere long enough to mix between the northern and southern hemispheres.[34]

Some critics say that the recent warming has been unexpectedly mild because aerosols have masked the contribution of CO_2 level increases by reflecting more incoming sunlight. Therefore, the observed temperature increase is mainly due to non-CO_2 greenhouse gases.[35]

---

31 Depiction created by Globalwarmingart.com. Data based on Hansen, 2006, IPCC, 2001a and Folland et al., 2001
32 Intergovernmental Panel on Climate Change, 2007b
33 Hansen et al. (2005) p. 1
34 IPCC, 2001a, pp. 107-110
35 Hansen, 2000 p. 9875

Climate models play an important role in predicting the future magnitude of global warming. The most prominent basis for climate predictions is the IPCC Special Report on Emission Scenarios (SRES). Depending on which scenario is used, and including the inevitable uncertainties, IPCC synthesized from 23 models a predicted warming of 1.1°C to 6.4°C by the end of 2100 relative to 1980-1999.[36]

The best-studied scenario is SRES A2, which assumes that no action is taken to reduce emissions and regionally divided economic development. Specifically, SRES A2 is characterized by a large global population (15 billion), high total energy use and a moderate level of fossil fuel dependency (mostly coal) by 2100. The results of this scenario predict a temperature increase by 2 to 5°C until 2100. All projections are relative to average global temperatures of 2000.[37]

1.1.1.3 Relationship between increased temperature and global climate

Having established that future temperature development is showing an alarming trend, the focus will now move to the question of how global warming will affect our climate.

Generally, scientists agree that depending on the temperature increase, the probability of unexpected and unprecedented consequences surges. These changes may be abrupt and irreversible on continental and global scales.[38]

One of the most popular publications on this topic is IPCC's fourth assessment report on climate change, which was published in 2007. To gain an initial understanding of how global warming will affect our planet, the depiction below shows a tremendous increase in the number of reported natural disasters; whereas the number of earthquakes remained pretty stable, the number of climate-related disasters has surged.[39]

36 Intergovernmental Panel on Climate Change, 2007b, pp. 12-15, Costello et al., 2009, p. 1698, Torn & Hart, 2006, p. L10703, Harte et al., 2006, p. 14001 and Scheffer et al., 2006, p. L10702
37 Intergovernmental Panel on Climate Change, 2007b, pp. 12-15
38 United States National Academy of Science, 2002
39 UNEP/GRID-Arendal

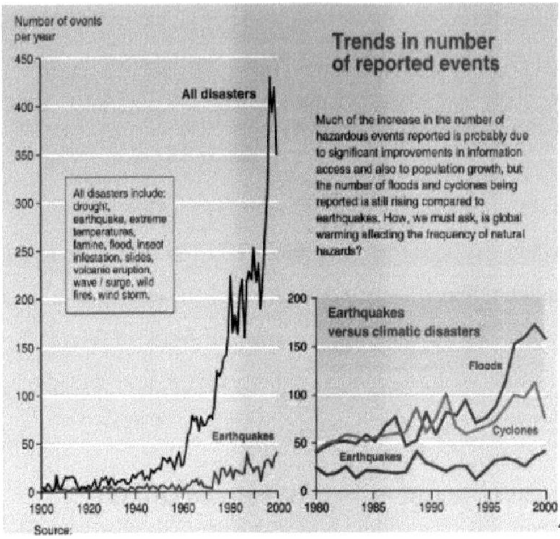

[40]

Figure 7: Development of global disasters

To provide a better overview of the implications of global warming, the following discussion is split by the major impact areas: atmosphere, oceans, glaciers and bio-diversity.

Atmosphere

Because increasing temperatures lead to more evaporation of oceans and lakes, the amount of rainfall will increase as well, and most scientists agree that this will not take the form of slight showers but of heavy rainfall and other extreme weather events, which will ultimately cause more erosion. Especially in tropical regions this could lead to desertification, while forests may grow in formerly dry regions.[41]

However, it must be noted that evaporation rates declined worldwide during the 20th century, which might be explained by the fact that other effects have outweighed the temperature increase.[42]

Oceans

40 UNEP/GRID-Arendal
41 Peterson & Golubev, p. 687 and Del Genio et al., 2007, p. L16703
42 Peterson & Golubev, p. 687

Because several effects take place within the oceans, only the two most important shall be focused on within this document:

First, rising sea levels can be attributed to global warming because oceans expand in volume with the addition of melt water that was formerly locked up in glaciers on land, e.g., in Greenland or the Antarctic. From 1900 to 2005, the sea level rose by almost 20 cm. For an illustration of this development, see Figure 8: [43]

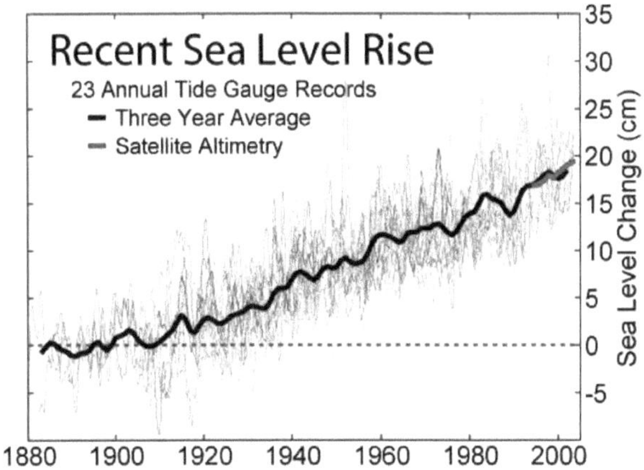

[44]

Figure 8: Development of sea level since 1880

Several scientists project a volume loss of glaciers of 60% by 2050. In the case of Greenland, this means 239 ± 23 cubic kilometers of melt water per year in the present day. Nevertheless, the Antarctic ice shield is expected to grow, mainly due to heavier precipitation. On a global scale, IPCC predicts that by the end of the century sea levels will rise by 0.22 to 0.44 m above 1990 levels. Unfortunately, the speed of the increase is accelerating. Whereas it averaged 1.7 mm from 1900 until 1993, it is currently about 4 mm per year.[45]

In 2007, Hansen et al. argued that ice at the poles does not melt in a gradual and linear manner, but in a sudden and non-linear way: [46]

43 Hansen et al., 2007 pp. 1925-1935
44 Depiction created by Globalwarmingart.com. Data based on Douglas (1997)
45 Schneeberger et al., 2003 p. 145 and Chen, Wilson, & Tapley, 2006, p. 1958
46 Hansen et al., 2007 p. 1925

"Our concern that BAU [business as usual] GHG scenarios would cause large sea level rise this century (...) differs from estimates of IPCC (...), which foresees little or no contribution to twenty first century sea level rise from Greenland and Antarctica. However, the IPCC analyses and projections do not well account for the nonlinear physics of wet ice sheet disintegration, ice streams and eroding ice shelves, nor are they consistent with the paleoclimate evidence we have presented for the absence of discernible lag between ice sheet forcing and sea level rise."[47]

Similarly, Carlson et al. (2008) used a paleo-climatic approach to predict the rise in sea level and arrived at comparable results to those of Hansen et al. (2007):[48]

"All these predictions are based on the assumption of a continued linear response between global temperatures and ice-sheet loss. This response is unlikely because of positive feedback loops in the global warming system, and sea level rise could thus be much higher. Some leading climate scientists have raised the concern that the IPCC 2007 predictions are too conservative."[49]

The issue of positive feedback loops (also referred to as tipping points) will be dealt with later in this chapter.

The second impact within oceans is acidification, which is not a direct consequence of increased temperatures but results from higher CO_2 concentrations in the air. Oceans soak up much of the CO_2 produced by living creatures, e.g., through skeletons of marine creatures that fall to the bottom, and from burning of fossil fuels, changing the ocean's pH[50]. Almost 50% of all CO_2 emissions produced by human activities (equaling approximately 118 petagrams as of 1994) have been absorbed by the oceans. Unfortunately, the CO_2 reacts with sea water and becomes weak carbon acid and has already lowered the pH value by 0.1 units to 8.2. The predicted emissions could lower the pH by an additional 0.5 units by 2100.[51]

This level of acidity has not been seen for hundreds of thousands of years. Additionally, it is occurring approximately 100 times faster than ever before. It is likely that this development has detrimental effects on the oceans' flora and fauna.[52]

47 Hansen et al., 2007 p. 1950
48 Carlson, et al. 2008 p. 620 and Pfeffer, Harper, & O'Neel, 2008, p. 1340
49 Costello et al., 2009, p. 1698
50 Laboratory measure of acidity
51 Sabine et al., 2004, p. 367
52 Sabine et al., 2004 pp. 367-371 and Walther et al., 2002, pp. 389-394

Glaciers

The third major impact area of global warming is mountain glaciers.

Although glaciers have always responded to alterations of the global climate by expanding and retreating in width and length, their appearance and disappearance have significant impacts on local weather and water supply conditions. For instance, the Little Ice Age, which lasted from 1550 to 1850, was the most recent period of global glacier growth. From then on, the glaciers retreated until 1940, when a slight global cooling occurred that lasted until the 1980s. Since then, glacier retreats have begun to happen more rapidly and are rather ubiquitous. Mass balance losses have been especially apparent for the glaciers in the Andes, Alps, Pyrenees, Himalayas, Rocky Mountains and Cascade Range. Many scientists see the future existence of glaciers as threatened by further global warming.[53]

This trend is alarming because the loss of glaciers can directly cause flash floods, landslides and glacial lake overflows. Additionally, the water supplies of heavily populated areas will become threatened. The impact of glaciers' disappearance on humans will be further explained in the next chapter.[54]

Bio-diversity

The fourth major impact area of global warming is bio-diversity. The situation is well described by Costello (2009):

"Global warming also threatens global biodiversity. Ecosystems are already being hugely degraded by habitat loss, pollution, and hunting. The millennium ecosystem assessment suggested that three known species are becoming extinct every hour, whereas the 2008 living planet report suggested that biodiversity of vertebrates had fallen by over a third in just 35 years, an extinction rate 10 000 times faster than any observed in the fossil record. Global warming is likely to exacerbate such degradation."[55]

53 Intergovernmental Panel on Climate Change, 2007b, pp. 350-359
54 Intergovernmental Panel on Climate Change, 2007b, pp. 350-359
55 Costello et al., 2009, pp. 1698–1699

Looking into the future, a similar picture is painted by scientists from the University of York: The global temperatures predicted for the coming centuries may trigger a new 'mass extinction event' where a large amount of animal and plant species would be wiped out.[56]

One prominent example of species at risk is the polar bear. Because the Hudson Bay is now ice-free 3 weeks longer every year than it was 30 years ago, polar bears find it more difficult to hunt prey.[57]

Additionally, Root (2003) mentioned in Nature that there have recently been changes in the range or seasonal behavior of flora and fauna. Approximately 80% have moved their ranges towards the poles or to higher altitudes, making them "refugee species".[58]

Nevertheless, the relationship between increased temperatures and bio-diversity is not as clear cut as it seems. According to Smith and Hitz (2003), the association between the two elements seems to be parabolic, meaning, first, an increase in CO_2 leads via better plant growth to more bio-diversity. But when a certain threshold is exceeded, increased temperatures will decrease bio-diversity. This relationship is also referred to as ecological productivity.[59]

The remaining part of this section shall focus on the implications of the temperature increase for the global climate.

As already described in this chapter, the relation does not have to be a linear one. Several scientists argue that there are certain regions that have started or could start a positive feedback loop. In other words, when the temperature has surpassed a certain threshold at which a certain mechanism is activated, global warming begins to accelerate. Once this threshold or tipping point has been reached, even the slightest perturbation can alter the state or development of the system tremendously.[60]

Some of the most prominent examples of positive feedback are as follows:

---

56 Mayhew et al., 2007, p. 47
57 Byers, 2010
58 Root et al., 2003, pp. 57-60
59 Smith & Hitz, 2003, p. 7
60 Costello et al., 2009, p. 1698

Water vapor feedback: As the temperature increases, oceans evaporate more water; but because water vapor is a GHG as well, the effect of global warming is enhanced, so even more water is evaporated.[61]

Reduced CO_2 absorption by the oceans: As the oceans warm, their ability to sequester CO_2 is reduced. This phenomenon occurs because nutrient levels in the mesopelagic zone (approximately 200 to 1,000 m deep) are reduced, creating a less friendly environment for diatoms that absorb CO_2. Therefore, less CO_2 is absorbed, and more stays in the atmosphere, heating it up even further.[62]

Ice-albedo feedback: As the planet warms, ice melts and land or open water appear. Because ice shields reflect much more solar radiation than land or open water can, a positive feedback loop begins, driving temperatures up even more and causing even more ice to melt.[63]

Arctic methane release: Because temperatures are rising even faster in regions that used to be very cold, like Siberia and Canada (mainly due to the ice-albedo effect), methane is being released from sources both on land (permafrost) and on the ocean floor. This also leads to an increased amount of GHGs in the atmosphere driving up temperatures even further.[64]

The latter two prominent feedback loops are also among the major global tipping points. This means that when their threshold is exceeded abrupt and devastating climate changes will occur which are irreversible.[65]

1.1.1.4 Climate change and its consequences for mankind

Having described the impacts of rising temperatures on global climate, the focus will now move to the question: "What implications will climate change have for mankind?"

Because "climate change is not just an environmental but also a health issue"[66], it will significantly affect everyday life in an unforeseeable manner.

---

61 Soden & Held, 2005, p. 3354
62 Buesseler et al., 2007, pp. 567-569
63 Stocker et al., 2001, p. 787
64 Westbrook et al., 2009, p. L15608 and Zimov, Schuur, & Chapin, 2007, p. 1612
65 Costello et al., 2009, p. 1698
66 Costello et al., 2009, p. 1697

Various models have tried to capture the impact of human behavior on nature and its consequences for society as a whole, but most remain very generic.[67]

This section is mainly based on the assessments of the Lancet Commission and the University College London Institute for Global Health Effects.

Even the authors see their report as conservative, but "First, even the most conservative estimates are profoundly disturbing and demand action. Second, less conservative climate change scenarios are so catastrophic that adaptation might be unachievable."[68]

As already mentioned, mankind has increased CO_2 emissions by more than 80 times since the beginning of the Industrial Revolution. Every year, 27.5 billion tons of CO_2 are released into the atmosphere. The impacts of such behavior will have to be handled not just by this generation but also by future generations.[69]

The assessment of the consequences of humans' carbon releasing behavior will be split into direct and indirect potential damages to human health.[70]

The direct consequences of climate change are segmented into health-related and economic effects. Note that some health effects have interdependencies and might therefore overlap.[71]

Health-related effects

The health effects themselves are further split into aspects of diseases, ecosystems, food, sea level and extreme weather events.

Starting off with the disease implications of global warming, it needs to be noted that the epidemiological outcome of climate change will be tremendous.[72] Developing countries lacking medical infrastructure will show the most negative effects. Because of heat waves, the incidences of cardiovascular and respiratory diseases will soar.[73]

67 Sarkis, 2001, pp. 671–672
68 Costello et al., 2009, p. 1697
69 Anschober & Ramsauer, 2007, pp. 122–124
70 Costello et al., 2009, pp. 1700–1701
71 Costello et al., 2009, pp. 1702–1708
72 Costello et al., 2009, pp. 1702–1708
73 Costello et al., 2009, pp. 1702–1708

For example, Europe's heat wave in 2003 killed approximately 70,000 people, most of them from heat stroke.[74]

History also shows that urban areas are by far more affected by cardiovascular and respiratory diseases than rural areas, mainly due to pre-existing respiratory diseases.[75]

Besides cardiovascular and respiratory diseases, the transmission rates of vector-borne and rodent-borne diseases such as malaria, dengue fever, schistosomiasis, fascioliasis, alveolar echinococcosis, leishmaniasis, Lyme borreliosis, tick-borne encephalitis, and hantavirus infections will also accelerate.[76]

This acceleration is due to the fact that rising temperature "affects rate of pathogen maturation and replication within mosquitoes, the density of insects in a particular area, and increases the likelihood of infection. Therefore, some populations who have little or no immunity to new infections might be at increased risk."[77]

To illustrate this, the development of malaria infections has been projected: Due to the warmer climate, the number of mosquitoes will grow because they will become able to reach higher altitudes (which have become warmer). It is expected that 260-320 million more people will be affected by malaria by 2080.[78]

As mentioned in the previous chapter, several aspects of ecosystems are at risk because of climate change. Unfortunately, in many cases these are the bases for food, work, recreation or other aspects of everyday life. If pushed out of balance, the consequences can threaten human lives extensively.[79]

For the third aspect of health-related consequences, namely food, the analyses show a rather heterogeneous picture of the impact of climate change on the global food supply. Some regions, mainly high-latitude countries such as Norway or Sweden, will benefit from global warming of 1-3°C, but beyond 3°C, agricultural production on a global scale will suffer.[80]

74 Costello et al., 2009, pp. 1702–1708
75 Costello et al., 2009, pp. 1702–1708
76 Costello et al., 2009, pp. 1702–1708
77 Costello et al., 2009, pp. 1702–1708
78 Costello et al., 2009, pp. 1702–1708
79 Schneider et al., 2007, p. 393
80 Schneider et al., 2007, pp. 8-12

But even below this threshold of 3°C, many regions, especially at low latitudes, will experience significant negative impacts of global warming. In particular, undernutrition and food insecurity will increase suffering.[81]

Undernutrition will manifest in low birth weight and suboptimal breastfeeding, which could lead to 3.5 million deaths of mothers and young children every year. In 2008, when the first global food crisis hit developing countries with soaring food prices, up to 1.6 billion people (almost one quarter of the world's population) suffered from hunger or food insecurity. This development is expected to worsen: different studies predict that by the end of the century, the world might face severe food shortages because yields of crops like rice and maize could fall by 20-40%. The sub-Saharan and south Asian countries are predicted to suffer most.[82]

Secondary effects of global warming such as rising sea levels and increased extreme weather conditions will further impact the global food supply. "Increases in extreme weather events will damage crops and disrupt farming. Sea level rise and flooding of coastal lands will lead to salination or contamination of fresh water and agricultural lands, and the loss of nursery areas for fishing. Drought, and changing patterns of plant and livestock diseases and pest infestations, reduction of income from animal production, decreased crop yields, lessened forest productivity, and changes in aquatic populations will all affect food production and security."[83]

Another major contributor to health-related issues is the water supply.

Accessibility and cleanliness of water and adequate sanitary conditions are the cornerstones for social and economic development. But even in 2002, 21% of the population in developing countries lacked sustained access to improved water sources.[84]

Due to the rising sea level and consequent contamination of ground water (through salt-water intrusion), the scarcity of fresh water will increase. Increased evaporation will mean more extreme weather events, making more water fall on hardened ground that is unable to absorb it and creating flash floods, exacerbating the lack of clean water.[85]

81 Costello et al., 2009, pp. 1702–1708
82 Costello et al., 2009, pp. 1702–1708
83 Costello et al., 2009, pp. 1702–1708
84 Costello et al., 2009, pp. 1702–1708
85 Costello et al., 2009, pp. 1702–1708

Additionally, the thawing of glaciers is reducing the global water supply even further. In the past, glaciers acted as a buffer of water supply shortages during warm months, but with the glaciers quickly retreating, run-offs are likely to eventually disappear. More than one sixth of the world's population depends on glacial-fed water catchments; South America and central Asia are particularly vulnerable to the disappearance of glaciers, which could lead to more droughts in these regions.[86]

To exemplify this, it is worthwhile to examine the case of central Asia, especially the Hindu Kush and the Himalayan regions. The glaciers in these mountains act as the dry-season water source for many major rivers in the central, south, east and southeast Asian mainland. Although melt water will lead to increased agricultural output in the short term, the risk of running out of water in the long term is credible. Unfortunately, the regions affected are the most populated in the world. A total of 2.4 billion people live in the drainage basin of the Himalayan rivers (Ganges, Indus, Brahmaputra, Yangtze, Mekong, Salween and Yellow) alone.[87]

Additionally, the Tibetan Plateau, which contains the third largest store of ice in the world, is experiencing temperature increases that are four times faster than in the rest of China. Unfortunately, running out of water is not the only problem these regions are facing; floods might also have a detrimental effect. For example, flooding of the Ganges alone could affect more than 500 million people.[88]

Besides floods, other aspects of extreme weather events such as a sea-level rise could negatively affect human health. As described in the previous chapter, sea-level rises occur mainly through two effects: Volume expansion and melting ice from the polar ice caps. [89]

To illustrate the consequences: "A more pessimistic scenario could occur if the observed temperature rise approaches the higher end of the IPCC expected scenarios. Sustained global temperature rises of 5–6°C could lead to the loss of both Greenland and the western Antarctic ice sheets by the middle of the next century, raising sea levels by up to 13 m.(…) However, a 13-m rise would cause the flooding and permanent abandonment of almost all low-lying coastal and river urban areas. Currently, a third of the world's population lives within 60 miles of a shoreline

86 Costello et al., 2009, pp. 1702–1708
87 Rühland et al., 2006, p. L15709 and Barnett, Adam, & Lettenmaier, 2005, pp. 303-306
88 Rühland et al., 2006, p. L15709 and Barnett, Adam, & Lettenmaier, 2005, pp. 303-306
89 Costello et al., 2009, pp. 1698–1699

and 13 of the world's 20 largest cities are located on a coast. More than a billion people could be displaced in environmental mass migration. A stable coastline would not be re-established for hundreds of thousands of years. The north Atlantic ocean circulation (which includes the Gulf Stream circulation) could collapse plunging western Europe into a succession of severe winters followed by severe heat waves during summer rise."[90]

Meanwhile, increasing ocean surface temperatures do not just lead to volume expansion and rising sea levels; they also increase the frequency of extreme weather events such as hurricanes. For example, MunichRe (one of the world's largest reinsurance companies) states that of the 238 great natural catastrophes that took place between 1950 and 2007, approximately 66% were extreme weather/climate-related events, mainly floods and windstorms. However, the number of great weather/climate events has risen from less than two per year in 1950 to more than six in 2007.[91]

Summing up the health effects of climate change, it can be said that the more temperatures rise, the worse the impact on humans is going to be. See Figure 9:

90 Costello et al., 2009, pp. 1698–1699
91 Costello et al., 2009, pp. 1702–1708

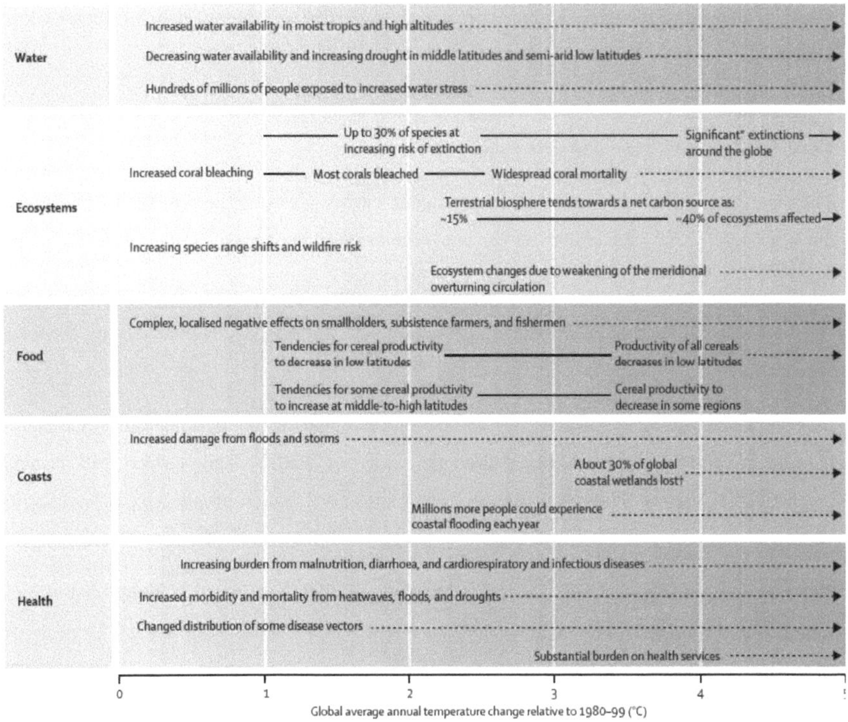

[92]

Figure 9: Effects of global average temperature change

Economic effects

Besides health effects, which will be quite detrimental, economic risks are also nonnegligible. Several papers have been written about the economic impact of climate change besides the most current one from the UNFCC, which is perceived as far too conservative.[93]

The best known is the Stern report, which states that if mankind does not cut back on carbon emissions and thereby mitigate climate change, the global cost will be approximately 5.5 trillion USD per year, or one fifth of global GDP. This number seems to be very conservative: the DIW

92 Costello et al., 2009, p. 1700
93 Friedmann, 2009, p. 1

shows that the damages solely within Germany could sum up to approximately 3 trillion EUR by 2100.[94]

In order to abate these costs, Stern suggests investing approximately 2% (previously 1%) of global GDP per year in cutting back emissions.[95]

The report has been heavily discussed in academic circles, accusing Stern of failing to consider the costs after 2200 and of not taking into account the appropriate discount rate for global damages.[96]

Having discussed the direct detrimental effects of global warming and climate change, the focus will now move on to the indirect (secondary) effects.

Indirect effects will further increase the burden for the remaining part of human society because, through different climatic events, substantial parts of Earth's land surface will become uninhabitable. Various analyses predict that approximately 1 billion people (i.e., 10% of 2050's world population of 10 billion) will become environmental refugees.[97]

Unfortunately, population explosion exacerbates the problems of global warming and climate change even further, pushing economic and health systems even closer to the edge.[98]

This statement holds especially true for developing countries, where the population is likely to increase from 5.4 to 7.9 billion people (2007-2050). However, through migration movements, developed countries will experience tremendous pressure on their own economic, social and health systems that might ultimately lead to violent conflicts over scarce resources, as has already happened in Darfur.[99]

Finally, in the last segment of this chapter, the distributions of direct and indirect effects of global warming and climate change shall be analyzed.

Unfortunately, the effects of climate change are not distributed on the basis of cause, nor are they evenly distributed. In fact, some regions (mainly high-latitude areas like Northern Europe, Russia

---

94 Anschober & Ramsauer, 2007, pp. 125–126
95 Costello et al., 2009, p. 1700
96 Tol & Yohe, 2006, pp. 233-245
97 Christian Aid, 2007, p. 1
98 Costello et al., 2009, pp. 1700–1701 and Costello et al., 2009, pp. 1702–1708
99 Costello et al., 2009, pp. 1702–1708

and Canada) will benefit from it in the beginning. As long as global temperatures do not rise more than 2-3°C, the world will be split between winners and losers of global warming; beyond this threshold, all will become losers.[100]

In the meanwhile, low-latitude areas like substantial parts of Asia, Africa and South America will suffer far more, although they have caused far less GHG emissions than industrialized parts of the world have. Therefore, more and more will see "The inequity of climate change—with the rich causing most of the problem and the poor initially suffering most of the consequences—will prove to be a source of historical shame to our generation.[101]

One might seek an explanation for this disturbing situation. Negative impacts on human health are not just driven by the magnitude of environmental consequences, but also by the means to cope with them, because there are different underlying vulnerabilities between more and less impacted regions of the world. Examples of this are "existing levels of heat and food stress, and exposure to disease vectors (…) and differing capacities to adapt to changing conditions (related to governance and resources nationally and individual incomes). (…) These differences in the effects of climate change are due to existing economic, social, and health inequities."[102]

1.1.2 Reaction of consumers and policy makers to environmental challenges

Having shown how detrimental climate change could be to human society, this section shall focus on the reactions of policy makers and consumers to this threat.

However, it must be noted that climate change and global warming are not the first environmental issues that have been on the minds of consumers and policy makers. To the contrary, "Concerns for environmental issues have consistently been one of the top ten topics for various societal stakeholders since the early 1970s […] With increasing affluence derived from rapid economic development, citizens in various parts of the world are becoming more and more

100 IPCC, 2007 and Schneider et al., 2007, pp. 8-15
101 Costello et al., 2009, p. 1694
102 Costello et al., 2009, p. 1701

concerned about the hazardous impacts of environmental deterioration on their enjoyment of life."[103]

Therefore, environmental issues have moved to the top of the list of priorities for national and international policymakers.[104] By consulting scientists to estimate the ecological impact of climate change on society, global leaders seek to understand how technology, economy, population and other factors will affect their countries.[105]

This led to various regulatory actions like the Kyoto Protocol, EU CO_2 certificate trading scheme and the restructuring of national energy supply.[106]

It is not just politicians who have updated their agendas; consumers also show increasing concerns about environmental deterioration and have become more aware of green products.[107]

Still, in 2007, surveys showed that the majority of consumers (51%) saw environmental problems, including climate change, as the most important issue for the next five years.[108]

Even in the US, climate change is seen as the most disturbing environmental problem for the upcoming years.[109]

---

103 Chan & Lau, 2002, p. 10
104 Saemann, 1992, p. 186
105 Sarkis, 2001, pp. 671–672
106 Cogan, 2006, pp. 11–13
107 Hokey Min & Galle, 2001, p. 1222 and Helmers, 2008, p. 24
108 Bonini, Hintz, & Mendonca, 2008, p. 2
109 Stauffer, p. 1

For an illustration, see Figure 10.

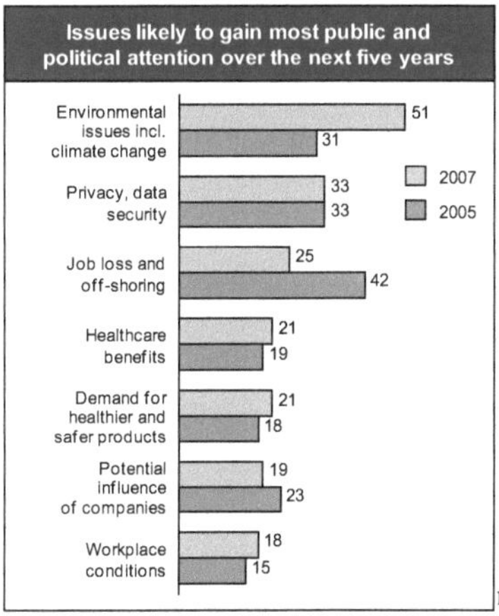

110

Figure 10: Future issues for consumers and executives

1.1.3 Implications of climate change for corporate leaders and investors

Knowing that policy makers and the general public are highly aware of the threat of climate change and willing to take action, corporate leaders and investors in companies (equity holders) face different risks.[111]

The first issue is regulatory risk. National and international organizations and governmental bodies are putting increasing pressure on companies to limit their GHG emissions during operations and to offer more climate-friendly products. Examples of this pressure are the European Cap and Trade system for CO_2 certificates, where companies will need to purchase documents that entitle them to emit GHGs. Developing countries like China have also passed emission reduction laws. CO_2 regimes are also being brought into place on the state level. California and ten other US states have limited the CO_2 emissions of cars sold within their state boundaries.[112]

110 Bonini et al., 2008, p. 2
111 Whereas risk is defined as the probability of occurrence multiplied by the possible damage. For further details, see Balderjahn & Mennicken, 1996, pp. 25–27
112 Cogan, 2006, pp. 11–13

An abundant number of other regulative actions exist to deal with this problem, but this brief overview should give the reader a first idea of what companies and their investors have to deal with.

Tightly linked to the regulatory risk is the competitive risk. Companies not fulfilling the explicit standards of regulatory bodies or the implicit expectations of their consumers may face higher costs, e.g., through penalties or lost revenues, because consumers turn to other companies. A good example of this is the US automotive industry, which relied heavily on gas-guzzling SUVs, but as consumer demand shifted, their market share and revenue fell.[113]

However, besides the regulatory and competitive risk, there is also the physical risk of climate change impacting corporate decisions. Examples of this impact are the intensity and frequency of extreme weather events, sea-level rise, droughts and floods. Hurricane Katrina, for instance, devastated huge areas of the Gulf Coast, damaging infrastructure and oil and gas rigs worth millions of dollars. Capital investment decisions need to reflect this development. Another example is the construction of a USD 7 billion pipeline in Canada that is dependent on the permafrost (frozen ground) for support. As the permafrost thaws, which has already begun, the pipeline structure becomes unstable and starts to sink into the ground, pushing a long-term investment project to the brink of abandonment. [114]

Taking all this together shows that pressure on companies to be environmentally responsible has increased significantly.[115] In particular with the beginning of the new millennium, economic, social and political pressure have increased tremendously.[116]

A valuable example of this new pressure is embodied in the following speech given by Klaus Töpfer (former Executive Director of the United Nations Environment Program): "many stakeholders are demanding greater responsibility and accountability of the private sector, in particular multinational corporations (…) The private sector is thus increasingly being held accountable to manage its operations in a manner that will enhance economic development, ensure environmental protection, and promote social justice."[117]

113 Cogan, 2006, pp. 11–13
114 Cogan, 2006, pp. 11–13
115 Stead & Stead, 2000, pp. 313–314, Wang, 2009, pp. 2-4 and Klassen & Vachon, 2003, p. 336
116 Kolk, Levy, & Pinkse, 2008, p. 720
117 Scherpereel, van Koppen, & Heering, 2001, p. 98

Facing these kinds of risks from climate change, companies have coped with the situation in different ways. Some have decided to form partnerships with other corporations to develop a blueprint for how to reduce GHG emissions, like the US Climate Action Partnership.[118] Others have set up a common knowledge database for eco-patents that are free to be used by all participating companies (e.g., IBM, Nokia, Sony) to spread knowledge on how to ease the environmental burden for society.[119]

Other companies have decided to develop responses on their own. For instance, BASF developed an eco-efficiency portfolio to assess corporate actions in a coherent tool covering economic and environmental concerns.[120] BP has invested heavily in low-emission products and technologies as a part of its new strategy, "Beyond petroleum".[121] Wal-Mart has set up an electronic indexing system to show the environmental impact of its products.[122]

Generally speaking, some companies see climate change just as a threat, but others also perceive a possibility. The decision how to cope with this challenge depends on corporate leaders.[123]

Unfortunately, the situation is not as clear cut as it might seem. Corporate leaders find it difficult to decide whether they should take their companies green or not, because they do not know how their stockholders will react. Although the decision, to move the company onto the path to a green future, might be the right thing for society and the planet, stockholders eventually will decide if this move created or destroyed company value and thereby if corporate leaders will keep their jobs.

This is where this dissertation will add value to the discussion. It will analyze how investors react when companies move towards a green future.

1.2 OUTLINE OF THE STUDY

In order to grasp the full extent of the major objectives of this dissertation, it is vital to lay a foundation by giving solid explanations of its governing principles.

118 Mufson, 2009, p. 1
119 Tripsas, 2009, p. 1 and Schmidt et al. 2004, p. 81
120 Rüdenauer et al., 2005, pp. 111–113
121 Kolk et al., 2008, pp. 720–721
122 Rosenbloom, 2009
123 Cogan, 2006, pp. 11–13

In the first step (**Chapter Two**), a literature review will describe the current state of theoretical frameworks, describing the relations between environmental disclosure, environmental performance and economic performance.

Purpose of Chapter Two: Illustrate how well existing theories can explain different corporate behaviors in terms of environmental disclosure, environmental performance and economic performance. Additionally, different shortcomings of current conceptual frameworks shall be addressed (research gap) while describing a new approach to old theoretical frameworks by combining them with theories of capital market research.

In **Chapter Three,** the main terms will be defined and explained. If necessary, different interpretations will be provided as well.

Purpose of Chapter Three: Provide explanations of terms necessary to understand the study.

In the next step (**Chapter Four**), the Carbon Disclosure Project (CDP) and its well-known report on the Global 500, upon which all analyses are based, are described. In particular, participation and key findings will be of great importance. Afterwards, a short critique of the CDP will be provided.

Purpose of Chapter Four: Describe CDP's report in terms of its uniqueness and global reach, which enabled this research project. Additionally, the variables that are later used in the study will be explained here.

Having described the current state of the literature and CDP's report, **Chapter Five** will describe the specific research questions to be answered within this study. It will also illustrate how theories were used to predict the outcomes of the analysis by developing a hypothesis. Further on, this chapter will describe how the research model is set up and which pathways can lead from an event to changes in financial valuation.

Purpose of Chapter Five: Describe key research questions and hypothesis to be tested.

Having described the CDP report on the Global 500 companies, **Chapter Six** will explain how this information is used by presenting the research methodology. It will include the necessary steps to conduct an event study as well as the pros and cons of different methods and approaches. Further on, it will describe the assumptions made and parameters set in this dissertation.

Purpose of Chapter Six: Introduce reader to the event study methodology and illustrate the strengths and weaknesses of this approach.

In **Chapter Seven,** the data set will be described. In particular, it will illustrate how the Global Fortune 500 sample is broken down into the relevant sample for further analysis. Additionally, major characteristics, such as revenue, profitability and share of institutional investors, shall be described.

Within **Chapter Eight**, the empirical result will be presented, giving answers to the defined research questions of Chapter Five. Further on, possible interpretations will be derived to explain the outcomes. However, interpretations will play only a minor part in this dissertation because they are beyond the scope of this study.

Finally, in **Chapter Nine**, the major findings will be summarized and their implications for management illustrated. Further on, limitations of the study will be shown and suggestions for further research addressed.

2 Literature review

This chapter shall be devoted to two aspects of the academic relevance of this dissertation.

First, the current state of the literature will be described, illustrating two relationships in particular: (A) The relationship between environmental disclosure and environmental performance and (B) the relationship between environmental and financial performance.[124] Each description will include a theoretical and an empirical part.

Second, the ultimate goal of this chapter is to identify a research gap based on the existing theoretical framework prescribed in Chapter 2.1 and 2.2.

2.1 RELATIONSHIP BETWEEN ENVIRONMENTAL DISCLOSURE AND ENVIRONMENTAL PERFORMANCE

2.1.1 Theoretical perspective

Two streams of academic literature attempt to explain the relationship between environmental disclosure and environmental performance. First, the socio-political theories, such as stakeholder or legitimacy theory, suggest that there is a negative association between the two elements. Second, disclosure theory suggests a positive relation between environmental disclosure and performance.[125]

These theories will be subject to elaboration of the following sections.

2.1.1.1 Socio-political theories

Starting off with the theoretical stream that suggests a negative association between environmental disclosure and environmental performance, socio-political theories such as the stakeholder theory and the legitimacy theory are well developed and mature. However, they are

124 The terms "financial performance" and "economic performance" will be used here interchangeably.
125 Clarkson et al., 2008, p. 308

not mutually exclusive, but show a rather high share of overlapping elements because they share one common thought: that environmental disclosure is a function of social and political pressure.[126]

This means that poor environmental performers will strengthen their efforts to disclose environmental information because they face severe political and social pressure that ultimately threatens their legitimacy. However, the company's main goal remains to alter the stakeholders' perception of their actual performance.[127]

In the following two segments, the two main socio-political theories (stakeholder and legitimacy) shall be described.

2.1.1.1.1 Stakeholder theory

As described in the previous section, the goal and relationship between environmental disclosure and environmental performance are essentially the same for stakeholder theory and legitimacy theory. The unifying goal is to alter the stakeholders negative perception of a company by disclosing environmental information. But the theories cover different aspects of this relationship. While the stakeholder theory concentrates on "any group that has a vested interest in the operations of the firm"[128], the legitimacy theory deals with the consequences of the interaction between companies and stakeholders.[129]

The following segment will describe different stakeholders and how they act to express and push through their interests. In the past, the main interest groups for a company were mainly internal (e.g., stockholders, employees and managers). But within the last decades, this restriction has been lifted, and other external parties have come to be seen as legitimate interest groups.[130]

This concept was mainly introduced by Freeman (1984), who defined stakeholders as: "any group or individual who can affect or is affected by the achievements of the firm's objectives".[131]

Since then, pressure on companies from external parties has increased even further, covering a huge number of different interest groups both inside and outside the company.[132]

---

126 Clarkson et al., 2008, p. 304
127 Clarkson et al., 2008, p. 304
128 Ellram & Birou, 1995, p. 155
129 Clarkson et al., 2008, p. 304
130 Staehle, 1992, pp. 68–81
131 Freeman, 1984, p. 25

Different frameworks can be used to gain an overview of the tremendous number of different stakeholders.[133]

Within this description, stakeholders are first divided into internal and external, and external is further split into market-oriented and non-market-oriented.[134]

INTERNAL	EXTERNAL	
	Non-market-oriented	Market-oriented
Corporate functions Subsidiaries Stockholders Bondholders Banks Employees Managers	Public/Media NGOs State •Executive •Judiciary •Legislature	Consumers Suppliers Competitors/JV Partners

Table 1: Overview stakeholders (adapted from Meffert/Kirchgeorg 1998)

The highlighted stakeholders (light grey) will be described in the next section.

In recent years, one new stakeholder has been defined as the ultimate stakeholder, "Planet Earth". Although it is not possible for this stakeholder to express his or her wishes, others might speak on his or her behalf. However, this is the opinion of a relatively small group of scientists.[135]

Stock- and bondholders

The potential of one of the most powerful stakeholder groups, equity and bondholders, to influence companies is quite significant, especially in the case of stockholders, who are actually the owners of the company. The reasons for equity and bond holders to care about environmental performance are twofold.[136]

First is the rational (profit-maximizing) perspective. Environmental developments such as climate change can have a significant impact on shareholder wealth. This can happen (A) through increased cost of purchased materials, such as oil, gas or emission certificates, or (B) through

132 Qinghua Zhu, Sarkis, & Geng, 2005, p. 450, Reese, 2007, p. 42, Klassen & Whybark, 1999a, p. 599, Azzone & Noci, 1996, p. 3055 and Cousins, Lamming, & Bowen, 2004, p. 557

133 Hall, 2001, p. 108, Scherpereel et al., 2001, p. 98, Gupta, 1995, p. 38, Michaelis, 1999, pp. 10–11, Baumast, 2001, p. 33, Deutschland / Bundesministerium für Umwelt, Naturschutz und Reaktorsicherheit, 2001, pp. 4–5, von Hauff, 1992, pp. 174–185 and Freimann, 1996, pp. 366–374

134 Meffert & Kirchgeorg, 1998, pp. 94–95

135 Stead & Stead, 2000, p. 313 and Stead & Stead, 2000, p. 321

136 Gert, 2009, p. 102, Wellington, 2005, p. 12 and Hoffmann & Busch, 2008, p. 506

decreasing revenues because product demand has fallen as a direct or indirect consequence of climate change.[137]

Second is the moral perspective. Since the beginning of the 20th century, ethical investments that attempt to avoid fund allocation in "sin stocks," e.g., alcohol, tobacco and gambling, have been on the rise. This designation was later extended to companies in the defense sector and has now reached to the environmental behavior of companies. At present, ethical funds make up approximately 10% of all investment funds.[138]

For bondholders and loan-granting banks, the reasons previously described also hold true, but this stakeholder group is mainly interested in the consequences of climate change for the company's risk to default, worthiness of collateral, and so on.[139]

Different approaches can be taken to create transparency of the risk posed by climate change for bond and stock holders of a company. For a detailed discussion, see CERES (2006) and PriceWaterhouseCoopers (2009). The CDP approach will be illustrated in Chapter Four.

Employees

Another important internal stakeholder group is employees, who are becoming increasingly sensitive about environmental issues within their company. This development, accompanied by the fact that the importance of work itself is becoming decreasingly rewarding, will lead employees to focus on other aspects within their work that make it more meaningful. Therefore, it is a great challenge for employers to attract new, adequately qualified employees by showing the company's environmentally friendly side.[140]

Public media and non-governmental organizations

Although public media and non-governmental organizations (NGOs) do not have direct influence on companies, their efforts can be quite effective. [141]

Polls have shown that people have become more concerned about the hazardous impact of environmental exploitation on their lives in recent decades,[142] increasing even further the scrutiny

137 Gert, 2009, p. 102, Wellington, 2005, p. 12 and Hoffmann & Busch, 2008, p. 506
138 Freimann, 1996, pp. 162–166
139 Wambach & Wunderlich, 2003, pp. 38–42
140 Freimann, 1996, pp. 190–197
141 Reese, 2007, p. 42

of companies' environmental behavior.[143] People are worried that companies' behavior might have negative consequences (directly or indirectly) on their health or that of their children or grandchildren, as described by Khoo, Bainbridge, Spedding, & Taplin (2001).

This scrutiny led to the foundation of various environmental NGOs whose goals were to disclose environmental scandals and inform about the shortcomings, risks and threats of particular products and production processes. Often, these protests were delivered in unusual ways, e.g., by blockages of streets and railways. A new approach of some NGOs is to participate in the solution process by working with foundations, e.g., the Climate Works Foundation, whose goal it is to share environmental best practices across industries.[144]

However, it shall be noted that environmental issues are not a constant worry of the public, but public attention towards certain environmental topics, e.g., climate change, is similar to the life cycle model of a product. It begins with the "latent phase," where the problem is first recognized just by a few individuals. Then it moves to the "emergent phase," where a wider portion of the public, including certain research scientists, begins to focus on the problem. However, at this stage, the problem is still mainly dealt with by scientists. Afterwards (the "upswing phase"), the environmental issue begins to be discussed in larger settings. Special interest groups and magazines like *National Geographic* or *GEO* focus on the topic. Politicians begin to pick it up as well. In the "mature phase," the environmental issue has reached the peak of public attention. All political groups have defined their positions towards the problem, but the media is already looking for new issues. In the "downturn phase," public attention towards the environmental issues erodes, laws have been passed and execution is pending. For a detailed description of the topic, see Deutschland/Bundesministerium für Umwelt, Naturschutz und Reaktorsicherheit (2001) and Meffert & Kirchgeorg (1998).

For a depiction of this development, see Figure 11:

142 Reese, 2007, p. 42
143 Chan & Lau, 2002, p. 10 and Hall, 2001, p. 108
144 Freimann, 1996, pp. 168–176, Delmas & Keller, 2005, p. 103 and Paddock, 2009, p. 1

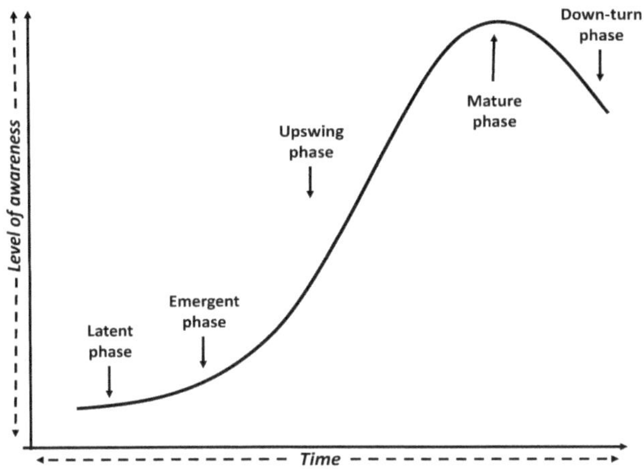

Figure 11: Life-cycle model of environmental issues

Government and regulatory bodies

Among the most powerful stakeholders are governments and regulatory bodies like the Environmental Protection Agency (EPA). Like other stakeholder groups, their pressure on companies has increased. This is described in Hokey Min & Galle, (2001), Srivastava (2007), Guide, J. (2000), and Hall (2001). Although the roles of governments and regulatory bodies in this situation may seem dissimilar, their ultimate goal is the same: to change companies' environmental behavior, for instance, by managing energy consumption and waste reduction. This is illustrated in Shrivastava (1995).

The general plan to change this behavior involves the internalization of environmental cost.[145] As explained by Hopfenbeck (1993), this strategy can take two forms: (A) "Ecological internalization: The polluter takes responsibility for cutting down pollution" [146] or (B) "Economic internalization: The polluter pays the cost and continues to cause the damage."[147] Ecological internalization is thereby a way to directly influence the company's behavior by restricting, e.g., the input or output of certain environmentally hazardous materials. One example of this strategy

145 Raffée, 1979, pp. 23–25 and Bickhoff, 2000, pp. 25–26
146 Hopfenbeck, 1993, p. 31
147 Hopfenbeck, 1993, p. 31

is the use of lead within the semiconductor industry in the EU.[148] However, this approach (also called technology-based) has been met with skepticism from scientists because it does not allow the market to find more efficient ways of avoiding certain kinds of pollution.[149] For economic internalization, governments take an indirect approach to changing the company's behavior by making them pay for the damage caused and thereby making it economically reasonable to find alternatives.[150]

For a detailed discussion of environmental policy measures, see Michaelis (1999), Deutschland/Bundesministerium für Umwelt, Naturschutz und Reaktorsicherheit (2001), and Meffert & Kirchgeorg (1998).

One new approach began in the US, where governmental agencies worked together with an automotive original equipment manufacturer (OEM) to develop a more environmentally-friendly car.[151]

Consumers

Among most powerful stakeholders on environmental issues are consumers, who can actually have a significant impact on the revenue side of a business. As described in academic circles quite extensively, the pressure on companies from these stakeholders has increased significantly (see Min & Galle (1997), Hokey Min & Galle (2001), Carter, Kale, & Grimm (2000) and Morton, Green, & New (1996)).

Although some of consumers' fears do not need to be rational, their influence has led to tremendous changes in the corporate world. (e.g., product innovation and changes in packaging and advertising approaches).[152]

Because their impact is so far reaching, it affects the whole supply chain of a product, not just the final assembler or retailer that is apparent to customers.[153] Consequently, consumers do not care at which step of the value chain environmentally detrimental actions took place; they want a

148 Trowbridge, 2001, p. 124
149 Bonifant & Arnold, 1995, p. 46
150 Darnall, Jolley, & Handfield, 2008, p. 36. However, environmental regulations do not always make sense. For a detailed evaluation of the German car scrap scheme, see Brake, 2009, p. 2.
151 Noci & Verganti, 1999, p. 10
152 Hall, 2001, p. 107 and Stead & Stead, 2000, pp. 322–323
153 Rao & Holt, 2005, p. 899

product that is entirely environmentally friendly.[154] Of course, this constitutes a risk for big companies that do not know the working conditions of all of their sub-suppliers but might be held responsible for them by their customers.[155]

For a detailed discussion on how companies deal with this challenge, see Hall (2001), Rao & Holt (2005), Rao (2002), Light (2002), Carter & Jennings (2004), Rao (2004) and Wang (2009).

However, customers do not just push companies to be more environmentally friendly; they also express their willingness to pay a mark-up of almost 25% for "green" products.[156]

Of course, not all customers are equally sensitive to green products. The typical Western consumer of green products is young, educated, urban and female.[157] Nevertheless, cultural differences impact the profile of green consumers and their perceptions of green advertising.[158]

For further elaboration of this cultural issue, see Chan & Lau (2002).

Additionally, studies have shown that there is a divergence between consumers' expressed willingness to buy green products and their actual purchasing behavior. Only a few cases report that consumers actually change their behavior.[159]

For detailed discussions, see Meffert & Kirchgeorg (1998), Berger & Corbin (1992), Ginsberg & Bloom (2004), Kates (2001) and Freimann (1996).

This complex situation (consumers requesting, but not buying, green products) makes it very hard for companies to find the right solution. Some start with "green washing" by promoting green features of old products. Others focus on the personal benefit of a green product to the customer, e.g., the health aspect.[160]

For further examples of how companies deal with "green" consumer requests, see Rosenbloom (2009) and Reese (2007).

154 Hall, 2001, p. 107
155 Rao, 2002, p. 632 and Light, 2002, p. 46
156 Schlegelmilch, Bohlen, & Diamantopoulos, 1996, p. 35, Ginsberg & Bloom, 2004, pp. 79–80 and Darnall et al., 2008, p. 37
157 Stafford et al., 1996, p. 67
158 Chan & Lau, 2002, p. 14 and Chan & Lau, 2002, p. 32,
159 Ginsberg & Bloom, 2004, p. 79, Freimann, 1996, pp. 155–162, Kates, 2001, pp. 393–394 and Berger & Corbin, 1992, p. 79
160 Stafford et al., 1996, p. 78

2.1.1.1.2 Legitimacy theory

Based on stakeholder theory, legitimacy theory focuses on the consequences of corporate interaction with stakeholders. Because stakeholders express their claims and thereby define society's environmental expectations toward a company, it is necessary for corporate leaders to align the company's goals with those of society. Otherwise, the company will lose its legitimacy as part of society, threatening its survival.[161]

Applying this theory to environmental disclosure, poor environmental performers will try to convince the public that their actions are not as environmentally detrimental as they might seem. In this way they will attempt to prove that they work within the same value system as the rest of society and ultimately regain their legitimacy.[162]

For further discussions, see Meffert & Kirchgeorg (1998) and Stahlmann (1994).

In sum, both theories (stakeholder and legitimacy) have as their starting point negative environmental behavior, and their ultimate goal is to alter this perception, but differ in the perspective on this relationship.[163]

2.1.1.2 Disclosure theory

As described in the previous section, different stakeholders have different requests, but all put enormous environmental pressure on companies. To deal with that pressure, companies disclose environmental information to alter the way they are perceived. This cause and effect relationship, starting off with the stakeholders' requests, holds true for the sociopolitical theories but exactly opposes the disclosure theory.

Here, the starting point is the company, which wants to transmit a positive image of its environmental performance by disclosing good environmental information voluntarily. The company will mainly focus on this information, which is not easy for inferior companies to mimic. According to the disclosure theory, these inferior firms will disclose less information or will not disclose any.[164]

161 Meffert & Kirchgeorg, 1998, pp. 55–56
162 Meffert & Kirchgeorg, 1998, pp. 55–56
163 Meffert & Kirchgeorg, 1998, pp. 55–56
164 Clarkson et al., 2008, p. 304

For further mathematical proof of the value of disclosing discretionary information (e.g., environmental information), see Dye (1985) and Verrecchia (1983).

But creating a positive image is not the only reason for companies to disclose environmental information. One significant benefit thereof is the reduction in the cost of capital[165] because information asymmetry between the management and stock/bond holders is reduced.[166]

Lang & Lundholm (1996) have shown a positive correlation between disclosure and superior earnings performance.

Therefore, in this theory, environmental disclosure follows good environmental performance.[167]

2.1.2 Empirical perspective

Having described the different theories (socio-political versus disclosure), empirical findings about the relationship between environmental disclosure and environmental performance shall now be discussed.

Because more and more companies have begun to use environmental information in marketing arguments, it is fairly interesting to ask if this just reflects "green washing" or indicates a serious commitment to environmental friendliness.[168]

Overall, empirical results about this relationship are mixed. The following section is split into three parts that describe a null, positive and negative association between environmental disclosure and environmental performance, respectively.

The first article on this topic was published by Ingram & Frazier (1980). They operationalized environmental disclosure by ranking companies' annual reports in twenty content categories covering four dimensions: Evidence, time, specificity and theme. Environmental performance, on the other hand, was approximated by an environmental performance rating conducted by the Council on Economic Priorities (CEP). They found no significant relationship between environmental performance and environmental disclosure.

---

165 Healy & Palepu, 2001, pp. 429–430 and Frankel & McNichols, 1995, p. 149
166 Clarkson et al., 2008, pp. 315–316
167 Clarkson et al., 2008, p. 304
168 DeCicco & Thomas, 1999, pp. 56–57

Similarly, Wiseman (1982), who used a study design almost identical to that of Ingram and Frazier (1980), found no significant association between environmental disclosure and environmental performance.

Freedman & Wasley, (1990), on the other hand, used a different research design, operationalizing environmental disclosure as information included in the annual report. However, they too failed to find a significant relationship.

However, there were also researchers who did find meaningful associations.

One such researcher was Rockness (1985), who used a field study approach operationalizing environmental disclosure as the assessment of the annual report by third parties (e.g., MBA students, environmental regulators, financial analysts and environmental protection agencies). The assessment group was asked to evaluate the environmental information included in the annual report. Environmental performance was scored, as previously, from CEP data. Rockness found a negative relationship, meaning the worse the company's environmental performance was, the better the assessment of the environmental disclosure and vice versa.

Similar results were achieved Yue Li, Richardson, & Thornton (1997) using a game theory approach and by Bewley & Li (2000), who used the Wiseman index as an indicator for environmental disclosure and by a request from the Ministry of Environment for a report of companies' pollution propensity.

One year later, Hughes, Anderson, & Golden (2001) published another article based on the Wiseman index and the environmental performance data of CEP. They also found a negative association between the two items.

Nevertheless, one article by Al-Tuwaijri, Christensen, & Hughes (2004) found a positive relationship between environmental disclosure and environmental performance. Environmental performance was measured as the percentage of materials recycled compared to total waste. Environmental disclosure was based on a content analysis of responsible party designation, toxic waste, oil and chemical spills and environmental penalties.

Thus, as this literature review has demonstrated, the results concerning the nature of this relation are very mixed.

2.2 RELATION BETWEEN ENVIRONMENTAL AND ECONOMIC PERFORMANCE

As in the previous chapter, this section is split into two segments. First, the theoretical perspective is presented, followed by the empirical perspective on the relation between environmental performance and financial performance.

2.2.1 Theoretical perspective

In general, three literature streams try to explain the different relations between environmental performance and financial performance. The traditional view suggests a negative association between environmental and financial performance; the revisionist view proposes a positive association; and a synthesized view combines the traditional and revisionist views.[169]

2.2.1.1 Traditionalist view

As noted above, the traditional view assumes a negative relation between environmental and financial performance. This argument is rooted in micro-economic theory because investments in the environment, e.g., in pollution abatement, will increase manufacturing costs and thereby cause increasing marginal cost and decreasing marginal benefits. This can be illustrated by Figure 12:[170]

169 Wagner, Schaltegger, & Wehrmeyer, 2001, pp. 97–101. Because environmental performance is a subset of Corporate Social Responsibility (CSR), this section will include relevant literature on CSR as well.

170 Wagner et al., 2001, pp. 97–101

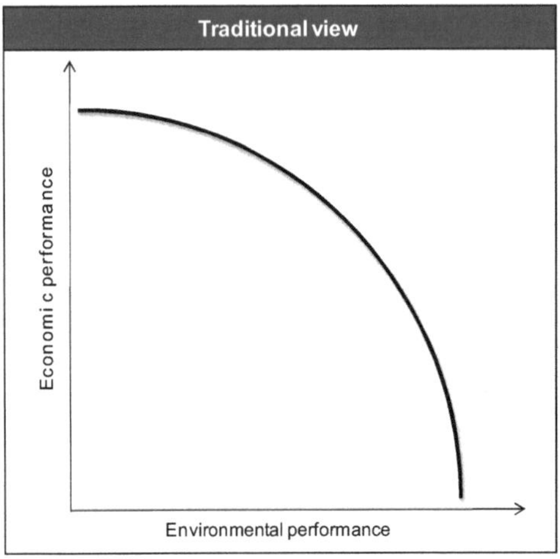

Figure 12: Traditional view of environmental and economic performance

Here, high environmental output leads to low economic output and vice versa. One might suggest that the relationship is monotonously decreasing, but this theory assumes (based on micro-economic theory) that the negative marginal impact of the environmental output on the economic performance is increasing.[171]

Ultimately, negative economic performance will lead to investors selling the company's stock and thereby decreasing its value.[172]

For a similar discussion on the relation between social responsibility and economic performance, see McGuire, Sundgren, & Schneeweis (1988).

2.2.1.2 Revisionist view

In the previous section, the traditional view was described, assuming a negative association between environmental performance and financial performance.

171 Wagner et al., 2001, pp. 97–101
172 Hassel, Nilsson, & Nyquist, 2005, p. 45 and Hassel et al., 2005, p. 56

Within the revisionist view, companies do not see ecological problems and their subsequent regulation as a threat but as an opportunity: the fight for resources (e.g., energy or water) and for green consumers may enable a corporation to gain competitive advantage.[173]

The revisionist view sees a lot of economic benefits to ecologically sound behavior.[174] The major benefits are as follows:

- ***Increase resource productivity:*** In order to protect the environment, less energy and other kinds of commodities are used, thereby reducing material consumption while increasing profits.[175]
- ***Extend and secure customer base:*** More consumers are interested in buying green products, and some are also willing to pay a premium. This might increase revenues and ultimately profits.[176]
- ***Minimize environmental liabilities:*** Because companies seek to avoid negative environmental impacts of their actions, e.g., by cutting CO_2 emissions, the probability of litigation and the likely amount of damages the company must pay will decrease.[177]
- ***Enhance corporate image:*** The public media might report less negative or even positive information about the company's environmental actions, which might have positive implications on other areas, e.g., consumers or financing.[178]
- ***Attract and motivate employees:*** Environmentally responsible companies are more attractive to potential employees and add more meaning to the work of existing employees.[179]

As described, the revisionist view sees a positive association between environmental and financial performance, meaning that an increase in environmental output leads to an increase in economic output as well. See Figure 13:

173 Shrivastava, 1995, p. 183, Helmers, 2008, p. 24 and Klassen & Whybark, 1999b, p. 602
174 Deutschland/Bundesministerium für Umwelt, Naturschutz und Reaktorsicherheit, 2001, pp. 6–10
175 Porter & van der Linde, 1995b, p. 133 and Porter & van der Linde, 1995a, pp. 105–106
176 Stahlmann, 1994, pp. 60–63 and Rao & Holt, 2005, p. 898
177 Shrivastava, 1995, p. 190 and Zabel, 1994, p. 14
178 Boström & Pöysti, 1992, pp. 3–4
179 Jahnke, 1994, p. 186 and Becke, 2000, pp. 10–15

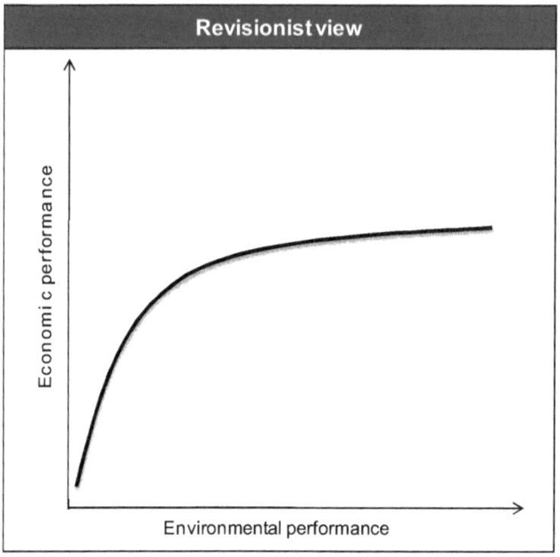

Figure 13: Revisionist view of environmental and economic performance

According to the revisionist view, the increase is not monotonously increasing (although the first derivative is positive); the second derivative is negative because this theory suggests that the marginal benefits of economic performance through environmental performance are decreasing.[180]

Because this attitude (revisionist view) gained significant popularity in recent decades, several new approaches were developed to integrate environmental concerns into the corporate world. The major ones are noted here:[181]

- Product stewardship[182]
- Eco-centric management[183]
- Lifecycle analysis[184]
- Design for environment/Green design[185]

---

180 Wagner et al., 2001, pp. 97–101
181 Sharma & Vredenburg, 1998, p. 730
182 Sarkis, 2001, p. 674
183 Shrivastava, 1995, pp. 183-200
184 Wang, 2009, p. 3, Fiksel, 1996, pp. 116–117, Ny, 2006, p. 2, Azapagic & Clift, 1999, p. 1510, Lei, Zhifeng, & Fung, 2003, p. 177, Menke, Davis, & Vigon, 1996, p. 1, Seppälä, 2003, p. 3, Guinée & Lindeijer, 2002, pp. 9–10, Baumann, 2004, pp. 19–20, Graedel, 1998, p. 18, Frankl, Rubik, & Bartolomeo, 2000, p. 2, Giudice, La Rosa, & Risitano, 2006, p. 96, de Udo Haes, 2002, p. 1, Owens, 1997, p. 38
185 Srivastava, 2007, p. 55, Zhang, Kuo, Lu, & Huang, 1997, p. 364, Angell & Klassen, 1999, p. 583, Sarkis, 1998, p. 160, Gupta, 1995, p. 44, Nochur, 1997, p. 69, Handfield, Walton, Seegers, & Melnyk, 1997, p. 298, Giudice et al., 2006, pp. 15-17 & 19-20, Loveday, 2000, p. 1,

- Green purchasing[186]
- Green supply chain management[187]
- Green manufacturing[188]

2.2.1.3 Synthesis of traditionalist and revisionist views

In the previous two sections, the two opposite views on the relationship between environmental and financial performance were described. However, the relationship need not be uni-directional and can take the form of a bell-shaped curve, as shown below:[189]

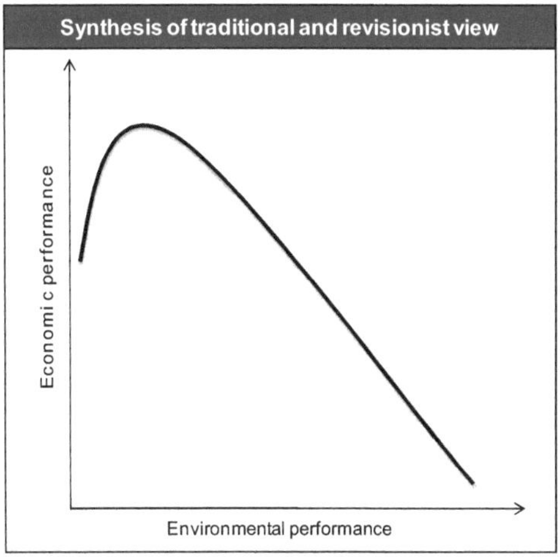

Figure 14: Synthesis view of environmental and economic performance

This means that until a certain point, increased environmental performance output (at low levels) can lead to increased economic performance, but beyond this point each additional unit of environmental output will actually decrease the economic value. Such a specification would also

Bullinger, Eversheim, & Haasis, 2000, pp. 27–46, Deutschland / Bundesministerium für Umwelt, Naturschutz und Reaktorsicherheit, 2001, pp. 272–277, Boström & Pöysti, 1992, pp. 95–103, Dyckhoff & Gießler, 1998, pp. 169–188

186 Rao & Holt, 2005, p. 901, Case, 2004, p. 30, 2007, p. 21, Case, 2005, pp. 10–11, Mebratu, 2001, p. 11, Hokey Min & Galle, 2001, p. 1222, 2000, p. 20, Min & Galle, 1997, p. 11, Vachon, 2007, p. 4372, Sarkis, 1998, p. 162, Carter, Kale, & Grimm, 2000, p. 220, 1993, p. 32

187 Rao & Holt, 2005, p. 899, Srivastava, 2007, pp. 53–54, Darnall et al., 2008, p. 33, Vachon, 2007, pp. 4359–4360, Qinghua Zhu et al., 2005, p. 451, Hines, 2000, p. 2, Zhu, Sarkis, & Lai, 2008, p. 262, Hervani, Helms, & Sarkis, 2005, p. 334, 2006, p. 797, Zhu & Sarkis, 2004, p. 267, 2008, p. 186, Dyckhoff, Lackes, Reese, & Fandel, 2004, pp. 14–19

188 Zabel, 1994, pp. 21–22, Zhang et al., 1997, p. 352, Shrivastava, 1995, p. 187, Spengler, Püchert, Penkuhn, & Rentz, 1997, p. 308, Dayna F Simpson & Damien J Power, 2005, p. 61, Rao, 2004, pp. 301–302, Rao, 2008, pp. 75–76, Michaelis, 1999, pp. 145–153, Schreiner, 1993, pp. 132–139, Technische Universität München., 2009, pp. 60–72, Fussler & James, 1999, pp. 120–121, Kreikebaum, 1994, pp. 105–107, Strebel, 1992, pp. 438–449

189 Wagner et al., 2001, pp. 97–101

be supported by micro-economic theory, taking into account the regulatory realities. Until state requests are fulfilled, all deviation from them would actually decrease company value because the company might face penalties or fines, but environmental protection beyond those limits would not add any more value to the company.[190]

2.2.2 Empirical perspective

Having described in the preceding sections theories that might explain different relations between environmental and financial performance, this chapter shall illustrate empirical findings on this topic. Overall, it can be stated that, similar to the relation between environmental disclosure and environmental performance, the results are mixed.[191]

Before moving to the empirical studies, a few unifying characteristics shall be described. First, all studies had to define their input parameters, which normally included some kind of environmental performance indicator and a dependent (output) variable, normally some kind of economic performance indicator. The input variables are very heterogeneous, and it is very rare that two studies consider the same kind of survey or member of certain environmental leadership groups. The output variables can be grouped into three segments: market-based, e.g., stock market performance; accounting-based, e.g., EBIT; or operations-based, e.g., lead time or product quality.

This chapter is split into three segments describing the empirical work showing a positive, negative and no association, respectively. In each segment, a distinction will be made between anecdotal evidence and results derived from larger samples.[192]

Positive association

Spicer (1978) was one of the first to tackle this relationship by analyzing a larger sample (18 companies from the pulp and paper industry). As input factors he used rankings of pollution control provided by the CEP. Different financial and investment indicators were used as output

190 Wagner et al., 2001, pp. 97–101
191 Al-Tuwaijri, Christensen, & Hughes, 2004, pp. 449–450, Christmann, 2000, p. 665 and Simpson & Power, 2005, p. 62
192 Bickhoff, 2000, pp. 29–34

factors, such as P/E ratios and companies' systematic risk. The result was that low polluters showed higher profitability.[193]

In 1996, Klassen and McLaughlin were among the first researchers to move away from classical anecdotal evidence and apply financial methodology (event-study approach) to describe a broader sample of firms that received positive or negative environmental press, e.g., because of environmental awards or pollution spills. These mentions in the press were used as input parameters, and the researchers then measured the abnormal performance of companies' stocks (output parameter) around the time of the relevant news. They found that stock markets reward positive news and punish negative news.[194]

In the same year, Florida (1996) analyzed how the use of new manufacturing and pollution prevention technology (as a proxy for environmental performance) impacted certain accounting numbers (economic performance), e.g., RoA (Return on Assets). The result showed a positive relationship as well.[195]

A similar step was taken by Gifford (1997), who analyzed the stock market performance of companies that invested heavily in environmental improvement measures. He found that after the investment, the riskiness of the stock decreased, and thereby the company's cost of capital was lowered. Consequently, the value of the firm rose.[196]

In 1997, Russo and Fouts used environmental ratings published by the Franklin Research and Development Group (FRDG) as indicators of environmental performance and RoA as an economic performance indicator. The results for 234 sample firms indicated a positive relationship between the environmental rating and the companies' economic performance.[197]

Judge and Douglas (1998) also found that the more environmental management was integrated into the companies' strategic planning process, the better the companies' financial performance became. Here, a survey was used to assess the quality of integration of environmental issues in

193 Spicer, 1978, p. 109
194 Klassen & McLaughlin, 1996, p. 1212
195 Florida, 1996, p. 82
196 Gifford, 1997, p. 11
197 Russo & Fouts, 1997, p. 534

the strategic planning process (input parameter), and Return on Sales (RoS) and RoA were used to evaluate the financial impact.[198]

Two years later, Dowell et al. (2000) analyzed the relationship between environmental performance ratings given by the Investor Responsibility Research Center (IRRC) and Tobin's q (a research indicator for economic performance) for 89 companies in the mining and production sector. They found a positive relation between these two variables.[199]

In the same year, Carter et al. (2000) and Hanna et al. (2000) started to analyze the economic impact of environmental actions of certain sub-functions, such as green purchasing. Both worked with surveys to assess the environmental performance of companies within their sub-functions. The economic performance was assessed with accounting numbers such as RoI, as used in Hanna et al. (2000), and net income or COGS, as used in Carter et al. (2000).[200]

A similar approach was taken by Melnyk et al. (2003), who analyzed how environmental management systems (EMS) affected operational performance indicators, e.g., lead time. As an approximation of environmental performance, they used a survey to assess the companies' quality of EMS.[201] Montabon et al. (2000) also analyzed the impact of ISO 14000 introduction on company performance (such as product quality and lead times) and found a positive relationship.[202]

In the same year, Hansmann et al. (2003) analyzed how companies within the Dow Jones Sustainability World Index (input parameter) performed versus the benchmark (Dow Jones Global Index). He found that during stock market upswings (1993-2000), the companies within the sustainability index performed better, but during the plunge from 1999-2003, they performed worse.[203]

As indicated in Chapter 2.1.2, Al-Tuwaijri et al. (2004) also studied the relationship between environmental and financial performance. They used CEP rankings as an approximation of

198 Judge & Douglas, 1998, p. 241
199 Dowell, Hart, & Yeung, 2000, p. 1059
200 Carter et al., 2000, p. 224
201 Melnyk, Sroufe, & Calantone, 2003, p. 344
202 Montabon, Melnyk, Sroufe, & Calantone, 2000, p. 4
203 Hansmann, Schlange, Seipold, & Wilkens, 2003, pp. 7–11

environmental performance and annual stock performance as an output variable for economic performance. They also found a positive relationship.[204]

Later, the first analyses on this topic were carried out in Asia. Rao and Holt (2005) studied how green supply chain management (GSCM) initiatives affected the economic performance of companies in southeast Asia. They used surveys to analyze the quality of green supply chains and compared their results with the companies' operational and accounting figures, e.g., profit margin, sales and market share.[205]

In 2004, Zhu and Sarkis analyzed the GSCM practices among Chinese manufacturers. Although GSCM was relatively immature in China at the time, they still found a positive relation with the company's operational performance, e.g., COGS.[206]

Besides those studies with large databases and statistical testing procedures, there is also anecdotal evidence within case studies describing how environmental performance positively affects financial performance. Jusko (2003) describes how the work of the EPA enabled GM to identify real opportunities. Shrivastava (1995) illustrates the Body Shop's positive experiences with applying a green strategy. Additionally, Geffen & Rothenberg (2000) describe how supplier interaction can actually reduce a company's environmental burden while maintaining cost and quality.

Negative association

Emission data from public sources, such as the Toxic Release Inventory published by the EPA, are commonly used to approximate environmental performance as an independent variable. Examples of this approach are Jaggi & Freedman (1992), Ahuja & Hart (1996) and Cordeiro & Sarkis (1997). However, the output parameters differed; whereas Jaggi & Freedman (1992) and Ahuja & Hart (1996) mainly used financial performance indicators such as RoA, RoS and net income, Cordeiro & Sarkis (1997) used analyst earnings projections for the next one to five years. All of them showed negative associations.

On the other hand, Christmann (2000) used a survey approach to check the quality of EMS and analyzed its implications for operational indicators (e.g., cost advantage).

204 Al-Tuwaijri et al., 2004, p. 447
205 Rao & Holt, 2005, p. 898
206 Zhu & Sarkis, 2007, p. 4352

One of the most recent studies on this topic is Hassel, Nilsson, & Nyquist, (2005), who analyzed how environmental performance (based on rankings by Caring Company Research) impacts several financial figures and stock market performance. They also showed a negative relationship.

No association

Within this section, studies that did not show a relationship between environmental and financial performance are described.

In 1975, Vance was one of the first to tackle the issue by comparing 14 companies that were previously described as highly socially responsible with the Dow Jones Industrial Average over several years. He found that it is not financially beneficial to behave in a socially responsible manner.[207]

In the same year, Fogler and Nutt (1975) analyzed how stock markets reacted when companies produced bad news regarding pollution of the environment. They found that no sell-off took place and company valuation remained largely unchanged.[208]

In several articles, authors have been very tentative in stating that there is no relationship, although they did not find any. As long as negative environmental performance does not exceed a certain threshold, investors do not care about environmental performance. For a detailed discussion of this argument, see Chen & Metcalf (1980) and Arlow & Cannon (1982).

On the other hand, some authors clearly state that there is no association between these two topics. See Cohen et al. (1997), who split the S&P 500 into high and low polluters and compared their stock market performance against each other.[209] Similar results were found by Luken (1997).

A completely different approach was chosen by Bowen et al. (2001), who checked the quality of GSCM within a survey and compared the results with the performance assessment of the participants (e.g., cost advantage) versus their competitors' and their own expectations.[210]

207 Vance, 1975, p. 18-23
208 Fogler & Nutt, 1975, p. 159
209 Cohen, Fenn, & Konar, 1997, p. 3
210 Bowen, Cousins, Lamming, & Faruk, 2001, p. 55

2.3 SUMMARY AND NEW APPROACH TO THEORETICAL FRAMEWORK

Summing up the major findings of the literature review on the relations between environmental disclosure, environmental performance and financial performance, it can be stated that existing results are inconclusive. Every theory that describes a certain association is backed by empirical studies.

There are four major reasons for this heterogeneous picture of relationships. The main focus of this segment explaining this heterogeneity will be on the relationship between environmental and financial performance, but the arguments hold true for the relationship between environmental disclosure and environmental performance as well.

First, the choice of input parameters (mainly environmental performance indicators) has an effect. Authors have used a wide range of different proxies for environmental performance, such as subjective environmental ratings of different organizations (e.g., IRRC and CEP), pollution control expenditures, emissions and so on. Of course, it can be questioned if variables like pollution control expenditures are an objective measure of environmental performance.[211]

Second, the same problem holds true for output parameters (economic performance), where even different categories of variables are used, such as accounting-based (e.g., RoS or RoA), market-based (stock market performance) or operations-based figures (e.g., lead time, product quality).[212]

Third, in most cases, moderating factors such as industry, firm size and profitability are not taken into account. Therefore, those variables could strongly influence the results.[213]

Fourth, in the majority of cases, environmental performance is used as the input parameter (independent variable) and economic performance as the output parameter (dependent variable). This need not be the case. Implicitly, researchers often assume that green behavior leads to good or bad economic performance. However, it could also be the case that good economic performance allows the company to behave in ways that are environmentally friendly. Therefore,

---

211 Wagner et al., 2001, p. 96
212 Wagner et al., 2001, p. 96
213 Wagner et al., 2001, p. 96

it is unclear which variables constitute cause and effect, respectively. This problem is called causality.[214]

In sum, it is not surprising to obtain inconclusive results if different problems are approached with different methodologies.[215]

This dissertation uses a new approach in an attempt to overcome some of the drawbacks (e.g., causality and lack of moderating factors) encountered in previous studies.

Generally speaking, most studies have employed a very classical mindset in combining the elements of environmental disclosure, environmental performance and financial performance.[216] The relations between these elements are depicted in Figure 15:

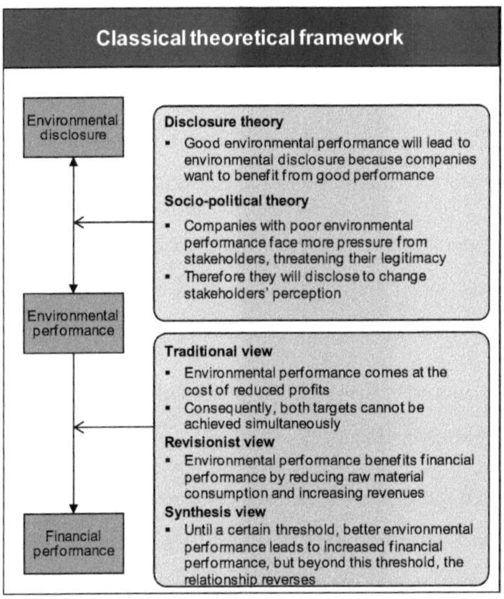

Figure 15: Classical theoretical framework

Here, the relation between the elements is assumed to be sequential. Environmental disclosure is related only to environmental performance and environmental performance only to financial

214 Wagner et al., 2001, p. 96
215 Wagner et al., 2001, p. 96
216 Except for Al-Tuwaijri et al. (2004), no one has checked for this relationship.

performance. Consequently all existing theories such as socio-political or disclosure theory, are developed in this sequential mindset.

Therefore classical theory does not suggest an association between environmental disclosure and financial performance.

However, market efficiency theory, based on Fama (1969) and Fama (1991), suggests that environmental disclosure is important to investors and might impact financial performance (here, stock market performance).

Therefore, a new approach to theory has been created. The new relationships are depicted in the picture below.

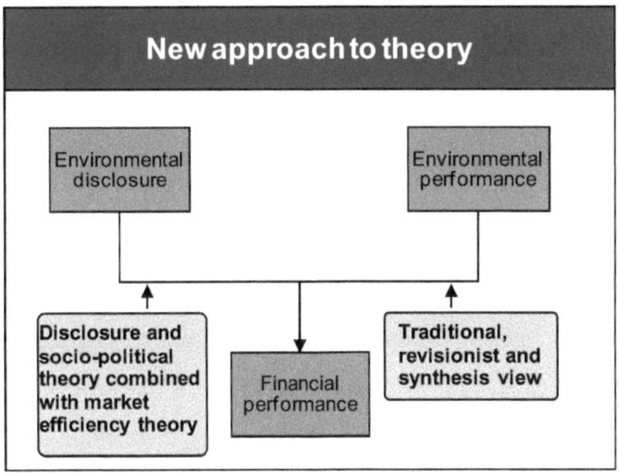

Figure 16: New approach to theory

Here, the old sequential relationship between the three elements is dissolved and changed to a setting where environmental disclosure and environmental performance can be examined separately in terms of their impacts on financial performance.

This newly created approach, together with the focus on CO_2 and its implications for stock market performance, have never been used before.

For further details, see Chapter Five for research questions, model set-up and hypothesis development.

3 Definition of terms

The previous two chapters described the need to conduct this study. Chapter 1 illustrated practitioners' interest in the topic, while Chapter 2 revealed the research gap. This chapter shall lay the foundations for the terms used later and provide the necessary context.

First, the term "sustainability" is defined and its different interpretations discussed. Based on that, "corporate social responsibility" (CSR) shall be defined, which is actually the derivation of sustainability for the business world. Afterwards, the term "environment" shall be focused on because it is the major concern within CSR. Drilling down even further, "environmental/green management" will be defined and the role of carbon consciousness discussed. Then, different definitions of "corporate success" will be provided and the term "event study" defined.

3.1 SUSTAINABILITY

There are many different definitions of the term "sustainability".[217] One of the best recognized[218] comes from the Brundtland report, which defines sustainability as "development that meets the needs of the present without compromising the ability of future generations to meet their own needs."[219]

Although this thinking was present in early forestry laws for decades, it became the basis for several environmental programs, e.g., that of the EU. In general, three major implications are derived from this definition.[220]

First, there is the aspect of integrating social, economic and environmental goals as equally weighted parts of the same development path of mankind. Second, intra-generational equity shall be achieved by allowing poorer countries to catch up to the standards of living of the industrialized world, even if this might come at the expense of reducing consumption in the first

217 Shrivastava, 1995, p. 184, Berry, 2002, p. 4 and Stahlmann, 1994, p. 72
218 Ny, 2006, p. 1, Wang, 2009, pp. 17–18, Ehrenfeld, p. 37 and Graedel, 1997, p. 53
219 Brundtland, 1987
220 Preuss, 2005, pp. 13–16

world. Finally, the inter-generational aspect of equity shall be addressed by using non-renewable resources in a responsible manner (i.e., consumption and pollution) so that future generations do not need to suffer from the actions of their ancestors.[221]

Although these implications are rather universal, four different types of interpretations of the Brundtland definition are common.[222]

The first is called the "treadmill" approach, which entails "business-as-usual" because mankind's ability to innovate is seen as paramount. Consequently, the problems of environmental pollution and scarce resources are perceived as merely in need of technical solutions. Therefore, sustainability in that sense almost means conventional growth.[223]

Within the second interpretation, the "weak form" of sustainability, environmental and social aspects of sustainability are integrated into everyday business so that the rate of depletion of non-renewable resources does not exceed its rate of replenishment. Thus, similar to the capital stock of a company, the environment's capital value is not depleted under this definition.[224]

Third, within the "strong form" of sustainability, authors suggest that a good environmental situation is a precondition for doing business. The circle of scientists who advocate for this definition (for example, see Berry (2002) is more focused on qualitative than on quantitative growth.[225]

Finally, within the fourth interpretation, the "ideal model" (also called the "deep ecology approach"), an abrupt change in social values is needed to radically improve the condition of the environment. This means restricting all economic growth; in other words, an increase in prosperity for the world's poorest has to be offset by a reduction in consumption by the industrialized world.[226]

Although the Brundtland definition is the best-known approach to sustainability, it is not free of criticism. Some researchers argue that it is highly focused on industrialized nations because it infringes upon the freedom of indigenous people to use as many resources as they like.

221 Baumast, 2001, p. 18, Bansal, 2005, p. 198, Berry, 2002, pp. 10–11 and Fussler & James, 1999, pp. 109–114
222 Preuss, 2005, pp. 13–16
223 Preuss, 2005, pp. 13–16
224 Baumast, 2001, p. 16, Angell & Klassen, 1999, p. 575, Giudice et al., 2006, pp. 3–4 and Faix, Kurz, & Wichert, 1995, pp. 15–16
225 Baumast, 2001, p. 16 and Giudice et al., 2006, pp. 1–2
226 Preuss, 2005, pp. 13–16

Additionally, it is seen as rather vague in that it sets no limits and does not provide a clear definition of "future needs".[227]

3.2 CORPORATE SOCIAL RESPONSIBILITY

Researchers have asked themselves how the social, ecological, and economic elements of sustainability can be translated to action plans for companies. Not surprisingly, they have used the same three principles to define the business analog, which is "Corporate Social Responsibility" (CSR).[228]

To understand these elements (social, ecological and economical), it is necessary to provide examples of what each could mean for a company.[229]

On a social level, CSR could mean that human capital is developed by extra training, balance of work and family, respect for the individual, self-directed work, and so on. It could also entail the development of social and cultural capital, e.g., strengthening of minorities' presence within the workforce and zero tolerance towards discrimination.[230]

On an ecological or environmental level, CSR could mean an increase in resource productivity, investment in renewable energy, or recycling. Its main goal is to reduce the ecological footprint of the company.[231]

And finally, on an economic level, CSR says that long-term wealth creation is more important than short-term profit maximization. Additionally, profits from financial products are considered with skepticism versus profits from real added value.[232]

3.3 ENVIRONMENT

This section shall focus on researchers' definition of the term "environment". Unfortunately, as for sustainability, there is no generally accepted definition. Instead, explanations and definitions

227 Preuss, 2005, pp. 13–16
228 Campino, pp. 63–64
229 Bansal, 2005, p. 199 and Ellram & Birou, 1995, p. 155
230 Campino, pp. 63–64 and Bansal, 2005, p. 198
231 Fischer & Schot, 1993, pp. 18–19, Campino, pp. 63–64, Bansal, 2005, p. 199 and Carter et al., 2000, p. 219
232 Campino, pp. 63–64 and Bansal, 2005, p. 198

of the term are abundant. Often the term has different meanings depending on the study (for example, see Baumann (2004), Michaelis (1999) and Meffert & Kirchgeorg (1998)). The same holds true for the term "ecology", which is often used as synonymous with "environment".[233]

Going forward, the definition of Hansmann and Voigt (1998) will be followed because it seems most adequate for the focus of the present study. Additionally, other authors, like (Peemöller, 2005), have used the same framework.

Within the approach of Hansmann and Voigt (1998), the term "environment" is defined as the specific vicinity of a system or a living unit, with which it is in a mutual relationship.[234]

In a business context, the corporate environment can be split into two segments. First is the anthropogenic environment (created by mankind), which can be grouped into:[235]

- Socio-cultural environment
- Political and legal environment
- Technological environment
- Economic environment

Second is the natural or ecological environment:

- Air
- Soil
- Water
- Creatures (plants, animals and humans)

In the past, research was mainly concentrated on the economic environment, but focus shifted when natural resources that were formerly available for free were used too extensively, leading to pollution and depletion problems such as air pollution, energetic emissions and liquid or solid pollution.[236]

Within this document, whenever the term "environment" is used, it is referring to the natural environment.

233 Streitferdt & Pfnür, 1998, p. 372 and Jahnke, 1994, pp. 176–177
234 Arentzen, 1997, p. 3868
235 Friedemann, 1998, p. 10 and Wagner, 1997, p. 2
236 Hansmann & Voigt, 1998, pp. 5–6, Schreiner, 1993, pp. 18–23 and Boström & Pöysti, 1992, p. 1

3.4 GREEN MANAGEMENT AND CARBON-CONSCIOUS BEHAVIOR

The situation for the term “green” or “green management” is similar to that of the term “environment”. Various definitions exist depending on the objective within each study, which makes its use rather ambiguous.[237] For example, in medicine, “greening” means minimizing the damage to human health, while in business, the term mainly refers to minimizing the environmental impact of economic actions. The main reason for this lack of clarity is the absence of a developed theoretical background.[238]

Some approaches have made initial attempts to resolve this ambiguity by splitting “greening” into two dimensions, relative and absolute. “Relative” refers to a comparison to the past or to a competitor (e.g., company X is green because its products are more environmentally friendly than company Y’s). However, these “green” products can still be detrimental to the environment. This is where the “absolute” meaning of greening comes into the picture. Here, a company or a product has no negative effects on the environment. Therefore, definitions of “green” or “green management” can be placed in either the absolute or the relative segment.[239]

To give a few examples, Bansal (2005) defined green or environmental management as an “effort by firms to reduce the size of their ‘ecological footprint’”.[240] Ellram and Birou (1995) saw it as a “philosophy of doing business in an environmentally friendly manner.”[241] Some authors also include societal issues in the term “green” as well. Peattie (1995) defined green management according to the following characteristics: “when its environmental and societal performance, in production, use and disposal, is significantly improved.”[242] For further definitions, see Meffert & Kirchgeorg (1998).

Summing up the different definitions of green management, it seems that the majority of definitions lean towards the relative interpretation of the term. The author did not find a single definition of green that could be considered absolute, probably because such a definition might be perceived as unrealistic.

---

237 Often, “green management” is also referred to as environmental management. Generally the two terms are synonyms.
238 Gupta, 1995, p. 36 and Zhu & Sarkis, 2004, p. 267. Generally speaking, the attitude towards environmental issues has developed quite significantly over time. For a detailed description of its historical development, see Peattie, 1995, p. 8 and Freimann, 1996, pp. 356–358
239 Deutschland/Umweltbundesamt, 1993, p. 40
240 Bansal, 2005, p. 199
241 Ellram & Birou, 1995, p. 157
242 Peattie, 1995, p. 181

However, even the relative definitions are rather abstract, so it is difficult for practitioners to make the best use of them. Therefore, this section shall briefly describe what green management could mean in practice.[243] More details are provided by Michaelis (1999), and Meffert & Kirchgeorg (1998).

As mentioned in the segment on consumers as stakeholders (chapter 2.1.1.1.1), customers want to know if a product is entirely environmentally friendly. This means that they are interested in the product's whole environmental life cycle, from the production stage (including all aspects of the supply chain) through the use phase and eventually to disposal. Therefore, green management must cover all functions of a company, such as design, production, procurement, logistics, quality, sales and after-sales. Nevertheless, green management does not stop at the borders of a company. Interactions with other parties, such as suppliers, consumers and recyclers, are vital as well. Consequently, green management is not just trying to reduce energy consumption and avoid waste on a vertical level (within the supply chain); it also tries to consolidate these efforts on an industry level if the environmental challenges are too substantial to be dealt with by one company.[244]

Companies can be classified in terms of the level of their green behavior based on their environmental efforts. As described by Peattie (1995), on the eco-performance continuum, companies like Body Shop, 3M and Norsk Hydro are labeled as green because they are environmentally excellent by current market standards. Worse environmentally performing companies are labeled light green, light grey, dark grey or black, where black corresponds to environmentally disruptive or societally unacceptable industries such as weaponry or tobacco.[245]

Another classification scheme is mainly used in the German-language literature, where there is a distinction between environmentally defensive and offensive companies. "Defensive" mainly refers to non-compliance with environmental standards, delaying necessary environmental actions and gaming the system. On the other hand, "offensive" means that the environment is a core element of corporate culture and philosophy (including goal setting), with top management

243 Because it is beyond the scope of this study, it will be not exhaustive.
244 Deutschland / Umweltbundesamt, 1993, p. 41, Stead & Stead, 2000, p. 324 and Carbon Trust, 2006, p. 1
245 Peattie, 1995, p. 182

paying attention to environmental issues, exceeding environmental standards and using green efforts to create a positive corporate image and promote products.[246]

Although the definitions and classifications of green and green management cover a good amount of the basic meaning of carbon-conscious behavior, they do not grasp the full extent of the term "carbon-consciousness".

Because this aspect of green management has not yet been analyzed, the author developed this concept from scratch.

Carbon-consciousness is a process starting with a very low level of consciousness about carbon and climate change and ending with a company that is totally aware of all of the risks and opportunities posed by climate change and acts accordingly. Within this study, not taking part in the CDP is perceived as an indication that the company is not carbon conscious at all. The first step of carbon consciousness is participation in CDP, which demonstrates to stakeholders that the company is aware of the problem. In the second stage, the company invests heavily in disclosing a large amount of high-quality data on company-specific CO_2- and climate-related issues. Eventually, the company is elected into the Carbon Disclosure Leadership Index (to be further described in Chapter 4). Reaching this level shows an even higher awareness of carbon issues. Finally, the disclosure of information is accompanied by high performance in the area of carbon management. This means that the company is not just disclosing information about its risk and opportunities through climate change, but actively reducing its carbon footprint and seizing its climate-related business opportunities, e.g., through appropriate products. If a company shows outstanding achievements in this area it is elected into the Carbon High-Performing Group.

For a depiction of the evolutionary model, see Figure 17:

246 Schreiner, 1993, pp. 46–55

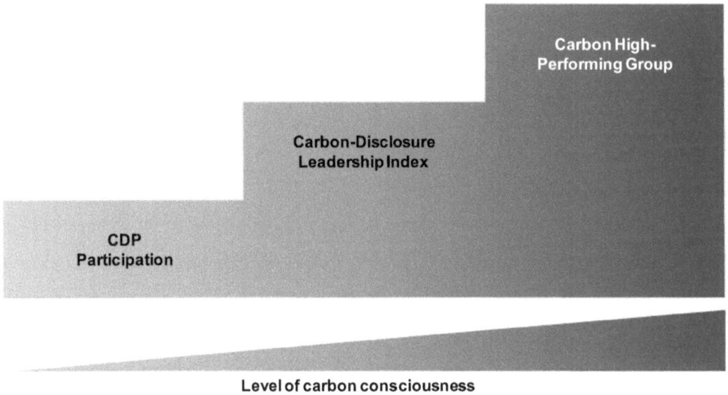

Figure 17: Level of carbon consciousness

Although it is highly likely, it must be noted that it is not necessary for a company to be a part of the Carbon Disclosure Leadership Index in order to become a member of the Carbon High-Performance Group.

Generally speaking, carbon-consciousness can be seen as an indicator of the maturity of a company's carbon behavior.

3.5 CORPORATE SUCCESS

Generally, success is defined as the extent to which a goal is achieved. However, in the case of a company, several goals are pursued rather than just one. This is called a multi-variable target system.[247]

In the classical economic literature, corporate success is narrowly defined mainly by profit as a residual of revenue and cost. However, some literature streams have moved to a broader definition of corporate success, such as Fritz (1992). Here, other goals besides profit maximization are integrated into the corporate target system, such as reputation, quality or employee motivation, etc.[248]

247 Bickhoff, 2000, pp. 80–85
248 Fritz, 1992, pp. 217–221

These goals are the result of different influencing factors, such as interest groups (e.g., customers, suppliers, or NGOs), situational factors (e.g., competition, product, or portfolio), ecological factors (e.g., resource efficiency or emission limits) and societal factors (e.g., workplace conditions, employee satisfaction).[249]

Of course, some of these targets are easier to measure than others that are more qualitative by nature. This disparity is the major reason why empirical studies mainly focus on financial goals (in particular, ROI). However this absence of other non-financial goals has been the subject of widespread criticism among researchers. Additionally, financial figures are not as objective as some readers might assume; instead, they need to be viewed rather skeptically because they might be the subject of manipulation through company-specific situations or different accounting standards. All of these concerns might deter the perceived objectivity of accounting numbers.[250]

To overcome this problem, researchers have developed several approaches to integrate different goals into quantitative frameworks. The work of Fritz (1992) shall be illustrated here as an example. He used a weighted index (called Total Company Target Fulfillment) to aggregate all 24 company goals (which he assumed to cover all possible company goals) into one number.[251]

$$TCTF_i = \sum_{j=1}^{n} B_{ij} * E_{ij} \quad \textbf{(1)}$$

$TCTF_i$: Total Company Target Fulfillment for company i

B_{ij}: Importance of target j for company i

E_{ij}: Target fulfillment of target j through company i

n: Number of targets in target system (here, n=24)

For this study, the focus will be on financial figures (i.e., stock market performance) because it is not known which goals are pursued by the company, how important each goal is and which level of fulfillment has been achieved. Additionally, stock market performance as a proxy for financial figures is not subject to manipulation because third parties (market participants) assess the impact of another party's (company) action. Further on, investors will implicitly consider other goals such as sustainability of a business strategy because they are interested in value creation, and not

249 Breidenbach, 1999, pp. 23–30
250 Fritz, 1992, pp. 221–223
251 Fritz, 1992, pp. 223–229

negative press (through environmental or societal scandals), which is damaging to a company's reputation and might eventually hurt the bottom line.[252]

3.6 EVENT STUDY

Event studies examine the effect on a company's asset prices (e.g., stock or bond prices) induced by a major corporate event (e.g., earnings or merger announcements, changes in dividend policy).[253]

However, this methodology cannot be used just for mean stock or bond price effects, but also for changes in return variance[254], trading volume[255], operating performance[256] and to test for market efficiency.[257]

One of this methodology's major benefits, which has been put to frequent use in scientific literature, is objective valuation through the marketplace.[258] Therefore, event studies do not rely on accounting numbers[259], which are subject to manipulation by insiders.[260] Furthermore, they have a clear cause and effect relationship.[261]

Due to this methodological superiority versus other research approaches, event studies are one of the most frequently used analytical tools in financial research.[262] Prior to their development, "there was little evidence on the central issues of corporate finance. Now we are overwhelmed with results, mostly from event studies".[263]

A more comprehensive description of event studies will follow in Chapter Six.

252 Zabel, 1994, pp. 8–9 and Kreikebaum, 1994, pp. 104–105
253 Campbell, Lo, & MacKinlay, 1997, p. 149, Binder, 1998, p. 111, Dwyer, 2001, p. 2, Dwyer, 2001, p. 1, Gebken, 2008, p. 24 and Fama, 1969, pp. 3–5
254 Beaver, 1968, p. 67 and Patell, 1976, pp. 246–248
255 Campbell & Wasley, 1993, pp. 73–75 and Beaver, 1968, p. 67
256 Barber & Lyon, 1996, p. 359
257 Kothari & Warner, 2006, p. 4 and Prabhala, 1997, p. 2
258 Mentz, 2006, p. 44
259 Benston, 1982, pp. 161–162
260 McWilliams & Siegel, 1997, pp. 626–627
261 Mentz, 2006, p. 45
262 Peterson, 1989, p. 36 and Kothari & Warner, 2006, p. 4
263 Fama, 1991, p. 1600

4 Carbon Disclosure Project and its Global 500 report

Because this study relies heavily on the outcomes provided by the CDP, this segment shall first describe what the CDP is and what it does. Second, it shall describe the CDP's Global 500 report published in 2009.

4.1 THE CARBON DISCLOSURE PROJECT AS AN ORGANIZATION

The CDP was founded in 2000 by institutional investors whose goal was to collect information about companies' risk associated with climate change[264] in an institutionalized manner.[265]

Over time, the number of institutional investors supporting the CDP (also called signatory investors) increased to 534, who have assets under management totaling USD 64 trillion. This equals approximately 91% of global GDP[266] or 125% of global market capitalization.[267]

As the number of signatory investors rose, so did the number of participating companies. As can be seen in Figure 18, within just six years, the number of respondents increased more than tenfold. Within this group, most of the biggest companies in the world are represented, such as Apple, Chevron, Wal-Mart, Dell, and Unilever.

264 PriceWaterhouseCoopers, 2009, p. 8
265 Stanny & Ely, 2008, p. 339
266 International Monetary Fund. Global GDP is assumed to be approximately 70 bn USD for 2009
267 PriceWaterhouseCoopers, 2009. Most current data on global market capitalization are from 2007.

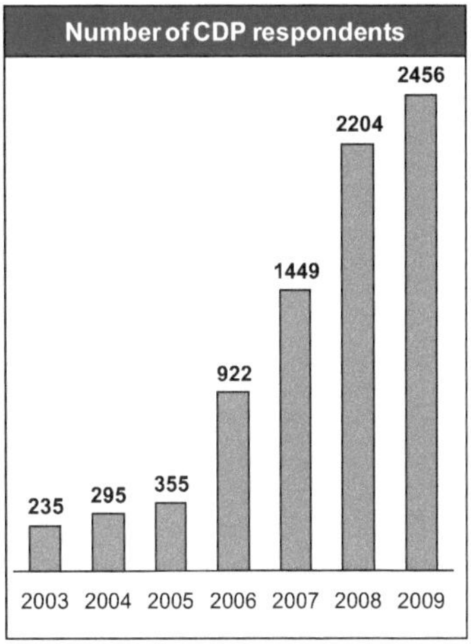

Figure 18: Number of CDP respondents by year (adapted from CDP website)

The track record of CDP's achievements is remarkable. CDP hosts the largest database of company-specific CO_2 emissions, representing 26% of global anthropogenic CO_2 emissions.[268]

Additionally, CDP has worked together with the major auditing companies (Ernst & Young, Deloitte, KPMG and PWC) to develop a standard carbon accounting system. Another example of the esteem with which CDP is regarded is shown by the fact that Bloomberg included the data in its Professional Service System.[269]

Further, CDP data are used to create "carbon betas", showing a company's sensitivity to carbon and climate change; for example, utilities or oil and gas companies have a high carbon beta, whereas banks would have a low carbon beta.[270]

This information, together with other CDP data, will be used to create ETFs (exchange traded funds) to enable investors to buy a group of companies based on the Carbon Disclosure Leadership Index (described later on).[271]

268 PriceWaterhouseCoopers, 2009, p. 13
269 PriceWaterhouseCoopers, 2009, p. 13
270 Kolk et al., 2008, p. 742
271 PriceWaterhouseCoopers, 2009, p. 13

Because of these achievements and its aspirational goals, CDP has also gained quite extensive political backing from Tony Blair (former UK prime minister), Dr. Angela Merkel (German chancellor), Ban Ki-Moon (UN Secretary General), and others.[272]

But not just politicians acknowledge the tremendous value CDP adds; institutional investors (according to recent studies) say that CDP data plays an important role in their investment decisions.[273]

4.2 GLOBAL 500 REPORT

4.2.1 Global 500, response rates and CO_2 emissions covered

The list of the 500 largest public companies changes almost every year due to economic circumstances, M&A activity, and other changes. A list of the included companies can be found in the appendix.

Taking a deeper look at the geographical composition of these companies, it is obvious that North America contains the most, with 222 (44%), Europe the second most, with 147 (29%), followed by Japan, with 58 companies.[274]

The response rate increased to 82% (representing 409 companies) from 77% in 2008.[275] The largest rise was in the utility sector, where the number of responding companies increased from 26 to 39. Overall, the information technology sector had the highest response rate, with 93%. More than one third of all participating countries (13 out of 36) had a response rate of 100%. These were Australia, Belgium, Brazil, Denmark, Germany, Ireland, Netherlands, Norway, Portugal, South Africa, South Korea, Sweden and Thailand.:[276]

272 PriceWaterhouseCoopers, 2009
273 Lee & Lee, 2009, pp. 1-2
274 PriceWaterhouseCoopers, 2009, p. 20
275 It shall be noted that the number of respondents (409) provided within the CDP report is slightly smaller than the number according to the data set the author received from CDP, which was 411. This difference probably stems from responses that were received late. Within this chapter, the number 409 will be used because it is the basis for the total report. For the analysis, 411 will be used, as it is the most current figure.
276 PriceWaterhouseCoopers, 2009, pp. 8–9

The largest non-respondent companies are mostly from the energy sector and/or from the BRIC region. For details, see Table 2:[277]

Sector	Company
Telecommunications	América Móvil
Energy	PetroChina
Telecommunications	China Mobile
Energy	China Petroleum & Chemical
Financials	Bank of China
Financials	Berkshire Hathaway
Consumer Staples	Philip Morris International
Energy	Reliance Industries
Energy	Rosneft
Health Care	Teva Pharmaceuticals Industries

Table 2: Largest non-respondents in 2009 (Source: CDP Global 500 Report)

Because the number of responding companies increased, so did the amount of disclosed CO_2 emissions, as seen in Figure 19:

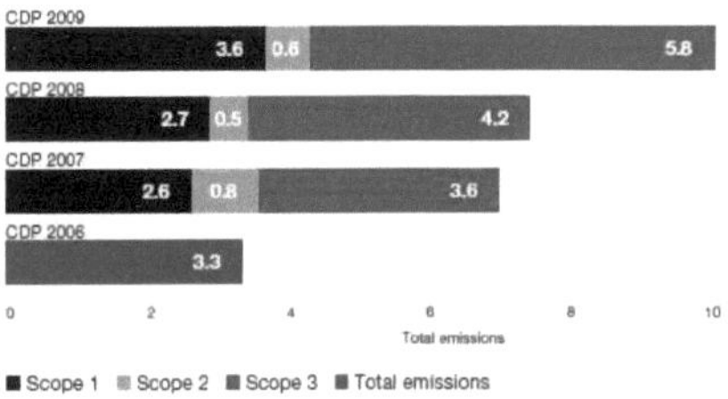

Figure 19: Total reported emissions (Scopes 1, 2 and 3) in billions of tons of CO_2 (Source: CDP Global 500 Report)

Scope 1 emissions, which are those emissions attributed to "sources that are owned or controlled by the institution, including: (…) stationary combustion of fossil fuels; mobile combustion of fossil fuels by institution owned/controlled vehicles"[278], increased by 34% versus 2008.[279]

Scope 2 emissions, which are those emissions attributed to "indirect emissions generated in the production of electricity consumed by the institution"[280], surged by 20% versus 2008.[281]

277 PriceWaterhouseCoopers, 2009, pp. 8–9
278 CampusClimateNetwork, 2008
279 PriceWaterhouseCoopers, 2009, p. 21
280 CampusClimateNetwork, 2008
281 PriceWaterhouseCoopers, 2009, p. 21

Scope 3 emissions, which include all other indirect emissions that are "a consequence of the activities of the institution, but occur from sources not owned or controlled by the institution such as commuting, air travel (…), waste disposal; embodied emissions from extraction, production, and transportation of purchased goods; outsourced activities; contractor owned- vehicles; and line loss from electricity transmission and distribution"[282], increased by 37% versus 2008.[283]

However, this development was only possible because in addition to the increased number of participating companies, companies also disclosed more emission data than they did in 2008, e.g., more emission forecasts. For an illustration, see Figure 20.

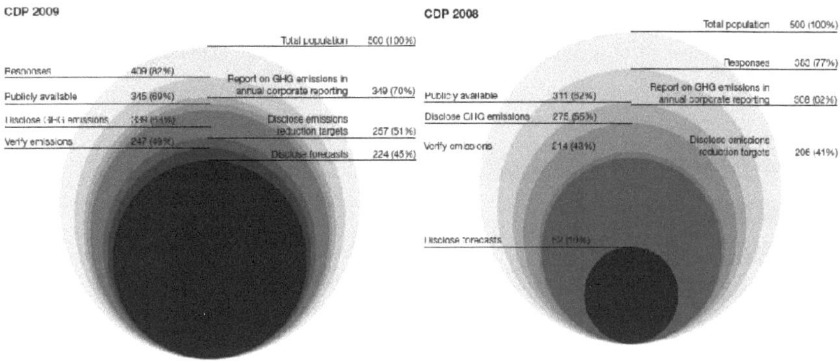

284

Figure 20: Proportion of Global 500 at each disclosure level - year-on-year (Source: CDP Global 500 report)

4.2.2 Carbon disclosure score

Generally, all companies that participate in the CDP are scored in terms of their quality of disclosure based on a standardized and transparent methodology.[285]

A high score reflects a company's ability to manage and report on carbon and climate change in relation to its business.[286]

---

282 CampusClimateNetwork, 2008
283 PriceWaterhouseCoopers, 2009, p. 21
284 PriceWaterhouseCoopers, 2009, p. 10
285 For further details on the methodology, see http://www.cdproject.net.

To put the score into perspective, it is necessary to note the following aspects.[287]

- The score is solely dependent on the company's disclosure information within the CDP response sheet.
- It does not consider other company efforts to provide carbon or sustainability information, such as environmental statements within the annual report or meetings with stakeholders.
- It is not a metric for a company's performance with regard to climate change management.[288]

In 2009, 10% of the Global 500, i.e., 50 companies, defined the Carbon Disclosure Leadership Index (CDLI). The companies within this index had to fulfill three prerequisites:[289]

First, they needed to belong to the best-scoring 10% of companies across all industries.[290] Second, the responses needed to be publicly available (companies could also request that their information be kept confidential). Third, they needed to use the online submission system.[291]

The major findings for the CDLI were, first, that almost all industries (9 out of 10) were represented. Only Telecommunication was absent. This shows that it is possible for all companies (irrespective of industry) to join this exclusive "club". The financial sector was best represented within the index (11 companies). Of those, four companies were Australian and just two American.[292]

Companies from nine countries showed up in the CDLI, four of which (Australia, Germany, UK and US) had more than five companies represented. The majority (almost 50%) came from the US. Only one Asian company (Samsung Electronics) was included.[293]

Critics might argue that this result is not surprising as industrialized regions (like Europe, North America and Australia) already have laws in place that force companies to disclose parts of the required information. However, it is worthwhile to highlight that the highest scoring companies

286 PriceWaterhouseCoopers, 2009, p. 9
287 PriceWaterhouseCoopers, 2009, p. 17
288 PriceWaterhouseCoopers, 2009, p. 17
289 PriceWaterhouseCoopers, 2009, p. 9
290 Therefore, no distinction is made between carbon-intensive and non-carbon-intensive industries. Consequently, companies were not penalized if they did not respond to questions because they were not relevant to their business.
291 PriceWaterhouseCoopers, 2009, p. 9
292 PriceWaterhouseCoopers, 2009, p. 18
293 PriceWaterhouseCoopers, 2009, p. 18

(Samsung Electronics, Vale, Anglo Platinum, Taiwan Semiconductor and Sasol) are based in countries that did not sign the Kyoto Protocol. For a full list of all companies represented in the Carbon Disclosure Index, see Table 3:[294]

Sector	Company	Score	Emissions Intensity*	Scope 1	Scope 2**	Scope 3***
Consumer Discretionary	Carnival	87	703	10,247,517	50,748	19,150
	BMW Bayerische Motoren Werke	79	17	375,425	875,036	395,297
Consumer Staples	Wal-Mart Stores	89	56	5,566,006	15,500,950	
	Woolworths	82	95	675,991	2,432,728	85,313,090†
	Reckitt Benckiser	80	44	125,795	165,264	18,215,832†
Energy	Chevron	88	267	62,978,970	5,216,351	382,000,000
	Spectra Energy	88	2,175	9,614,164	1,421,690	4,419
	Hess	86	274	10,714,780	574,092	78,037,693
	Total	81	275	57,900,000	3,500,000	603,100,000
	Anadarko Petroleum	79	610	8,284,413	641,458	0
	Transocean	79	170	2,148,208	4,762	1,803,735
Financials	HSBC Holdings	92	7	102,933	771,506	107,445
	Bank of Montreal	87	3	15,898	32,980	14,690†
	Simon Property Group	86	189	26,068	689,914	2,876
	Allianz	83	4	73,762	396,833	187,962
	Australia and New Zealand Banking Group	82	8	14,615	184,422	18,789
	National Australia Bank	82	6	15,337	208,468	16,107†
	Commonwealth Bank of Australia	81	6	10,933	137,046	0†
	Aviva	80	13	61,886	204,521	26,409
	Lloyds Banking Group	80	22	97,700	357,942	25,129
	Westpac Banking	80	6	6,316	121,108	20,126
	Allstate	79	7	33,575	178,892	57,071
Health Care	Bayer	95	165	4,000,000	3,570,000	21,900,000
	Allergan	85	24	45,643	58,567	32,548
	Schering-Plough	85	54	446,987	557,157	32,416
	Biogen Idec	83	24	49,459	47,438	4,234†
	Johnson & Johnson	83	21	356,729	970,543	369,673
	GlaxoSmithKline	79	85	945,678	1,133,549	4,911,482
Industrials	Boeing	87	28	575,000	1,104,000	280,140
	Burlington Northern Santa Fe	85	844	14,889,927	323,267	27,715
	Siemens	85	33	1,480,000	2,060,000	1,051,200
	United Parcel Service	82	257	12,148,866	1,105,134	2,357,467
Information Technology	Cisco Systems	88	15	51,620	546,762	197,951
	Samsung Electronics	87	97	4,043,115	5,276,142	96,104,520
	Hewlett-Packard	86	21	303,844	2,145,534	5,926,506
	EMC	82	25	35,850	335,770	60,500
Materials	BASF	94	320	23,531,528	4,156,188	113,184,000
	Rio Tinto	87	927	30,300,000	20,000,000	657,555,000
	Lafarge	84	4,489	108,879,000	9,889,000	2,264,000
	Praxair	83	1,244	3,695,830	9,732,516	265,292
	BHP Billiton	82	1,131	23,093,870	28,798,955	318,872,809
	E.I du Pont de Nemours	80	437	9,336,753	4,002,807	74,957
Utilities	PG&E	88	235	1,903,901	1,535,505	22,569,017
	Public Service Enterprise Group	88	1,962	24,287,856	1,851,103	42,593,087
	Union Fenosa	86	2,008	19,034,052	1,036,883	10,583,502
	Centrica	84	520	10,871,403	232,294	23,317,006
	RWE	83	3,743	172,100,000	75,080,000	68,145,400
	FPL Group	82	2,813	46,007,608	168,880	14,987
	Consolidated Edison	79	351	4,211,511	557,918	0†
	Fortum	79	2,324	17,903,090	308,000	4,078,570

Table 3: Carbon Disclosure Leadership Index 2009 (Source: CDP Global 500 report)

4.2.3 Carbon performance score

The Carbon performance score was set up for the first time in the 2009 report and was therefore still in a pilot phase.[295]

294 PriceWaterhouseCoopers, 2009, p. 18
295 PriceWaterhouseCoopers, 2009, p. 27

Its goal is to assess the impact of climate change actions and activities and consequently award performance points for managing regulatory, physical and commercial risks. Differently, the disclosure score also assigns points if a company discloses that it does not have a certain kind of strategy or plan, e.g., an emission reduction plan.[296]

For example, performance points can be awarded for business continuity plans for natural disasters (e.g., flooding) impacting production sites, implementing regulation and policy monitoring teams, introducing new products and services to capitalize on changes in consumer behavior due to climate change, setting emission reduction targets, or engagements with policy makers.[297]

Although the performance scoring does not impact the disclosure scores, performance scores can only be awarded if the information is disclosed. Therefore, a certain correlation is a given. Additionally, in this CDP report, performance scores will be provided only on an aggregated level, such as country- or sector-specific.[298]

The major findings for the performance score were:[299]

A high percentage (78%) of respondents had emission reduction targets, whereas just 54% of BRIC companies had emission reduction targets. Companies in Europe and North America showed high engagement with policy makers (77% and 65%, respectively). Asian companies are still lagging behind in this respect (49%). The leadership group (containing 12 companies) showed a strong focus on Europe, where more than half had their origins. Fur a full list, see Figure 21:[300]

296 PriceWaterhouseCoopers, 2009, p. 28
297 PriceWaterhouseCoopers, 2009, p. 29
298 PriceWaterhouseCoopers, 2009, p. 11
299 Lee, 2009, p. 1
300 PriceWaterhouseCoopers, 2009, p. 11

Company	Sector	Region
Accenture	Information Technology	North America
Allianz	Financials	Europe
BASF	Materials	Europe
Boeing	Industrials	North America
Cisco Systems	Information Technology	North America
Consolidated Edison	Utilities	North America
EMC	Information Technology	North America
Nokia Group	Information Technology	Europe
Reckitt Benckiser	Consumer Staples	Europe
Royal Dutch Shell	Energy	Europe
Siemens	Industrials	Europe
Swiss Re	Financials	Europe

Figure 21: Carbon High Performance Group (Source: CDP Global 500 Report)

On a sector level, the information technology industry is surprisingly also represented by four companies (as in the CDLI, although this group is more than four times larger).[301]

Additionally, it seems that there is a strong link between good disclosers and good performers because almost 70% of the Carbon High Performance Group member companies were also members of the CDLI. These were Allianz, BASF, Boeing, Cisco Systems, Consolidated Edison, EMS, Reckitt Benckiser and Siemens.[302]

4.2.4 Geographic and industry overview

In order to give more meaning to the results, it is worthwhile to take a geographic and an industrial perspective on the results.

Overall, it can be stated that the total disclosed scope 1 emissions equal 11.5% of global anthropogenic CO_2 emissions.[303]

The key facts on a country level can be taken from Figure 22:

301 PriceWaterhouseCoopers, 2009, p. 11
302 PriceWaterhouseCoopers, 2009, p. 28
303 PriceWaterhouseCoopers, 2009, p. 26

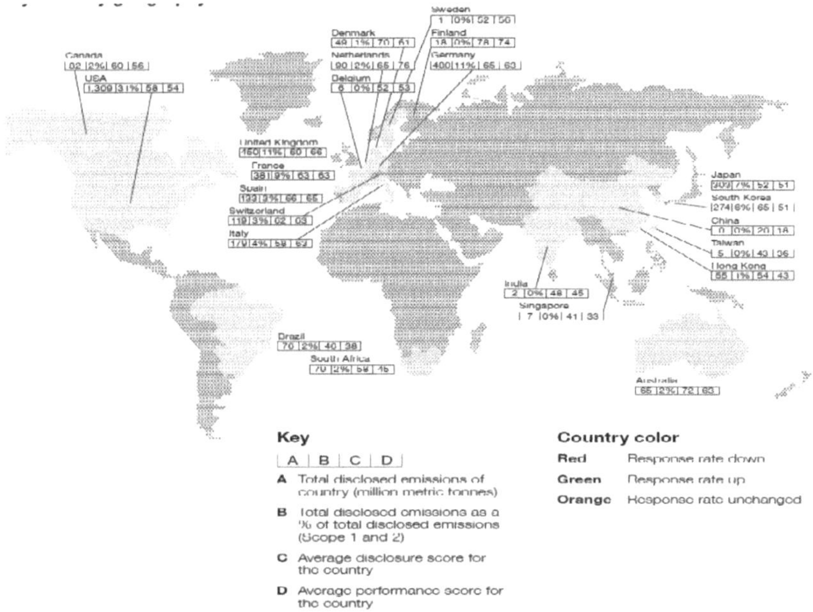

Figure 22: Key facts by geography (Source: CDP Global 500 Report)

Here, the first field (A) shows the disclosed emissions (Scopes 1 and 2) of the companies originating from that country (in millions of metric tons). The second field (B) shows the share of these disclosed emissions compared to the global disclosed emissions of companies. The third field (C) shows the average disclosure score and the fourth field (D) the average performance score. The color of the country indicates if the response rate went up (green)[304], down (red)[305] or remained unchanged (orange)[306].[307]

One of the major findings is that companies in just five countries (US, Germany, UK, France and Japan) account for 70% of the disclosed emissions. However, only the UK companies also ranked among the top five for disclosure scores. Furthermore, Europe is the region with the highest

304 Green: US, Canada, Brazil, Italy, Spain, France, Germany, Denmark, Belgium, India, China, Singapore, Taiwan, Hong Kong, South Korea
305 UK, Switzerland, Finland and Japan
306 Sweden, South Africa and Australia
307 PriceWaterhouseCoopers, 2009, p. 26

disclosed emissions, despite also having the highest average disclosure and performance scores.[308]

As previously noted, overall disclosure levels increased in 2009. However, there is still significant variation on a sector level. For an overview, see below:

Sector	Year	Total population	Responded	Publicly available	Report on GHG emissions in annual corporate reporting	Disclose GHG emissions	Verify emissions	Disclose emissions reduction targets	Disclose forecasts
Consumer Discretionary	CDP 2009	37	28	78%	88%	83%	64%	61%	64%
	CDP 2008	33	32	72%	84%	88%	63%	59%	18%
Consumer Staples	CDP 2009	51	45	88%	95%	89%	63%	78%	63%
	CDP 2008	92	37	89%	80%	81%	68%	61%	11%
Energy	CDP 2009	54	39	88%	95%	98%	68%	69%	59%
	CDP 2008	56	30	87%	82%	69%	64%	48%	10%
Financials	CDP 2009	109	90	77%	83%	79%	62%	53%	53%
	CDP 2008	91	93	84%	74%	65%	45%	44%	3%
Health care	CDP 2009	43	37	90%	80%	89%	51%	71%	57%
	CDP 2008	47	31	81%	77%	71%	52%	58%	16%
Industrials	CDP 2009	54	41	78%	88%	78%	59%	63%	40%
	CDP 2008	54	37	68%	51%	57%	35%	60%	14%
Information Technology	CDP 2009	40	37	86%	88%	92%	74%	71%	65%
	CDP 2008	44	32	84%	69%	69%	66%	50%	22%
Materials	CDP 2009	36	30	90%	97%	93%	80%	77%	90%
	CDP 2008	36	32	78%	94%	91%	78%	63%	13%
Telecoms	CDP 2009	33	23	91%	91%	100%	64%	72%	46%
	CDP 2008	31	24	75%	92%	88%	67%	56%	21%
Utilities	CDP 2009	44	30	84%	100%	100%	86%	78%	81%
	CDP 2008	57	26	89%	81%	85%	69%	62%	19%
Global (G500)	CDP 2009	500	409	84%	86%	83%	60%	63%	55%
	CDP 2008	500	383	81%	80%	77%	60%	58%	15%

Table 4: Change in level of disclosure by sector (Source: CDP Global 500 Report)

The responses on an industry level can be grouped into three buckets (risks and opportunities, emission reporting and governance).[309]

Risks and opportunities

Generally, all sectors identified industry-specific risk and opportunities. Whereas energy, utilities and health care saw more risks than opportunities, consumer staples, industrial and information technology saw more opportunities.[310]

In particular, carbon-intensive sectors such as utilities, energy and materials saw great risk through regulatory action. In terms of physical risk, sectors such as telecommunication, materials, utilities and financials saw themselves as most threatened.[311]

As expected, the three most carbon-intensive sectors, energy, utilities and materials, are above the average disclosure score. Financials also scored well in this regard.[312]

308 PriceWaterhouseCoopers, 2009, p. 26
309 PriceWaterhouseCoopers, 2009, p. 26
310 PriceWaterhouseCoopers, 2009, p. 26
311 PriceWaterhouseCoopers, 2009, p. 26
312 PriceWaterhouseCoopers, 2009, p. 26

Reporting of emissions

Scope 1 and 2 level disclosures were well performed across all sectors. However, scope 3 emissions are still the weakest area for all sectors. This pattern likely exists because companies report only emissions that are under their control. [313]

Governance[314]

Generally, all sectors performed well in disclosing this information. The highest scoring sectors in this area were once again utilities, materials and health care. Additionally, utilities and materials showed the highest shares of companies having a board-level member responsible for climate change. [315]

4.3 CRITIQUE OF THE CARBON DISCLOSURE PROJECT

Of course, besides all of the positive aspects of the CDP that create transparency for investors on businesses' climate issues, several points have raised skepticism among researchers assessing the validity and usefulness of the CDP's report.

One aspect that is mentioned quite often is the fact that signatory investors (e.g., investment banks, insurance companies, pension funds) do not need to disclose their own carbon information, which raises the possibility that they are motivated to become signatory investors just for image reasons.[316]

However, checking the response rate of all financial companies in the Global 500 sample, it can be seen that more than 80% participated in the CDP in 2009. Therefore, the response rate is just slightly below the general response rate of 82%.

Another negative aspect that has been brought forward is the fact that data are not comparable between companies. Two major reasons for this are, first, that carbon accounting standards are

313 PriceWaterhouseCoopers, 2009, p. 26
314 Governance refers to all organizational aspects, such as climate-friendly incentive systems and board-level responsibility for climate issues.
315 PriceWaterhouseCoopers, 2009, p. 26
316 Kolk et al., 2008, p. 731

not universal and there is no standard for calculating GHG emissions. Second, in many cases, emission data are not verified by independent third parties.[317]

Picking up on the aspect of lack of external validation, this argument seems valid as just half of all respondents validated their emissions. However, the percentage increased from 43% in 2008 to 49% in 2009. The lack of uniform and standard carbon accounting principles seems a valid point that needs to be resolved as soon as possible to guarantee comparability across firms. [318]

The third negative aspect is that CDP does not provide a risk measure to quantify a company's exposure to climate risk. This makes it hard for investors to compare financial risk scenarios across firms.[319]

Additionally, readers should be aware of the fact that CDP has changed the questionnaires over time, making it hard to compare current disclosure scores with past publications.[320]

In sum, the CDP methodology still needs improvement, and carbon accounting standards must become more widely accepted. However, the information provided by CDP is the best available to investors and, as recent studies indicate, is an important contributor to the decision process. Researchers should bear in mind that even with widely accepted accounting standards, such as US-GAAP or IFRS, companies have many chances to manipulate their accounting figures.

317 Kolk et al., 2008, pp. 733–736
318 Kolk et al., 2008, pp. 733–736
319 Kolk et al., 2008, pp. 736–740
320 Kolk et al., 2008, pp. 733–736

5 Research questions, model setup and hypothesis development

This chapter shall illustrate how the title of the document, "Does carbon-conscious behavior drive firm performance?" is disaggregated into its three main research questions, which directly relate the companies' CDP activity.[321]

Later, survey-specific research questions will be described. In the next step, the pathways from carbon-conscious behavior to financial performance shall be described. Depending on which theory is assumed, different outcomes within the model will occur. The predicted outcomes based on different theories shall be described in Chapter 5.4. Having defined which theory will be followed, hypothesis will be derived from the research questions.

5.1 RESEARCH QUESTIONS ON CDP ACTIVITY

As indicated previously, the title question, "Does carbon-conscious behavior drive firm performance?" can be split into three key research questions. This disaggregation is based on the evolutionary model of carbon-consciousness explained in Chapter 3.4. For an overview, see Figure 23:

321 Sachs & Hauser, 2002, pp. 31–45

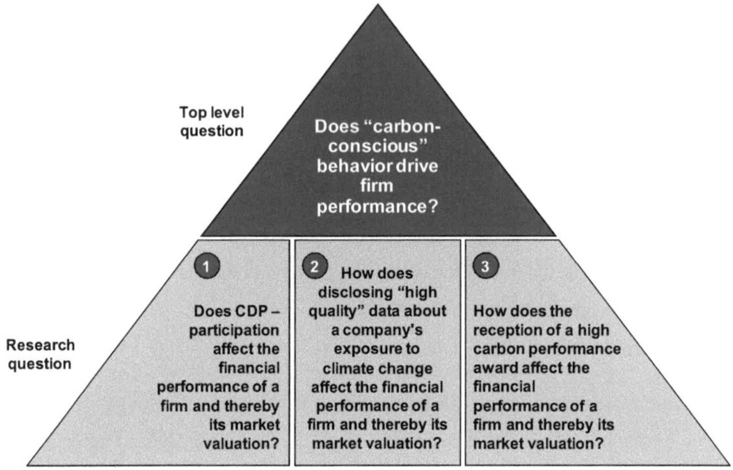

Figure 23: Splitting up of title question into three key research questions

R_1: Does CDP participation affect the financial performance of a firm and thereby its market valuation?

The determining input factor for this research question is: Did the sample company participate in the CDP 2009? The only possible answers to this question are yes and no. Additionally, it was further checked if the company was participating for the first time. Therefore, a sub-question of research question one is:

R_{1A}: Is there a different reaction if companies participate for the first time?

The second major research question is on the level of disclosure of carbon information:

R_2: How does disclosing "high-quality" data about a company's exposure to climate change affect the financial performance of a firm and thereby its market valuation?

To check for this relationship, two alternative operational variables were chosen: the disclosure score and the CDLI.

The third research question deals with the actual carbon performance of companies:

R_3: How does the reception of a high carbon performance award affect the financial performance of a firm and thereby its market valuation?

This is operationalized by membership in the Carbon High Performance Group.

5.2 RESEARCH QUESTIONS ON SURVEY-SPECIFIC ITEMS

Besides key variables like CDP participation, disclosure scores and performance awards, three additional, less aggregated research questions shall be answered. These survey-specific questions concern single items within the CDP survey and were selected because they seemed most interesting to the author. Because these research questions are highly specific no meaningful theoretical framework could be discovered and is therefore left to further academic research.

R_4: Does setting emission reduction targets affect financial performance?

R_5: Does having a board-level member responsible for climate change affect financial performance?

R_6: Does having an incentive system to support climate-friendly behavior affect financial performance?

5.3 MODEL SETUP

The general setup of the model is straightforward. Different events (based on research questions 1 to 6) shall be analyzed for their impacts on financial performance while taking into account how moderating factors influence the results. Different variables influencing the relationship have been chosen:

- Region
- Industry
- Carbon intensity
- Financial leverage
- Business model
- Profitability

- Share of institutional investors

The reasons for choosing these moderating factors are the following:

"Region" was selected to find out if different geographical patterns can be identified; e.g., are companies in Europe and North America behaving differently than those in the rest of the world?

"Industry" was chosen to identify differences in the way companies in different sectors react to the announcement; e.g., how do utilities behave compared to financial companies?

"Carbon intensity" was selected to find out if highly carbon-intensive companies behave differently than less carbon-intensive companies. This moderating factor is similar to "industry," but it is still used because it is quantifiable.

"Financial leverage" was chosen because the more geared up a company is, the more risk it is exposed to if cash flows change too much because of changes to cost or revenue resulting from climate change. For example, a highly indebted company will find it more difficult to compensate for lost revenue due to changed customer preferences than a less geared-up company because the former still has to pay interest and repay the principal. Therefore, the leveraged company is more risky and is expected to behave differently than the less leveraged one.

"Business model" was selected because it is assumed that there is a difference between a company that is mainly in the B2B[322] sector and one in the B2C[323] sector.

"Profitability" was chosen because it is worthwhile to analyze if only highly profitable companies put effort into disclosing because they have more resources or if less profitable companies behave similarly.

"Share of institutional investors" was selected because it might be assumed that companies with a high share of institutional investors are more severely scrutinized as institutional investors are more professional than private investors are. Thus, if companies do not act as desired by institutional investors (through CDP), they might be punished more rigorously than companies with a lower share of institutional investors would be.

For an overview of these relationships, see Figure 24:

322 B2B: Business to Business
323 B2C: Business to Consumer

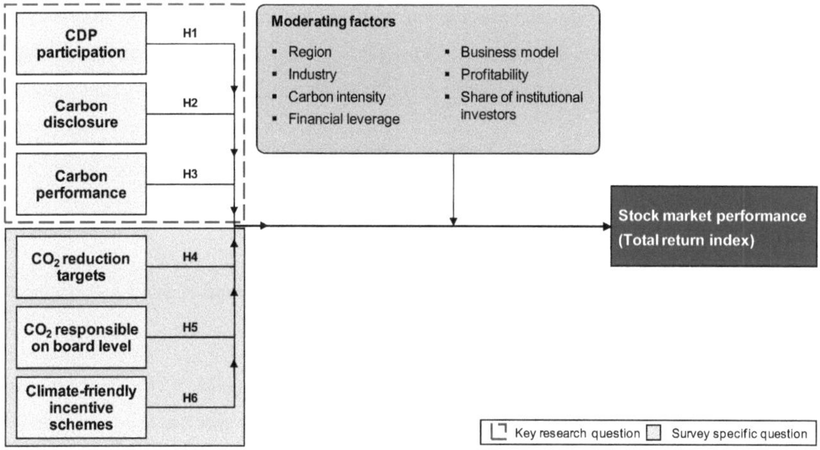

Figure 24: Simple model setup

Several aspects of this approach are advantageous:

First, the input variables (CDP participation, disclosure score, CDLI and High Performance Group) are not subject to manipulation because the information is announced by an independent third party that used outside reviews by experts and specialists with access to detailed company information. This setup enhances the reliability and validity of this study.

Second, the reaction to these developments is reflected by the stock markets, which is a standard proxy for the financial performance of a firm. Because this approach is market based, it can also be seen as independent. Stockholders are, similar to the CDP, independent third parties assessing future cash flows based on a company's attitude towards carbon-conscious behavior and discounting it to present value. Thus, if new information reaches the market, it will be incorporated instantly, and the change in stock price indicates the assumed impact on the company's value as a result of the announcement or event.[324]

Third, because an event-study approach is chosen (further explained in Chapter Six), causality can be inferred.

324 Klassen & McLaughlin, 1996, p. 1204

Although the approach enables the assumption of causality, it is nevertheless necessary to describe the pathways by which carbon-conscious behavior (e.g., CDP participation, disclosure scores or high carbon performance) can affect financial performance.

In order to explain the model more easily, a positive association (revisionist view) will be assumed. However, the pathways would work quite similarly in a negative relation.

This model is adapted from Klassen and McLaughlin (1996).

In general, there are two pathways (revenue and cost) from carbon-conscious behavior to financial performance.

First, on the revenue side, if a company becomes more carbon conscious, it changes its product portfolio to become more climate-friendly, e.g., by offering products that use less energy and/or emit less CO_2. This change could have two positive effects. First, the company could sell more units and consequently increase its market share. Second, the company could charge more for its products (increasing prices). Both cases would have a positive impact on the bottom line.[325]

Second, on the cost side, carbon-conscious companies will try to reduce energy consumption, emit less and avoid waste. All of this will eventually lead to lower operational costs, positively affecting profits. Additionally, by limiting their CO_2 emissions, companies reduce the risk of lawsuits and the potential amount of damages, which would also otherwise consume management resources.[326]

For an overview of these pathways, see the Figure 25:

325 Klassen & McLaughlin, 1996, p. 1201
326 Klassen & McLaughlin, 1996, p. 1202

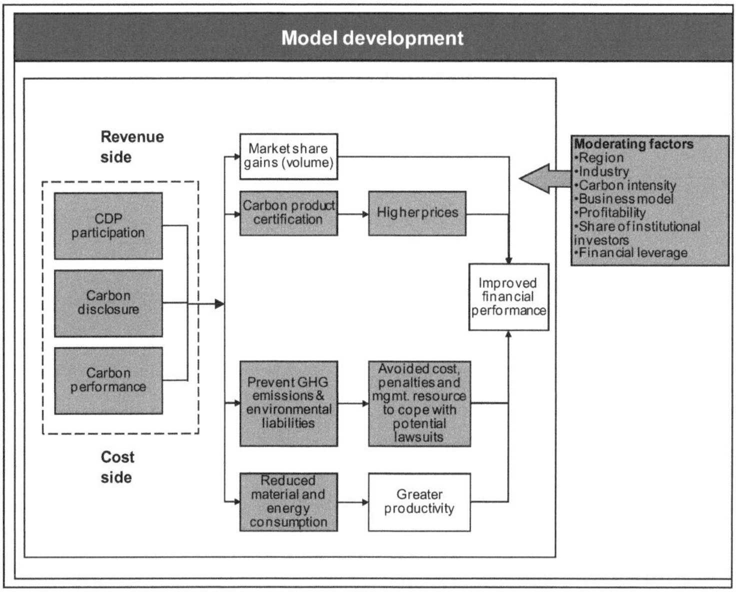

Figure 25: Model with pathways

For the sake of readability, just the key research questions are denoted.

5.4 PREDICTED RESEARCH OUTCOME BASED ON THEORIES AND HYPOTHESIS DEVELOPMENT

As described in the previous section, the first research question covers participation in the CDP, while the second research question covers the quantity and quality of disclosed carbon information. Therefore, the disclosure elements of the two questions are theoretically covered by the disclosure theory and socio-political theories.

Nevertheless, the existing theoretical framework does not provide clear answers to how stock markets might react if companies disclosed carbon information.

However, based on the general view within these theories, the disclosure theory might suggest a positive relation between carbon disclosure and financial performance because companies would positively distinguish themselves from weak performers. Investors should also perceive this as a good sign, and the stock price should react accordingly (at least based on the disclosure theory).[327]

Following the reasoning of the socio-political theories, it is harder to predict a clear outcome. Basically, socio-political theories argue that companies disclose due to social pressure. Therefore, an action to disclose carbon information is not a way for a company to positively distinguish itself from inferior competitors, but just a way to alter negative public perception. If the released information is better than expected, the public might not believe it because it was disclosed under pressure and might have been manipulated. Therefore, this might not have an impact. But if the information is worse than expected, the outcome would be negative, and investors might punish the stock. Following the socio-political theories, it is hard to predict if there is no or a negative relation between carbon disclosure and financial performance, but this relation is likely not positive.

For the third research question on the association between carbon and financial performance, inferences from theories are easier. Based on the traditional view, a negative relation would be suggested. Based on the revisionist view, a positive relation would be assumed, with a similar reasoning as used in the model setup.[328]

A summary of the predicted outcomes can be found in Figure 26:

327 Knowing that investors value environmental information, as different studies suggest. See Blacconiere & Patten, 1994, Cormier & Magnan, 1997 and Cormier, Magnan, & Morard, 1993

328 The synthesis view will not be discussed here because it is just a combination of the traditional and revisionist views.

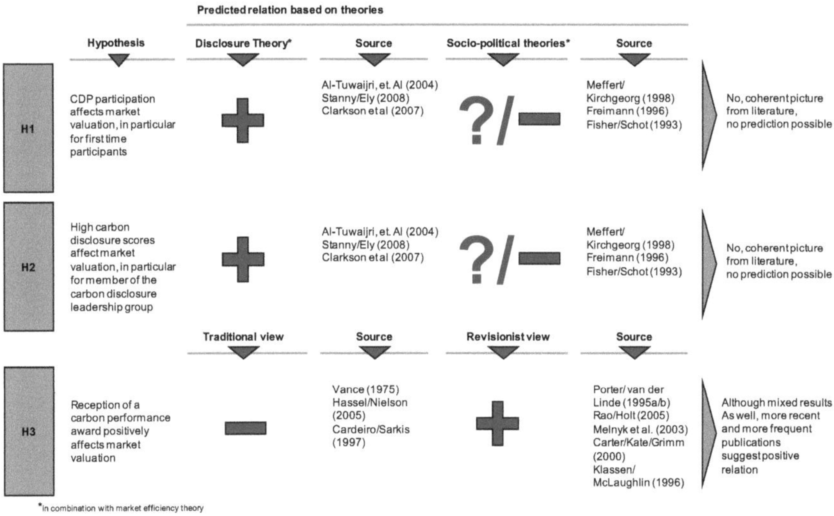

Figure 26: Overview of predicted outcomes based on theory

Although different theories suggest different outcomes, it is necessary to decide on one to derive a hypothesis for each research question. Because the disclosure theory is, at least, more clear on its predicted outcome than the socio-political theories are, the author will assume a positive relationship between carbon disclosure and financial performance. This choice leads to the first three hypotheses (including a sub-hypothesis for research question 1) based on the disclosure theory:

H_1: Participating in the CDP positively affects financial performance.

H_{1A}: Companies participating in the CDP for the first time should experience an even more positive effect.[329]

H_2: Disclosing "high-quality" carbon information positively affects financial performance.

329 Announcement would be truly unexpected compared to companies that have taken part several times before, which makes it more likely that they will participate again.

Because empirical evidence for a positive relationship between environmental and financial performance is a bit more extensive, the author will follow the revisionist view and define the third hypothesis as follows:[330]

H_3: The reception of a carbon high performance award positively affects financial performance.

330 All survey-specific questions, like emission reduction targets, carbon dioxide responsibility on the board level and climate-friendly incentive systems, are subsets of carbon performance management, so a positive relationship for these items is assumed.

6 Research methodology

In this chapter, the scientific method is further elaborated in order to explain the results. As for most methodologies, there is no one perfect method for answering the research questions.[331]

The following chapter is split into three segments: research approach, describing step-by-step the setup of an event study; data collection, showing how the financial and climate data and news were collected; and critique of event studies, illustrating the shortcomings of this research approach. Finally, a summary of the event study methodology is given.

6.1 RESEARCH APPROACH

Within this section, the major elements of an event study are described. The setup is similar to the methodological approach used by Campbell (1997).[332]

The section begins with the history of event studies and the academic fields in which they have been applied, followed by the question of what actually defines an event and what assumptions are made when an event study is conducted. The following sections describe the reasoning behind the companies chosen as well as the major variables for determining the estimation and event window. Afterwards, the importance of confounding effects will be explained. Then, different models to calculate normal and abnormal will be discussed. This discussion is followed by the choice of the right benchmark. Afterwards, different statistical testing methods will be described to find one suitable for this dissertation's setting.

6.1.1 History of event studies and academic fields of application

Event studies have a long history in capital market research. In 1933, James Doley conducted his work on the price effects of stock splits.[333]

---

331 Ny, 2006, pp. 11–12
332 Campbell et al., 1997, pp. 151–152
333 MacKinlay, 1997, pp. 13–14

From the 1930s to the 1960s, the level of sophistication of event studies increased significantly.[334] Examples of this development are Ball & Brown (1968), Barker (1956), Barker (1957), Barker (1958) and Myers & Bakay (1948). One of the major enhancements of the methodology was the removal of market price effects and the consideration of confounding effects.[335] From there on, the methodology has remained largely unchanged.[336]

Therefore, event study methodology is quite mature, with easily more than 500 publications in A-journals.[337] The main reason for this is that "the conditions under which event studies provide information and permit reliable inferences are well-understood."[338]

Consequently, event studies have become one of the most important research approaches in corporate finance.[339] Or, as mentioned by Harrington & Shrider (2007), "Over 35 years following its introduction by Fama, Fisher, Jensen, and Roll (1969), the short-horizon event study remains a workhorse of empirical finance in general and corporate finance in particular."

But not only capital market research has benefited from the event study methodology.[340] Other aspects of management research have studied the effects of endogenous corporate events such as "divestiture from South Africa, corporate control changes, corporate refocusing, CEO turnover, the use of affirmative action programs, layoffs, plant closures, corporate illegalities, product recalls, customer service changes, diversification programs, strategic investment decisions, and the formation of joint ventures" [341] or of exogenous events such as "the enactment of major legislation, the appointment of top executives to cabinet positions, and the deaths of CEOs."[342]

Furthermore, event studies have been used outside of their original domain, including in the field of law, e.g., to determine insider trading or to measure the economic effect of regulatory changes[343] or legal liability cases.[344]

---

334 MacKinlay, 1997, p. 14
335 Campbell et al., 1997, pp. 149–150 and Binder, 1998, p. 112
336 Campbell et al., 1997, pp. 149–150, Kothari & Warner, 2006, pp. 7–8 and Gebken, 2008, pp. 24–25
337 Kothari & Warner, 2006, p. 5 and Mentz, 2006, pp. 44–45
338 Kothari & Warner, 2006, p. 5
339 Gebken, 2008, p. 24
340 Gebken, 2008, p. 24
341 McWilliams & Siegel, 1997, p. 626
342 McWilliams & Siegel, 1997, p. 626
343 Schwert, 1981, pp. 121–122
344 Mitchell & Netter, 1994, p. 545, MacKinlay, 1997, p. 13, Kothari & Warner, 2006, pp. 4–5 and Campbell et al., 1997, p. 149

6.1.2 Assumptions of event study

In order to rely on the inferences of event studies, three major assumptions have to be met: (1) efficient markets, (2) unanticipated events and (3) no confounding events during the event window. Besides these assumptions, there is a set of issues related to research design, e.g., length of event and estimation windows, that also must be considered.[345]

First, one of the major pillars of the event study methodology is the assumption that markets are efficient. In other words, current prices reflect all information available to the market participants, and new information to investors will be reflected in the stock price immediately. However, in most situations it is difficult to pinpoint exactly when investors received and acted upon that new information, e.g., in the case of M&A announcements. Often, investors know the fact prior to the announcement, and stock prices react accordingly. This kind of leaking makes the event date difficult for researchers to define (for further details, see the next section). In order to overcome this problem, researchers extend event windows to capture the event, but this action implicitly violates the assumption of efficient markets. Therefore, semi-efficient markets are assumed to justify event windows of a few days.[346]

Second, in order to be able to infer valid statements from event studies, it is necessary that the event was unanticipated by market participants and therefore represents new information to investors. Consequently, "Abnormal returns can then be assumed to be the result of the stock market's reacting to new information."[347] However, as previously mentioned, it is very difficult for researchers to define the exact moment when markets became aware of the new information. In many cases, information leaked prior to the announcement or was anticipated by investors.[348]

Third, in several publications it is noted that data sets need to be controlled for confounding effects. In other words, researchers need to isolate the event effect by excluding observations that experienced other events, e.g., earnings announcements, dividend declarations, or M&A activity. However, this assumption is challenged by recent articles in A-journals that did not control for confounding events. There are two possible reasons for not excluding observations with

345 McWilliams & Siegel, 1997, pp. 629–630
346 McWilliams & Siegel, 1997, p. 630 and Mentz, 2006, p. 43
347 McWilliams & Siegel, 1997, pp. 630–634
348 McWilliams & Siegel, 1997, pp. 630–634

confounding events. First, the definition of confounding events is arbitrary, and second, in large samples, positive and negative effects should cancel each other out.[349]

6.1.3 Event definition

One of the first steps when conducting an event study is the definition of an event. What seems rather trivial at first glance might be rather challenging when attempted in detail.[350] Not only is it rather difficult to determine the exact point in time when the market participants became aware of the new information (as previously described), but selecting an event severely restricts the range of possible hypotheses to be tested.[351]

As Brown and Warner (1980) pointed out, event studies are very sensitive to the precision of the event date definition. To illustrate this, assume you want to analyze the effect of changes in dividend policy on shareholder value. In this case, it would not be appropriate to use the date when the dividend was paid, and perhaps not even the date the announcement was made, because some information might have previously been leaked.[352]

Within this study, the event date is September 20th, 2009, at 9:00 pm ET. This was the time when the first information about the CDP 2009 Global 500 report was released in New York.

6.1.4 Selection of companies

After successfully defining the event, it is necessary to determine which companies shall be included in the data set. The first selection comes with the event itself; afterwards, data availability, e.g., total return prices, will further restrict the set of data. Then, whether the relevant samples and subsamples are still large enough for meaningful significance tests to be conducted must be determined. A minimum of 25 observations should be sufficient. Further on, the sample should be described in terms of its characteristics so that possible biases can be spotted.[353]

349 McWilliams & Siegel, 1997, p. 634. Interestingly, the author did not find a single article justifying why it did not control for confounding events.
350 MacKinlay, 1997, p. 14
351 Bowman, 1983, p. 563 and Dwyer, 2001, p. 4
352 Mentz, 2006, p. 53, Dwyer, 2001, p. 3 and Gebken, 2008, p. 25
353 MacKinlay, 1997, p. 15 and Bartholdy, Olson, & Peare, 2007, p. 227

6.1.5 Event and estimation window

Having defined the event and the companies to be observed, it is now necessary to define the appropriate event window, meaning how long the researcher assumes it takes the capital market to incorporate the new information. Following the assumption of market efficiency, security prices should reflect new information instantly.[354]

Dann, Mayers, and Raab (1977) found that market prices reflect new information after 15 minutes, and Mitchel and Netter (1989) found that stock prices adjusted within 90 minutes after an announcement.[355]

However, in practice, event windows are extended by far more than just the trading day. Event windows of 181 trading days (which equals approximately nine months) are not uncommon.[356]

Although there might be reasons to extend the event window to several days, e.g., to capture the effect on a global scale or if the researcher is unsure when the markets became aware of the new information, long event windows of several months are viewed highly critically in academic circles.[357] It is much more difficult to control for confounding events over a long than a short event window.[358] As Brown and Warner (1980) pointed out, the reliability of tests decreases as the event window enlarges. Therefore, scientists prefer short horizons of event windows because they represent the "cleanest evidence we have on efficiency"[359].

The question of estimation windows plays a role for two models where variables need to be estimated. These are the constant-mean and the market models (both of which will be described later). In general, estimation windows include 100-300 trading days and do not overlap with the event window.[360] In most cases, they are prior to the event window, and in some cases post-event returns (i.e., outside of the event window) are included as well.[361] The main reason why overlapping windows should be avoided is the objective of isolating effects during the event

354 McWilliams & Siegel, 1997, pp. 636–637
355 Dann, Mayers, & Raab, Jr., 1977, p. 20 and Mitchell & Netter, 1989, pp. 37–39
356 MacKinlay, 1997, p. 15
357 Gebken, 2008, p. 25 and Peterson, 1989, p. 37
358 Kothari & Warner, 2006, p. 8 and Kothari & Warner, 2006, p. 17
359 Fama, 1991, p. 1602
360 Peterson, 1989, p. 38
361 Mikkelson & Partch, 1986, pp. 39–43

window.[362] If the event is included in the estimation window, it might distort the estimated variables, which could lead to false inferences.[363]

Another issue with estimation windows, as with event windows, is their length. Although a long estimation window might increase the precision of the variables estimated, it simultaneously increases the risk that the variables are out-of-date, e.g., due to a change in the gearing of the relevant company.[364]

Within this study, the event window equals the day of the event (September 20, 2009) plus 4 trading days (until September 24, 2009) because the author wished to include all Japanese companies within the sample. The last day of the event window was the first regular trading day in Japan after a three-day close due to holidays. The estimation window within this study includes 250 trading days, which is quite customary for event studies (see above). The author tried different event windows, even adding another 20 trading days, and the results were similar.

6.1.6 Correction for confounding events

As previously described, it is highly important for event studies to use short event windows to better control for confounding events. In many publications, confounding events were not appropriately considered or were not considered at all.[365]

Confounding events are effects that might distort the event effect, e.g., earnings announcements or dividend payments. Consequently, these effects make it difficult to isolate the event effect.[366]

There are four different ways to deal with confounding effects: (1) Eliminate firms from the sample; (2) group firms that have experienced similar types of events; (3) eliminate a firm only on the day it experienced the confounding event; or (4) subtract the impact of the confounding effect from the abnormal return.[367]

However, as previously noted, a tremendous number of event studies do not consider confounding events. In most cases no explanation is given, but two possible interpretations could

---

362 MacKinlay, 1997, p. 15 and Peterson, 1989, pp. 37–38
363 Mentz, 2006, pp. 55–56
364 Armitage, 1995, p. 34 and Masulis, 1980, pp. 153–156
365 McWilliams & Siegel, 1997, p. 637
366 Bowman, 1983, p. 564 and Salinger, 1992, p. 671
367 Foster, 1980, pp. 54–56 and McWilliams & Siegel, 1997, p. 637

be that (1) the definition of confounding events is arbitrary[368] and (2) in large samples, negative and positive confounding events should cancel each other out.

Within this event study, confounding effects were controlled. The following types of confounding events were used to exclude a company from the sample:

- Analyst up-/downgrades
- Earnings announcements
- M&A activity
- Changes in board structure
- Dividend announcement
- Contracts awarded
- Transaction of company shares by board members

However, even with the exclusion of confounding effects, the results were similar.[369]

6.1.7 Estimation of abnormal returns

Having elaborated the necessary assumptions and adjustments for a meaningful event study, this and the following section will describe how to calculate the impact of an event on shareholder wealth. The general logic is the same for all methods and models.

The impact effect on shareholder wealth, which is conditioned through the event, is called the abnormal return. The normal effect without the event is called the normal or expected return. Therefore, the relation can be described as follows:[370]

$$AR_{it} = R_{it} - R_i^e \quad \textbf{(2)}$$

AR_{it}: Abnormal return for security i at time t

R_{it}: Actual return for security i at time t

R_i^e: Normal/expected return for security i

368 McWilliams & Siegel, 1997, pp. 637 & 640

369 Further results will be shown, including companies with confounding effects, because of the similarity of results and for sample size reasons.

370 Kothari & Warner, 2006, p. 9, MacKinlay, 1997, p. 15, Gebken, 2008, p. 26 and Brown & Warner, 1980, p. 205

This means that the abnormal return is the difference between the actual return and the expected/ normal return.

At first glance, this might seem trivial; however, most work employing the event study methodology aims to estimate the "right" normal return. The number of different models and adjustments is tremendously high. The following chapters will present the major models, including their assumptions, benefits and drawbacks.[371]

To be able to test different hypotheses, it is necessary to aggregate abnormal returns. Normally, this starts with an aggregation over time for each security. This process can be described as follows:

$$CAR_i(T_1, T_2) = \sum_{T1}^{T2} AR_{it} \qquad \textbf{(3)}$$

CAR_i: Cumulative abnormal return for security i

AR_{it}: Abnormal return for security i at time t

T_1: Start of event window

T_2: End of event window

This means the cumulative abnormal return is the sum of all abnormal returns during the event window.[372]

Afterwards, the cumulative abnormal returns are aggregated by securities. Mathematically speaking:

$$CAAR = \frac{\sum_{i=1}^{N} CAR}{N} \qquad \textbf{(4)}$$

CAAR: Cumulative average abnormal return

CAR: Cumulative abnormal return

N: Number of observations

371 Brown & Warner, 1980, pp. 205–207
372 MacKinlay, 1997, pp. 21–22, Kothari & Warner, 2006, pp. 10–11 and Mentz, 2006, pp. 56–58

This means that the cumulative average abnormal return is the sum of all securities' cumulative abnormal returns divided by the number of observations (securities).[373]

6.1.8 Estimation of normal returns

As previously mentioned, there is a variety of different models available to estimate the normal return of a security. These models can be grouped into two different categories.

First, there are statistical approaches that do not rely on economic arguments at all but just on statistical assumptions on the behavior of asset returns. [374]

Second, there are economic approaches that rely on assumptions regarding the investor's behavior and not solely on statistical assumptions. Nevertheless, readers should be aware of the fact that, in practice, economic models still need statistical assumptions. Therefore, their benefit does not lie in the absence of statistical assumptions but in the ability to calculate normal returns more precisely. However, the importance of economic models has diminished in recent decades.[375]

On the following pages, the most important models of each group (statistical and economic) will be presented.

6.1.8.1 Statistical models

In academic circles using the event study methodology, three models are perceived as the most important ones. The simplest is (1) the constant-mean model, then (2) the index model and the most commonly used (3) market model.[376]

6.1.8.1.1 Constant mean model

The constant mean model assumes that the best predictor of a company's normal return is the company's average security return prior to the event calculated for an estimation window of, e.g., 250 trading days.[377] This predictor can be described as:

373 Campbell et al., 1997, pp. 157–162, Peterson, 1989, p. 45 and Bowman, 1983, p. 569
374 MacKinlay, 1997, p. 17 and Campbell et al., 1997, pp. 153–157
375 MacKinlay, 1997, p. 17 and Campbell et al., 1997, pp. 153–157
376 Armitage, 1995, pp. 27–28
377 Binder, 1998, pp. 117–118

$$R_i^e = \frac{\sum_{E_1}^{E_2} R_i}{E_2 - E_1} \qquad \textbf{(5)}$$

R_i^e: Normal/expected return for security i

R_i: Daily actual return for security i during estimation window

E_1: Start of estimation window

E_2: End of estimation window

Putting equations (2) and (5) together yields:

$$AR_{it} = R_{it} - \frac{\sum_{E_1}^{E_2} R_i}{E_2 - E_1} \qquad \textbf{(6)= (5) in (2)}$$

The major benefit of this model is, first, that just one variable needs to be estimated; the market model requires two variables. Second, there is no need for market data.[378] Although it is the simplest model, Brown and Warner (1980/1985) found that the constant mean model often yields similar results to the more advanced models.[379] In fact, variance is not tremendously reduced by more sophisticated models.[380]

One of the model's major drawbacks is its lack of control for market movements and therefore variance increases. Or, as Binder (1998) pointed out: "What does not disappear even in large samples is the additional noise in the abnormal return estimator because the event period market return is not controlled for. Therefore, these abnormal return estimators have considerably greater variance than the market model disturbances."[381]

6.1.8.1.2 Index model

In contrast to the constant mean model, the index model does not assume normal returns to be predicted by the historic average of companies' securities return, but simply by the market portfolio. Consequently,

378 Gebken, 2008, pp. 27–28
379 Brown & Warner, 1980, pp. 207–208
380 Mentz, 2006, pp. 51–52, Bowman, 1983, p. 567 and MacKinlay, 1997, p. 17
381 Binder, 1998, pp. 117–118

$$R_i^e = R_{mt} \quad \textbf{(7)}$$

R_{mt}: Return of the market portfolio m at time t

Putting equations (2) and (7) together yields:

$$AR_{it} = R_{it} - R_{mt} \quad \textbf{(8) = (7) in (2)}$$

Therefore, the abnormal return is just the actual daily return minus the return of the market portfolio.[382]

Consequently, the benefit of this model is obvious. Unlike in the constant mean model and the market model, parameters do not need to be estimated.[383]

However, one major problem with the index model is its assumption that the systematic risk of all securities is constant and equals one.[384]

6.1.8.1.3 Market model

One of the most common approaches in event study methodology is the market model, mainly because "evidence suggests that the market model will perform as well as, if not better than, any alternative in most circumstances."[385] Other scientists share this point of view.[386]

In general, the market model is similar to the index model because it incorporates market movements into the predictions of the normal return. However, it does not assume the relation of every security to the market portfolio to be one and constant. In contrast, the market model says that every security is individually sensitive to the market movement. This sensitivity is expressed in the estimated variables α and β. Therefore, the normal return according to the market model is as follows:[387]

$$R_i^e = \alpha_i^e + \beta_i^e R_{mt} \quad \textbf{(9)}$$

α_i^e: Estimated regression intercept for security i

382 Brown & Warner, 1980, p. 208 and Funke, 2005, p. 4
383 Binder, 1998, p. 118 and Gebken, 2008, pp. 28–29
384 Mentz, 2006, p. 52
385 Armitage, 1995, p. 26
386 McWilliams & Siegel, 1997, pp. 628–629, Armitage, 1995, p. 31 and Binder, 1998, p. 119
387 Karpoff & Malatesta, 1989, pp. 306–307, Campbell, Cowan, & Salotti, 2010, pp. 6–7, McGuckin, Warren-Boulton, & Waldstein, 1992, p. 2 and Klassen & McLaughlin, 1996, p. 1205

β_i^e: Estimated regression slope coefficient for security i

R_{mt}: Return of the market portfolio m at time t

Putting equations (2) and (9) together yields:

$$AR_{it} = R_{it} - (\alpha_i^e + \beta_i^e R_{mt}) \qquad \textbf{(10)=(9) in (2)}$$

This means that the abnormal return from the market model is the difference between the actual return and the linear specification, based on ordinary least squares (OLS), of the market return and the security return.[388]

As previously mentioned, the market model is perceived by scientists as superior to the index and the constant mean models[389] because it includes the security's sensitivity to market movements. The main benefit of this model upgrade is the reduction in return variance, which makes it more likely to detect abnormal returns.[390]

Nevertheless, there is one major drawback within the market model that has led to contentious discussions in academic circles: the parameter estimation of α and β. β could change over time if overly long estimation periods are chosen. However, this discussion was resolved with the advent of the Capital Asset Pricing Model (CAPM), to which the market model has strong ties. Although the CAPM has similar beta estimation problems this methodology remains one of the most widely applied in corporate finance.[391]

As described, α and β need to be estimated. Normally the OLS method is used for this. The estimation window for the regression is usually 100-300 trading days.[392] Although OLS has its problems, like non-synchronous trading (i.e., securities that seem to be traded at the same time as the market are actually traded prior to or later than the relevant market), in general OLS is seen in academic circles as sufficiently efficient.[393]

388 Funke, 2005, p. 3, Funke, 2005, p. 4, Bowman, 1983, p. 568, MacKinlay, 1997, p. 18 and Gebken, 2008, p. 28
389 Brown & Warner, 1980, p. 209
390 Campbell et al., 1997, pp. 162–163 and Mentz, 2006, p. 48
391 Binder, 1998, p. 118 and Brown & Warner, 1980, p. 208. Nevertheless, incorrect estimation of β can still be a problem.
392 Bartholdy et al., 2007, p. 228, Funke, 2005, p. 4 and Peterson, 1989, p. 38
393 MacKinlay, 1997, p. 20, Peterson, 1989, p. 39, Mentz, 2006, pp. 46–48 and Salinger, 1992, p. 671

6.1.8.1.4 Other statistical models

Most other statistical models try to enhance their explanatory power by incorporating additional factors, e.g., changes in interest rates, dividend yields, price-earnings ratios. This enhancement can be described as follows:[394]

$$R_i^e = (\alpha_1^e + \beta_1^e R_1) + (\alpha_2^e + \beta_2^e R_2) + \cdots \qquad \textbf{(11)}$$

α_i^e: Estimated regression intercept for security i with factor R

β_i^e: Estimated regression slope coefficient for security i with factor R

Putting equations (2) and (11) together yields:

$$AR_{it} = R_{it} - (\alpha_1^e + \beta_1^e R_1) - (\alpha_2^e + \beta_2^e R_2) - \cdots \qquad \textbf{(12)=(11) in (2)}$$

The ultimate goal of building such a multi-factor model is to reduce the variance of the observation and thereby detect abnormal returns more easily.[395]

Consequently, the market model is actually a special case of factor models with just one factor. One common approach is to include industry-specific movements by adding an industry index.[396] Another approach is to include the return of a portfolio of companies of similar size,[397] where size is defined as the market value of the respective company. An example of the use of alternative statistical models is Dyckman and Smith (1979).[398]

However, in simulations, these more sophisticated models yield only marginal benefits.[399] "The reason for the limited gains is the empirical fact that the marginal explanatory power of additional factors the market factor is small, and hence, there is little reduction in the variance of the abnormal return."[400]

394 Basu, 1983, pp. 133–137, Keim, 1983, pp. 17–19, Litzenberger & Ramaswamy, 1979, pp. 165–169 and Miller & Scholes, 1982, pp. 1120–1125
395 Mentz, 2006, pp. 48–50 and Dimson & Marsh, 1986, pp. 114–115
396 MacKinlay, 1997, pp. 18–19 and Sharpe, Alexander, & Bailey, 1999, p. 303
397 Banz, 1981, pp. 4–6 and Reinganum & Shapiro, 1987, pp. 284–285
398 Dyckman & Smith, 1979, pp. 49–52
399 Mentz, 2006, p. 50, Dimson & Marsh, 1986, p. 114 and Brown & Weinstein, 1985, pp. 491–493
400 MacKinlay, 1997, pp. 18–19

6.1.8.2 Economic models

Two economic models are commonly used.

First, the CAPM is actually an equilibrium theory where the normal return (here: expected return) for a given security is a linear function of its covariance with the return of the market portfolio. It is one of the best-known theories in corporate finance and stems from Sharpe (1964) and Lintner (1965). Mathematically speaking, it says:

$$E(R_{it}) = R_{ft} + \beta_i[E(R_{mt}) - R_{ft}] \quad \textbf{(13)}$$

$E(R_{it})$: Expected/normal return for security i at time t

R_{ft}: Risk-free lending interest rate, e.g., 10-year US Treasury bill

β_i^e: Covariance between R_{it} and R_{mt} during the estimation period

$E(R_{mt})$: Expected return of the market portfolio

Beta is actually the measure of how much risk a certain security adds to a certain investor holding the market portfolio. Appropriately, the investor will ask for a higher return if beta increases. Consequently, the abnormal return is:[401]

$$AR_{it} = R_{it} - R_{ft} - \beta_i[E(R_{mt}) - R_{ft}] \quad \textbf{(14) = (13) in (2)}$$

As is obvious, this is fairly similar to the market model. In fact, the market model is a version of the CAPM, just with looser restrictions, where α can be interpreted as:[402]

$$\propto = R_{ft}(1 - \beta_i) \quad \textbf{(15)}$$

The other well-known economic model, the arbitrage pricing theory (APT), which is attributed to Ross (1976), describes the normal/expected return as a multifactor model.[403] Although the APT has strong theoretical end empirical backing, its benefits to event study methodology, like the other multi-factor models, is marginal.[404]

401 Armitage, 1995, pp. 28–29 and MacKinlay, 1997, p. 19
402 Binder, 1998, p. 118 and Dwyer, 2001, p. 7
403 Ross, 1976, pp. 346–348
404 Dwyer, 2001, p. 8, Binder, 1998, p. 119 and MacKinlay, 1997, p. 19

The main reason is that the additional factors do not show more explanatory power than simpler models do. Unfortunately, this is also the reason why the use of economic models within the event study methodology has almost ceased.[405]

Concluding this chapter, it should be noted that, within this study, the index and market model were used to calculate abnormal returns and yielded similar results. However, because the market model is more common in the academic literature and perceived to be superior, the following results are based on the market model.

6.1.9 Benchmarks

Whatever models researchers decide to adopt for an event study, except for the constant mean model, all require some kind of benchmark.

As Brown and Warner (1980) indicated, the choice of benchmarks has a significant impact on the results of event studies. In this context, three questions need to be answered.[406]

First, is it better to use an industry index or a broad market index? Scientific circles are not sure if one index is superior. Initial analysis show that industry indices do not yield more precise results than do market indices. For industry indices, it needs to be considered if certain companies will bias the index too much.[407]

The second question deals with the question of whether equally weighted indices perform better than value-weighted indices. The literature shows mixed results in this area. Whereas older publications, such as Brown and Warner (1980), prefer equally weighted indices, more current publications see value-weighted indices as a reasonable alternative.[408]

Third, it is disputed in academic circles if price or performance indices should be used. Performance indices control for dividend payments, whereas price indices show decreases at the time of ex-dividend dates. Until now, no simulation (at least to the knowledge of the author) has tested which index will perform better.[409]

---

405 Mentz, 2006, p. 50
406 Mentz, 2006, pp. 53–54
407 Mentz, 2006, p. 54
408 Mentz, 2006, pp. 54–55, Funke, 2005, p. 4, Boone & Mulherin, 2007, p. 858 and Armitage, 1995, pp. 33–34
409 Mentz, 2006, pp. 54–55

Fourth, in multi-country event studies it is questionable if global market indices perform better than multi-country indices. As for the previous question, no simulation that has tested this situation is known.

Within this study, a global benchmark (MSCI All World Index Large, Mid, Small Cap) was chosen. It represents a value-weighted index covering approximately 8,500 securities from 45 countries.[410] This index was the broadest (in terms of company size and industry) that was available to the author. The main reason for choosing this index compared to several local indices was that Global 500 companies might influence their local indices too much. However, the analysis was carried out with local indices (e.g., S&P 500, DAX, CAC40, NIKKEI) as well, and the results were similar. Because academic circles do not object to the use of a global index, further results are based on the MSCI All World Index Large, Mid and Small Cap.

6.1.10 Statistical testing methods

Having calculated the abnormal returns, whether the results are statistically significant and if inferences can be drawn will be tested. This chapter is split into three segments. Within the first segment, it will describe how to test if the abnormal return is statically significantly different from zero. The second section will show how to test two mean abnormal returns for equality. In the third section, it will demonstrate how to test for statistical significance if the assumptions for the first two test statistics are not met.

In general, all test statistics work similarly, whether they are t-tests (based on the normal distribution assumption) or non-parametric tests (based on the alternative distribution assumption). First, the test statistic is calculated, then compared to the assumed distribution under the null hypothesis that the average abnormal return is equal to zero.[411]

If the calculated test statistic exceeds a pre-determined critical value, the null hypothesis is rejected. This pre-determined critical value usually corresponds to the 10%, 5% or 1% tail region.[412]

410 MSCI website, 2010
411 Gebken, 2008, p. 29
412 Gebken, 2008, p. 29

6.1.10.1 T-test for significance of abnormal returns

One of the first steps in testing for significant abnormal returns is the definition of a hypothesis. This process begins with setting up a null hypothesis (H_0), which describes that the abnormal return does not result from the systematic impact of an event on the stock price. The alternative hypothesis (H_A) states that there is an abnormal return that is significantly different from zero. Mathematically speaking:[413]

$$H_0 \qquad E(CAAR_{it}|\eta, y_t) = 0 \qquad \textbf{(16)}$$

$$H_A \qquad E(CAAR_{it}|\eta, y_t) \neq 0 \qquad \textbf{(17)}$$

η: Expectation model

y_{it}: Information from η for firm i at time t

Second, it is necessary to determine which kind of t-test should be conducted and what level of confidence should be applied.

Regarding the first aspect (type of t-test), the literature suggests using a two-tailed test unless there are strong arguments that you can be sure about the direction of the effect.[414] However, using a two-tailed instead of a one-tailed test significantly reduces the power of the test because, for a 10% level of confidence, the percentage is split into 5% for each side of the distribution in a two-tailed test. Therefore, a one-tailed test would have twice the probability of detecting an abnormal return as a two-tailed test.[415]

Regarding the second aspect (level of confidence), management research views an error probability of 5% as sufficiently large. Therefore, within this study, a level of confidence equaling 95% is chosen.[416]

In the next section, different ways of calculating t-statistics will be described. However, the focus will be on the most common t-test, the cross-sectional. Unfortunately, testing procedures within

413 Mentz, 2006, p. 60 and Bowman, 1983, p. 565
414 Brown & Warner, 1980, p. 227
415 Brown & Warner, 1980, p. 227
416 Salin, pp. 1–2

the event study methodology are far from homogeneous.[417] All try to address different statistical shortcomings, but overall it seems that no testing method is superior to the others.[418]

Starting off with the standard test statistic, the cross sectional t-test:

$$t = \frac{CAAR(T_1, T2\,)}{\sigma(CAAR(T_1, T_2))}\sqrt{N} \qquad \textbf{(18)}$$

$$\sigma^2(T_1, T_2) = L\sigma^2(AR_t) \qquad \textbf{(19)}$$

t:	Test statistic
CAAR:	Cumulative average abnormal return
T_1:	Start of event window
T_2:	End of event window
N:	Number of observations
σ:	Cross-sectional standard deviation
σ^2:	Cross-sectional variance

This means that the test statistic is the cumulative average abnormal return divided by its standard deviation multiplied by the square root of the number of observations. On the other hand, the longer the event window, the higher the variance of abnormal returns and the harder it becomes to detect abnormal returns.[419]

The hypothesis and testing procedure are summarized in Figure 27:

417 Gebken, 2008, pp. 26–27
418 Bartholdy et al., 2007, p. 227
419 Kothari & Warner, 2006, pp. 12–13 and Gebken, 2008, p. 30

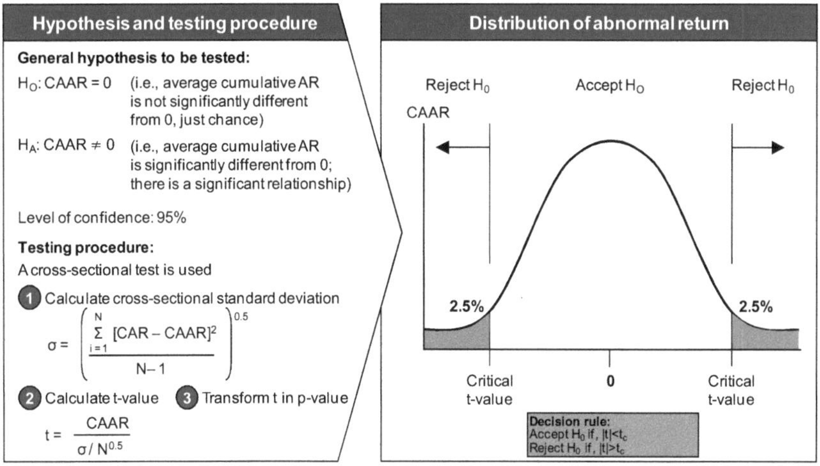

Figure 27: Summary t-test of abnormal returns

Besides the cross sectional t-test, there is the time-series method, which is similar to the previous method except that the t-test is done for each security individually.

$$t = \sum_{i=1}^{N} SE_{it}/\sqrt{N} \qquad \textbf{(20)}$$

N: Number of observations

SE: Standard error for each security i at time t

As previously noted, there is a tremendous number of testing procedures, especially for estimating the standard deviation. The ultimate goal of all of these procedures is to overcome four main drawbacks that need to be considered when choosing the right testing procedure.[420]

First is the issue of cross-correlation. Most testing procedures implicitly assume independently distributed returns with regard to time and industry.[421] If this assumption is violated, e.g., all companies belong to the same industry or event windows overlap (like in case of governmental

420 Brown & Warner, 1980, p. 233
421 Armitage, 1995, p. 37 and Giroud & Mueller, 2010, p. 328

regulations or changes in accounting methods),[422] the variance will be artificially reduced and thereby lead to higher t-statistics.[423] Consequently, there is an increased likelihood of falsely rejecting the null hypothesis and committing a type-1 error.[424]

Another major issue with testing procedures is heteroskedasticity (unequal variance) during time and within samples. Heteroskedasticity in time is mainly referred to by event-induced variance, which says that the event itself changes the variance compared to what it would have been had the event not taken place. This misspecification of variance could also lead to false inferences about the test statistics.[425]

Heteroskedasticity and the possible lack of independence among sample firms have already received scientific attention. Jaffe (1974), Mandelker (1974) and Fama (1976) provide evidence that market model residual variances differ across firms.[426]

Fourth, there is the issue of non-normality of abnormal returns. Most test statistics assume normally distributed returns. Although daily returns differ quite significantly from normal distributions, the average abnormal returns converge to normality if the number of securities exceeds a critical value.[427] As Brown and Warner (1980) stated: "For samples of size 50, the mean excess return seems close to normal."[428]

In the final segment, the issues about choosing the right testing procedures shall be evaluated. Many simulations have sought to determine if these theoretical drawbacks really affect performance and if adjustments yield significant benefits to the scientific community.[429]

As indicated, there is no testing procedure that represents "the silver bullet" to solve all statistical problems. In fact, simulations show that in practice these problems are quite minor or that new testing methods do not detect abnormal returns better.[430] As in the case of cross-sectional dependence over time (which is present in this study), it seems not to influence the results, at

422 Peterson, 1989, p. 53 and Kothari & Warner, 2006, pp. 13–14
423 Gebken, 2008, pp. 30–31 and Brown & Warner, 1980, pp. 232–233
424 MacKinlay, 1997, p. 27, Campbell et al., 1997, pp. 166–167 and Bernard, 1987, pp. 1–4
425 Boehmer, Musumeci, & Poulsen, 1992, pp. 259–260, Gebken, 2008, p. 31, Kothari & Warner, 2006, p. 18 and Patell & Wolfson, 1979, pp. 121–130
426 Binder, 1998, p. 114, Binder, 1998, p. 115, Mandelker, 1974, pp. 315–317 and Jaffe, 1974, pp. 415–418
427 Mentz, 2006, pp. 61–62
428 Gebken, 2008, pp. 31–32
429 Brown & Warner, 1980, p. 233, Brown & Warner, 1985, p. 5 and Kothari & Warner, 2006, p. 12
430 Binder, 1998, p. 116

least as long as the securities are chosen randomly.[431] Additionally, the market model seems to overcome the lack of independence, in contrast to the constant mean model. [432] Even the classical cross-sectional t-test, which is used in this study, is still sufficient in case of clustering.[433]

6.1.10.2 T-test for equality of abnormal returns

In order to be able to compare two groups with different cumulative average abnormal returns and to detect underlying influencing factors, it is necessary to split the sample into two subsamples. First it is necessary to define the hypothesis, type of test and level of confidence. This procedure begins with setting up a null hypothesis (H_0), which describes that the difference in abnormal returns between the two groups is not the result of systematic impact of an event. The alternative hypothesis (H_A), on the other hand, states that there is a significant difference in abnormal returns. Mathematically speaking:[434]

H_0 $$E(CAAR_{A,t}|\eta, y_t) = E(CAAR_{B,t}|\eta, y_t) \quad \textbf{(21)}$$

H_A $$E(CAAR_{A,t}|\eta, y_t) \neq E(CAAR_{B,t}|\eta, y_t) \quad \textbf{(22)}$$

$CAAR_{A,t}$: Cumulative average abnormal return for sample group A at time t

$CAAR_{B,t}$: Cumulative average abnormal return for sample group B at time t

η: Expectation model

y_{it}: Information from η for firm i at time t

If H_0 is rejected, it can be inferred that the underlying factor has a significant impact. Similarly to the previous test, a two-tailed test is chosen and the level of confidence is set at 95%.[435]

Basically, the testing procedure of two average cumulative abnormal returns is a two-sample t-test with unequal sample size and equal variance:[436]

---

431 Binder, 1998, p. 116
432 Brown & Warner, 1980, p. 235 and Brown & Warner, 1980, pp. 233–234
433 Boehmer et al., 1992, pp. 266–267
434 Mentz, 2006, pp. 66–67 and Gebken, 2008, pp. 33–34
435 Mentz, 2006, pp. 66–67
436 Gebken, 2008, pp. 33–34

$$t = \frac{CAAR_A - CAAR_B}{\sqrt{\left(\frac{N_A\sigma_A^2 + N_B\sigma_B^2}{N_A + N_B - 2}\right) * \left(\frac{N_A + N_B}{N_A * N_B}\right)}} \quad \textbf{(23)}$$

N_A: Sample size of group A

N_B: Sample size of group B

σ_A^2: Variance of group A

σ_B^2: Variance of group B

The hypothesis and testing procedure of the t-test for equality are summarized in Figure 28:

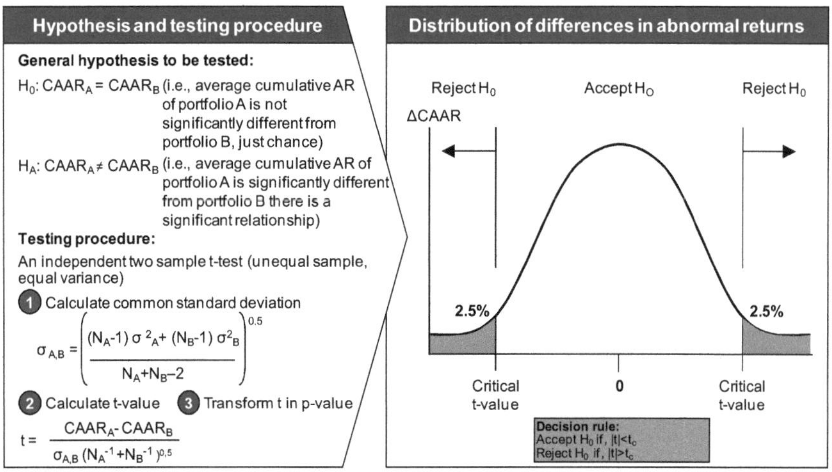

Figure 28: Summary t-test of equality

6.1.10.3 Non-parametric tests

As previously described, one of the major drawbacks of t-tests is the lack of normality of the returns. Even though abnormal returns tend to converge to normal distributions, the power of outliers can significantly distort mean abnormal returns. Therefore, to identify those outliers and to reduce their biasing influence, testing procedures that are based on calculations with medians are illustrated within this segment. Often, these methods are referred to as "non-parametric" because they do not rely on the assumption of a normal distribution.[437]

There are many different non-parametric tests, but the focus here will be on the two most common ones. For one sample, we will examine the Wilcoxon signed rank test, which is the analogue to the one-sample t-test. Second, we will focus on the Wilcoxon rank sum test, which is the analogue to the independent two-sample t-test.[438]

	Normal test	Rank test
One sample	One-sample t-test	Wilcoxon signed rank test
Two independent samples	Two-sample t-test	Wilcoxon rank sum test

[439]

Figure 29: Comparison of tests based on normal distribution with nonparametric tests for similar settings

For the Wilcoxon signed rank test, first, it is necessary to rank all observations by their absolute value. Afterwards, the signs of the original observations are attached to their respective ranks. Next, the sum of all positive-signed observations, $\sum ri+$, is calculated and put into the test statistics:[440]

$$z = \frac{\sum r_i^+ - \mu}{\sigma} \tag{24}$$

$$\mu = N * (N + 1)/4 \tag{25}$$

$$\sigma^2 = N * (N + 1) * (2N + 1)/24 \tag{26}$$

This holds true if the total number of observations is sufficiently large. Simply speaking, the Wilcoxon signed rank test can be defined as follows: "In the sign test for a given sample, the null hypothesis is that the proportion of sample securities having positive measures of abnormal

437 Moore & McCabe, 2006, p. 2 and McWilliams & Siegel, 1997, pp. 635–636
438 Moore & McCabe, 2006, pp. 2–3 and Moore & McCabe, 2006, p. 2
439 Moore & McCabe, 2006, p. 3
440 Gebken, 2008, pp. 32–33, MacKinlay, 1997, p. 32 and Campbell et al., 1997, pp. 168–175

performance (e.g., positive residuals) is equal to 0.5; the alternative hypothesis (for any particular level of abnormal performance) is that the proportion of sample securities having positive performance measures is greater than 0.5. In the Wilcoxon test, both the sign and the magnitude of the abnormal performance are taken into account in computing the test statistic."[441]

The last non-parametric test that should be illustrated here is the Wilcoxon ranked sum test, also called the Mann-Whitney U test. It begins similarly as the Wilcoxon signed rank test by ranking the combined data set and then summing all ranks of the corresponding samples. Then, the smaller sum, W, is put into the test statistic.[442]

$$z = \frac{W - \mu}{\sigma} \quad \textbf{(27)}$$

$$\mu = Ns * (Ns + Nl + 1)/2 \quad \textbf{(28)}$$

$$\sigma^2 = Ns * Nl * (Ns + Nl + 1)/12 \quad \textbf{(29)}$$

However, even these test statistics have their drawbacks. Scientists often assume that because non-parametric tests do not rely on the normal distribution assumption, they are free in terms of distributions assumed. However, Wilcoxon tests do rely on a symmetrical distribution assumption, which is invalid in the case of event studies, where abnormal return distributions are slightly skewed to the right.[443]

6.2 DATA COLLECTION

For this study, different data sources were used to compile a coherent data set.

Information about Global 500 companies, e.g., names and origins, were provided by the CDP. Additionally, the CDP provided survey-specific information such as the response status (AQ equals "answered questions", IN equals "incomplete", NR equals "no response" and DP equals "declined participation") and the list of members of the Carbon Disclosure and High Performance Group. For further analysis, two groups of response status were defined: AQ, which equaled

441 Brown & Warner, 1980, pp. 217–218, Peterson, 1989, p. 54 and Mentz, 2006, p. 65
442 Gebken, 2008, pp. 33–34
443 Armitage, 1995, pp. 42–43 and Bowman, 1983, pp. 571–573

"answered questions", and NAQ, "not answered questions" (which included "no response", "declined participation" and "incomplete").

Bloomberg was the main source for financial and accounting data, such as sales, EBIT, share of institutional investors and financial leverage. As the basis for the securities price reaction, a total return index for each company was selected to control for the effect of dividend payments. In case such information was not available, the respective company was excluded from the sample. The same procedure was applied if companies were acquired by September 20, 2009. In order to avoid the problem of infrequently traded securities, the stock prices were always taken from the exchange with the highest trading volume. Further, Bloomberg was the source for industry classifications of the relevant companies, based on the Global Industry Classification Standard (GICS) sector scheme. Within this scheme, companies are assigned to one of ten industries (energy, materials, consumer staples, consumer discretionary, telecommunication services, IT, health care, financials, industrials and utilities). The standard was developed by Morgan Stanley Capital International and Standard & Poor's. Additionally, some climate-relevant information was received from Bloomberg, such as CDLI score, CO_2 emissions (scopes 1 and 2), CO_2 reduction targets, board-level responsibility for climate change and climate-specific incentive systems.

Information about the business model was integrated by the author himself.

All companies were checked for information about 2009 CDP participation in order to better control for possible leakages (analyzing the time frame from January 1, 2009, to September 18, 2009). The search key used was "Carbon Disclosure Project" and the company name. Additionally, confounding events were controlled for during the event window. In both cases, the LexisNexis database was the source for newspaper releases.[444]

6.3 CRITIQUE OF EVENT STUDIES

Although some drawbacks have already been presented for the event study model and testing procedure, some issues are over-arching.

444 Klassen & McLaughlin, 1996, p. 1206

First, event studies do not just check for significant abnormal returns but implicitly check the hypothesis of normal returns as well. Checking these two hypotheses at once is referred to as a joint-hypothesis problem. This means that if no significant abnormal returns are found, it cannot be stated that none exist. It could also be the case that the normal returns are just wrong. However, in simulations with daily returns, this problem seems negligible.[445]

In some cases, event studies are conducted where securities are not traded for several days. Cumulative abnormal returns for these securities could be too high because they could include other factors as well.[446] This is not a problem within this study because all companies showed high trading volumes.

6.4 SUMMARY

Concluding this chapter on research methodology, it can be stated that event studies are a highly developed and mature research approach. Event study models, estimation techniques and testing procedures have been refined over the last thirty years. This work has enabled the event study methodology to become one of the most highly recognized tools in financial economics.[447]

445 Mentz, 2006, pp. 69–72 and Fama, 1991, pp. 1576–1577
446 Scholes & Williams, 1977, pp. 315–318, Mentz, 2006, pp. 69–72 and Campbell et al., 1997, pp. 175–178
447 Mentz, 2006, pp. 72–73

7 Description of data set

Before moving to the empirical results of the study, it is necessary to gain a better understanding of the data set. First, the major characteristics (industry and regional segmentation) of the Global 500 will be shown. Then, a breakdown will be provided, showing why 387 companies remain in the relevant sample although the overall data set contained 500. Afterwards, different characteristics, such as industry and regional segmentation, will be provided, followed by financial and operational figures such as sales, EBIT, and leverage.

7.1 REGIONAL AND INDUSTRIAL SEGMENTATION OF GLOBAL 500

Within the basic population, which is the Global 500, it is obvious that besides an overweighting of financial companies (banks, investment groups, insurers and re-insurers) of almost 22% of the basic population, all other industries are well represented and rather equally distributed.

On a regional level, the dominance of the Western industrialized regions, such as North America (US and Canada), Europe (extended European Union) and Australia, is prevalent, at more than 75% of the population.

A depiction can be found in Figure 30:

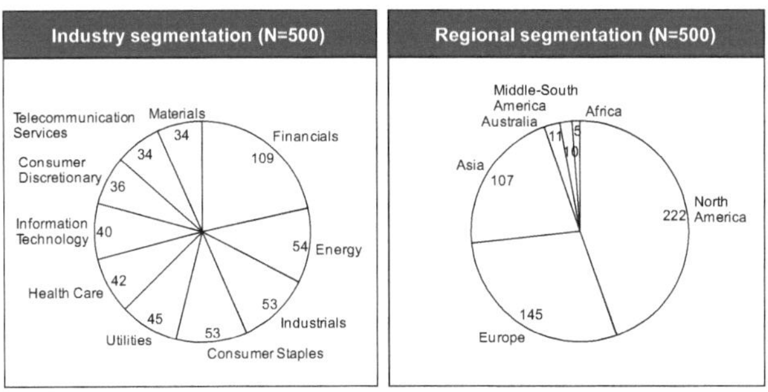

Figure 30: Regional and industrial segmentation of Global 500

7.2 BREAKDOWN OF GLOBAL 500 DATA SET INTO RELEVANT SAMPLE

This section describes why the basic population of 500 companies was reduced to the relevant sample of 387 companies. Of the 500 companies invited to participate in CDP's 2009 survey, 13 companies declined participation, 21 provided an incomplete data set and 55 did not respond at all, leaving 411 participating companies.[448]

However, some effects still have to be taken into account before starting the analysis. Fourteen companies within the sample were subsidiaries of a company within the sample and were therefore excluded. This effect can be explained mainly by M&A activities or special cases such as Wal-Mart Mexico, Unilever Hindustan or Yahoo! Japan. Additionally, for 10 companies no share prices were available. Removing these yielded 387 companies within the relevant sample. Out of these 387, 31 companies were first-time participants in the CDP.

For a graphical depiction, see Figure 31:

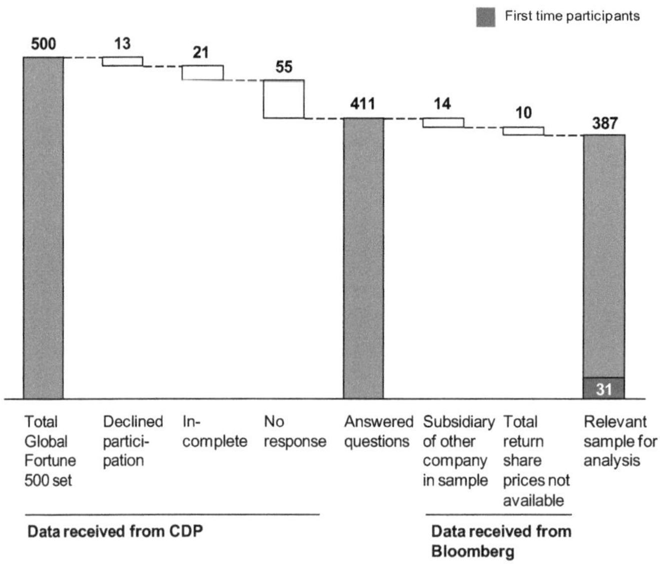

Figure 31: Breakdown of basic population to relevant sample

448 This number was provided by CDP.

7.3 REGIONAL AND INDUSTRIAL SEGMENTATION OF RELEVANT SAMPLE

Compared to the industrial segmentation of the basic population, the relevance of the financial sector in the relevant sample has decreased just a bit. However, the financial sector remains overweighted. All other sectors are more or less evenly distributed.

In contrast to the industrial segmentation, the regional segmentation shows an even stronger dominance than is found in the basic population. In particular, Western industrialized nations (EU, North America and Australia) now represent more than 80% of the relevant sample. This shows that, as previously indicated, the non-respondents mainly come from Asia, Middle and South America and Africa.

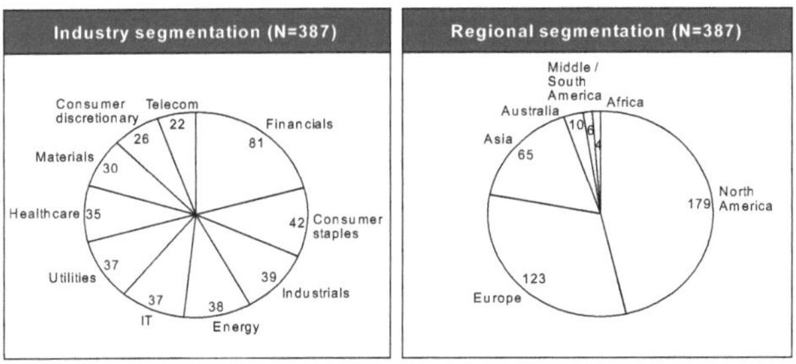

Figure 32: Regional and industrial segmentation of relevant sample

7.4 FURTHER CHARACTERISTICS OF THE SAMPLE

Within this section, other characteristics of the sample shall be described in order to better understand the setting up of moderating factors.

The focus will now be on sales by sector. As the biggest companies by sales are oil and gas firms such as Royal Dutch Shell and BP, it is not surprising that the industry with the highest average sales is energy (more than 95 billion USD). The average across all industries is 44.3 billion USD. Further details can be seen in Figure 33.

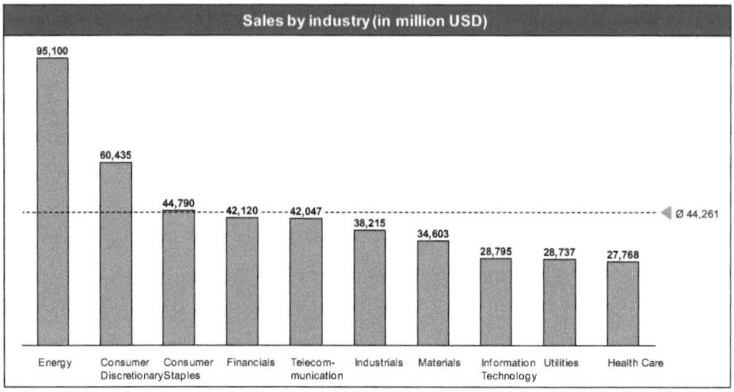

Figure 33: Average sales by industry

In the next step, how the moderating factors are structured will be described. This means that all companies are split into three equally sized buckets (in general, low, medium and high) in order to spot differences in the outcomes. Additionally, all moderating factors are then described by showing an industry split to get a better understanding of the relevant data set.

First, it seems interesting to understand how profitability (here, EBIT margin) might impact later results. Therefore, all relevant companies providing profitability numbers (N= 311) were grouped into three almost equally sized buckets. EBIT margin groups were bigger than 22.5%, between 22.5% and 12.0% and smaller than 12.0%. For a better understanding of the distribution of margins, see Figure 34:

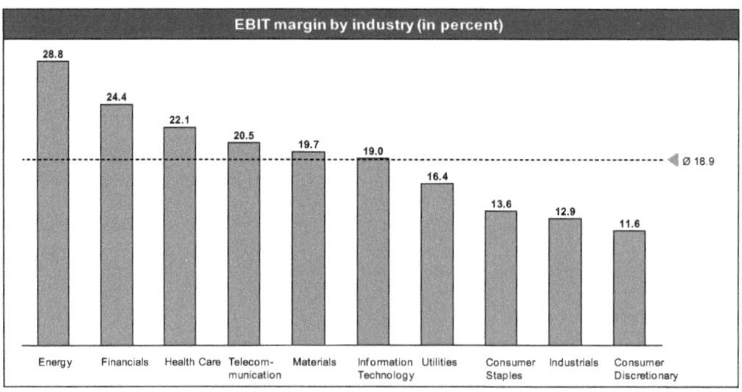

Figure 34: Average EBIT margin by industry

As illustrated, the energy sector is the most profitable one, with nearly a 29% EBIT margin, whereas the average EBIT margin lies for the overall sample at 18.9%. One of the major reasons for this is probably the high oil prices during 2008, which boosted earnings for energy companies.

Second, the importance of leverage (share of debt to total assets) shall be analyzed further. Therefore, similar to the case of profitability, three equally sized buckets are formed. High leverage is above 28.8%, medium between 28.8% and 15.4% and low leverage below 15.4%. The most indebted sector is the utility industry, with a leverage of 36.2%. The average indebtedness is 24.6%.

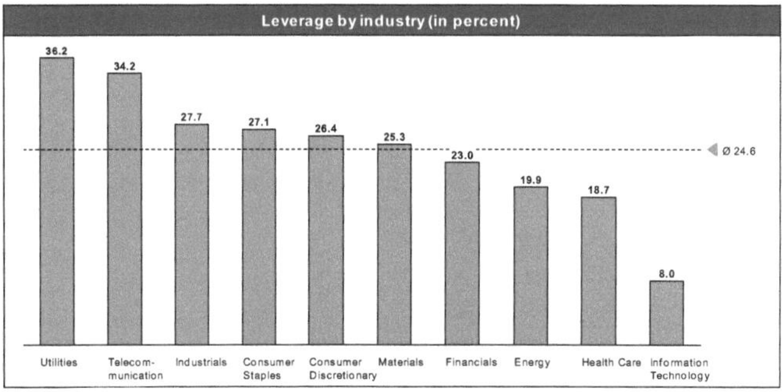

Figure 35: Leverage by industry

Third, the share of institutional investors might also play an important role. Therefore, the bucket boundaries are: High share of institutional investors equals more than 74.8%, medium share between 74.8% and 43.8% and low share below 43.8%. The average share of institutional investors across all industries is 57.9% (N=380). The industry with the highest level of institutional investors is the health care industry, with 67.2%. For further details, see Figure 36:

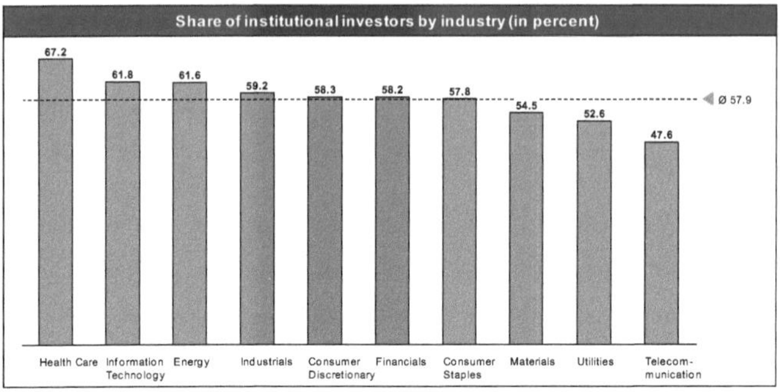

Figure 36: Share of institutional investors by industry

Fourth, to analyze how carbon intensity (CO_2 emissions[449] in tons per million USD of revenue) influences empirical results, three equally sized buckets are formed. High carbon intensity is assigned if a company emits more than 122 tons of CO_2 per million USD in revenue, medium intensity if emissions are between 20 and 122 tons and low carbon intensity if below 20 tons is emitted per million USD in revenue. The total basic population for this analysis is 329. The average carbon intensity is more than 740 tons of CO_2 per million USD in revenue. However, it should be noted that this number is extremely skewed due to the high carbon intensity of the utilities sector (4.278,1 tons CO_2).

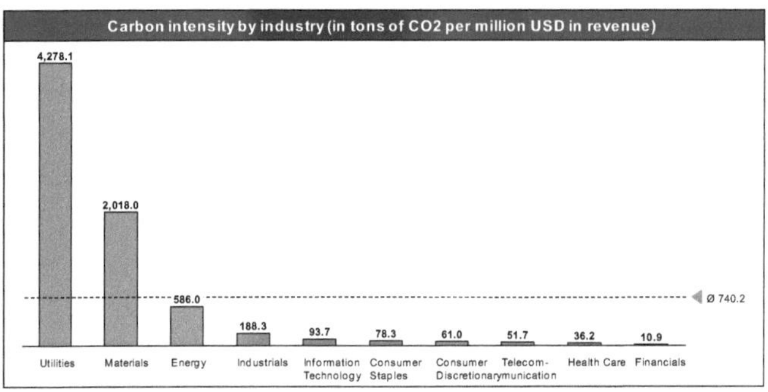

Figure 37: Carbon intensity by industry

449 Scope 1 and 2

The last moderating factor that should be considered is the business model, namely whether each company is consumer or business oriented (B2C vs. B2B) or something in between (Mid). The basic population is 387 companies, which are (unintentionally) almost evenly spread.

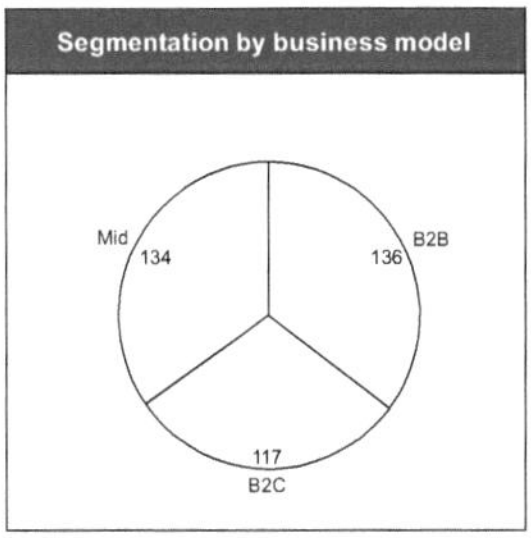

Figure 38: Segmentation by business model

8 Empirical results and interpretation

The following section shall provide the empirical results to all research questions posed. Each research question will be covered by one sub-chapter along with a brief interpretation of the results. However, as mentioned, interpretation is not a focus area of this document and is left to further research.[450] Sections 8.1 to 8.3 will cover the key research questions, while 8.4 to 8.6 cover the survey-specific research questions.

8.1 IMPACT OF CDP PARTICIPATION ON FINANCIAL PERFORMANCE

Surprisingly, the analysis revealed a negative relationship between participation in CDP (here: "AQ") and financial performance, i.e., an abnormal return of -0.2%, which was significant. Although not taking part (here: "NAQ") yielded an even stronger negative abnormal return (-0,5%), this value was not significant.

On a regional level, this significant negative reaction towards CDP participation was particularly strong in Western regions. Europe showed a very significant negative reaction of -0.6% and North America similarly of -0.4%. In contrast, Asia showed a significant positive abnormal return of +0.9%. Additionally, even in comparison to Asian companies that did not take part in CDP (abnormal return: -0.6%), they yielded a significant abnormal return, showing that in Asia it pays off to take part in CDP by generating an abnormal return of +1.5% (0.9%+0.6%).

Taking a sector perspective, only consumer staples and energy showed significant changes in stock prices. While consumer staples showed a positive abnormal return (+0.8%) for companies participating in CDP, energy showed a negative abnormal return (-0.9%).

For an illustration of these empirical results, see Figure 39:

450 As mentioned in Chapter 6.1.4, if the analysis involved sub-samples of fewer than 25 companies, the results were ignored even if they might have been significant. Consequently, if results are not significant, they will not be mentioned.

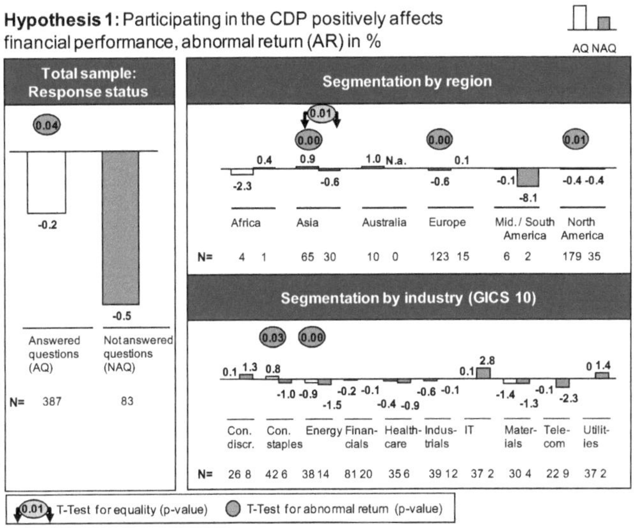

Figure 39: First part of empirical results on research question 1

Some readers might assume that consumer-oriented companies show positive reactions towards participation in CDP. However, on an aggregated level (business model as moderating factor), this cannot be confirmed. Only companies in the B2B segment show a significant relationship for participation versus non-participation. Here, not taking part is "punished" by investors by an abnormal return of -1.0%, whereas taking part yields a negative abnormal return of "just" -0.7%.

Checking for carbon intensity also revealed interesting results. Only highly carbon-intensive companies showed significant abnormal returns of -0.7%. Here, non-participating companies could not be compared with participating ones because only those that took part in CDP released their CO_2 emissions data in a comparable manner.

Comparing the results by level of profitability also showed significant results only for highly profitable companies that participated in CDP, with an abnormal return of -0.8%.

Another moderating factor was the level of institutional investors. Interestingly, companies with high shares of institutional investors seemed to react more strongly to the information on participation or non-participation. Investors severely punished companies that did not take part.

The abnormal return of -1.2% for those companies was significant, compared to the "only" -0.6% abnormal return for the companies participating in CDP. The participating companies thus benefit from a relative advantage of +0.6%.

Finally, the aspect of financial leverage should be covered as well. Here, only companies showing a medium value of leverage showed a significant abnormal return of -0.6%.

For an illustration of the results according to business model, carbon intensity, profitability, share of institutional investors and financial leverage, see Figure 40:

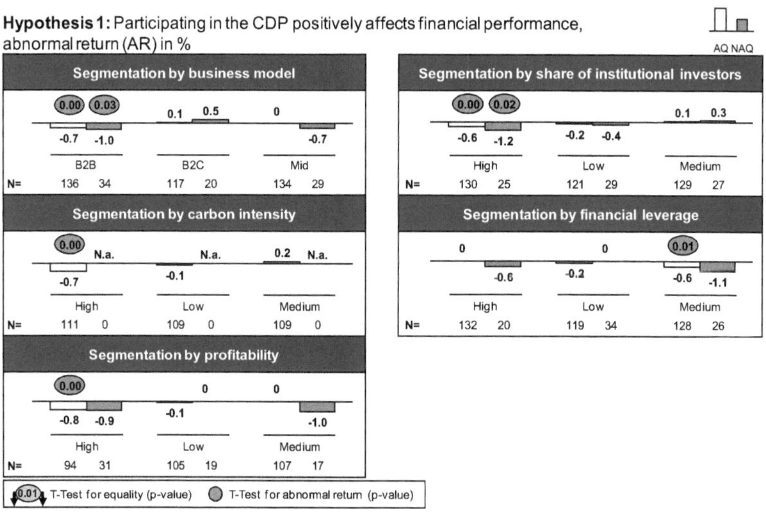

Figure 40: Second part of empirical results on research question 1

Because the impact of participation should be isolated as far as possible, the second section of this chapter focuses on the stock market reaction of just those companies participating in the CDP for the first time. The effect should be stronger here because companies that might have been assumed to be taking part in CDP again are excluded.

In fact, the results showed a stronger reaction for companies participating for the first time than for those that were not "first-timers". As illustrated in the picture below, first-timers showed a strongly significant abnormal return of -1.0% that is significant even compared to the non-first-timers.[451]

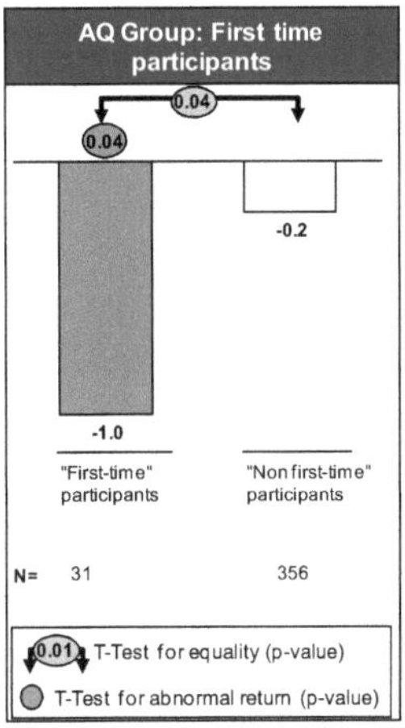

Figure 41: Empirical results for research question 1A

Generally, it seems that investors do not value participation in CDP. Perhaps they see this as a company's first step towards a green corporate policy, which might eventually hurt profitability. This would mean that investors follow the traditional approach, suggesting a reciprocal relation between carbon disclosure/management and economic performance. Alternatively, investors could also perceive participation in CDP as a costly PR move.

However, it seems that there are differences in the reactions of investors depending on their level of professionalism. Whereas companies with high shares of institutional investors reacted in the way assumed (participation in CDP rewarded by investors compared to non-participation, which was punished), companies with lower shares of institutional investors did not show this response.

Another aspect that is worth interpreting is the fact that there are strong regional differences in the ways in which CDP participation was perceived. While Asia rewarded this behavior, Western regions (North America and Europe) punished companies for participating. One possible explanation could be that North America and Europe are more short-term oriented, while Asian

451 Because the group of first-timers is small (just 31 companies), no further analysis of moderating factors was carried out.

companies (mainly Japanese) are more long-term oriented. Therefore, including carbon and environmental issues into planning is more natural to Asian companies and does not mean sacrificing profits but creating real opportunities.

8.2 IMPACT OF MEMBERSHIP IN CARBON DISCLOSURE LEADERSHIP INDEX ON FINANCIAL PERFORMANCE

Within the second research question, the focus was on the potential financial impact of providing high-quality data on the company's exposure (risk and opportunities) to climate change. Here, two operational variables came into play: membership in the CDLI and the disclosure score.

On an aggregated level, membership in the CDLI does not show any significant impact on financial performance. Members of CDLI even show a more negative abnormal return (-0.4%) than do non-members (-0.2%). However, all changes are nonsignificant.

Even within the regional or the industry splits, not a single group showed significant results for members of CDLI. However, not being a member yielded some significant results. On a regional level, Asia showed a positive abnormal return (+1.0%), while Europe and North America both showed negative abnormal returns of -0.5%. The industry perspective also revealed a positive abnormal return for consumer staples (+0.8%) and a negative one for energy of -0.8%.

For an illustration of these empirical results, see Figure 42:

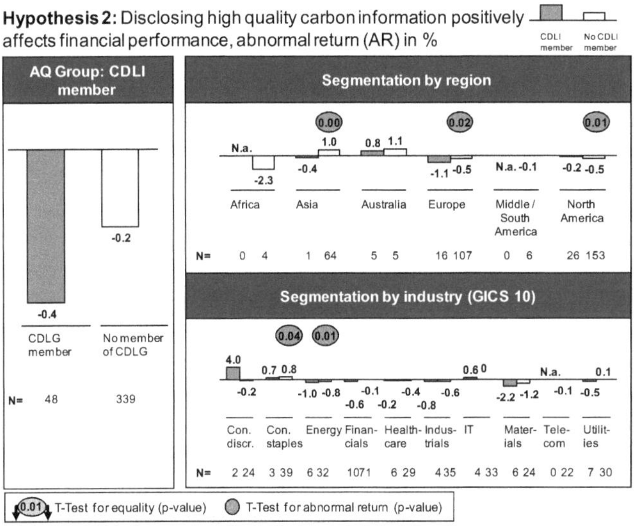

Figure 42: First part of empirical results on research question 2

When analyzing the sample on the basis of business model, it was revealed that only in the B2B segment, not being a member significantly reduces firm value (-0.6%). However, investors in other segments do not seem to react.

Interestingly, the situation looks different when it comes to the moderating factor of carbon intensity. Here, highly carbon intensive companies that are members of the CDLI show significant abnormal returns of -1.1%, while not being a member yielded a significant negative abnormal return of "just" -0.7%.

On the level of profitability, it seems that only highly profitable companies that are not members of CDLI show significant abnormal returns (-0.9%).

Also, the share of institutional investors seems to play a role, but just for companies with high shares of institutional investors. Here, not being a member of the CDLI leads to an abnormal return of -0.6%.

Also, medium leveraged companies show a significant abnormal return of -0.7%.

For an illustration of the results relevant to the business model, carbon intensity, profitability, share of institutional investors and financial leverage, see Figure 43:

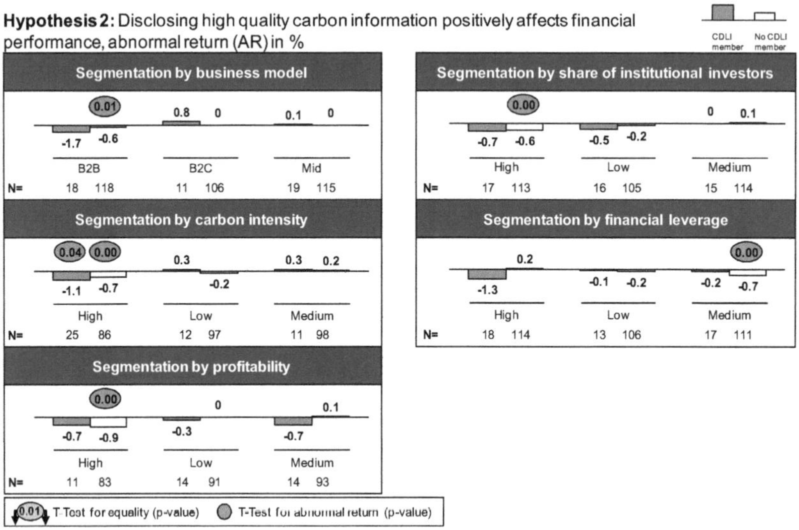

Figure 43: Second part of empirical results on research question 2

In order to verify the overall finding that the quality of carbon disclosure does not seem to impact financial performance, another variable (disclosure score) shall illustrate this with a regression.

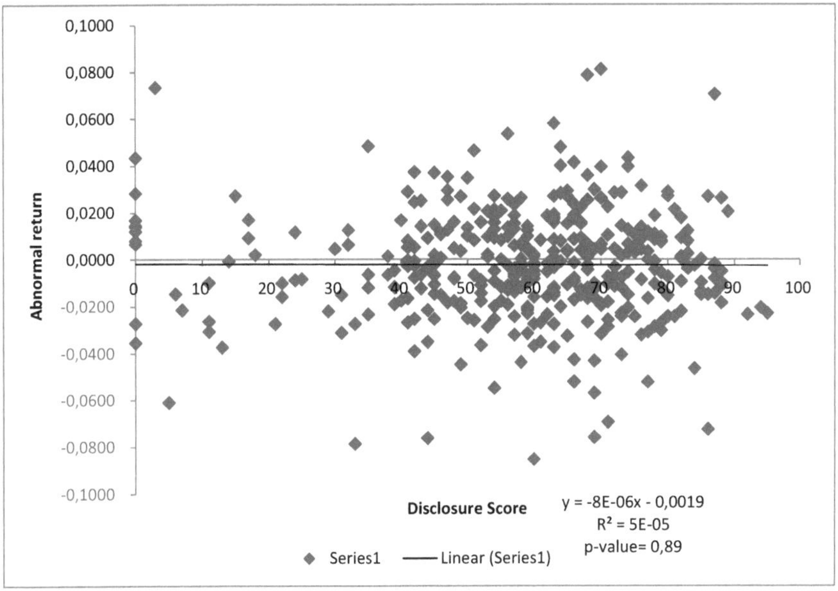

Figure 44: Regression analysis on disclosure score and abnormal return

As is obvious from the picture above, there is virtually no correlation between disclosure score and abnormal returns. The regression coefficient is close to zero and the p-value almost 90%.

Wrapping up this chapter, it can be said that whether companies disclose their exposure to climate risk seems insignificant to investors, at least on an aggregated level. Even excellent disclosing companies (that are part of the CDLI) do not seem to matter. One interpretation of this might be that the investors do not see value creation in disclosing information, so no significant abnormal return is observed. However, they might value it in nonfinancial terms.

Interestingly, the only case where membership in the CDLI showed significant results was for carbon-intensive companies, where an even stronger negative abnormal return was observed than for those that were not members of the CDLI. One reason for this might be that in a situation where companies are ex-ante known to be highly exposed to regulative actions, e.g., utilities, the detailed disclosure of the full amount of data can include negative surprises.

8.3 IMPACT OF CARBON PERFORMANCE AWARD ON FINANCIAL PERFORMANCE

One of the major research questions was the impact of carbon performance awards on financial performance. Interestingly, the receipt of carbon performance awards itself does not seem to impact market valuation (abnormal return: +0.1%). However, not receiving such an award seems to have a significant impact (-0.3%).[452]

For an illustration of the empirical result, see Figure 45:

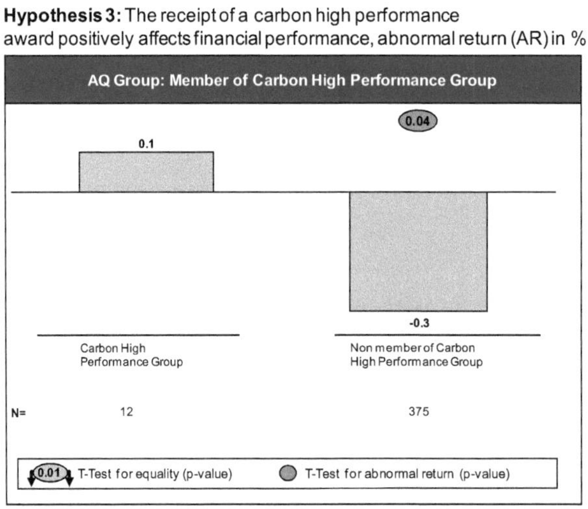

Figure 45: Empirical results for research question 3

Because just the companies not receiving an award showed significant abnormal returns, the relationship might be perceived as a hygiene factor. This means that investors expect companies to behave in a carbon-friendly manner and consequently do not reward this. However, if companies are labeled as not climate friendly, they might be punished for that.

452 Because just twelve companies belong to the Carbon High Performance Group, no further splits (regional, industry, etc.) were conducted as they would lead to small sample sizes.

8.4 IMPACT OF SETTING CO_2 REDUCTION TARGETS ON FINANCIAL PERFORMANCE

This sub-chapter is the first that covers survey-specific research questions. Because not all companies participating in the CDP answered the question on the setting of CO_2 reduction targets, the total population for this analysis is just 296.

Comparing the sample of those companies that have set CO_2 reduction targets (255 observations) to those without such targets (41 observations), the analysis reveals that, on an aggregated level, investors do not see to care about this fact. Although the difference is quite big (0.6%), it is still not significant.

On a regional level, companies from Asia show a significant positive abnormal return of 1.5% for having CO_2 reduction targets, while companies in Europe show a significant negative abnormal return of -0.7% for the same behavior. Interestingly, North American firms only show a significant negative abnormal return (-1.1%) for those companies that do not set CO_2 reduction targets. This result is significant even in comparison to the North American group that did set targets (abnormal return: 0.0%). This means that for US companies, it creates value to set emissions targets compared to not setting them because otherwise they might be punished by investors.

On an industry level, only consumer staples show a significant positive abnormal return (1.0%) for setting CO_2 emission targets.

For an illustration of the results, see Figure 46:

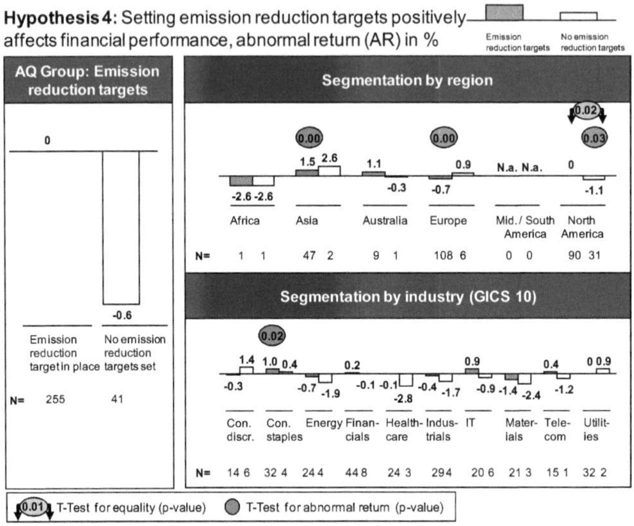

Figure 46: First part of empirical results on research question 4

Checking other moderating factors like business model reveals that setting CO_2 reduction targets in the B2B segment leads to significant abnormal returns (-0.7%).

Similarly, highly carbon-intensive companies also show significant negative abnormal returns (-0.6%) for setting those targets, as do highly profitable companies with a significant abnormal return of -0.6%.

An illustration of those results see Figure 47:

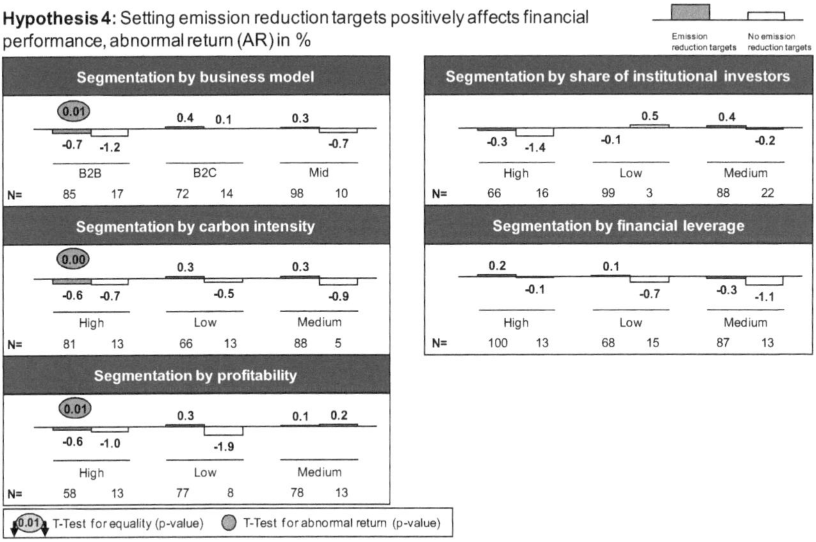

Figure 47: Second part of empirical results on research question 4

Although there are certain situations (e.g., particular regions) where CO_2 emission reduction targets seem to matter, on an aggregated level, investors do not care about them. Therefore, it can be stated that these targets are not important to investors in general. This is surprising because governments are moving toward a cap and trade system of CO_2 emissions that should eventually make companies pay for their emissions (as indicated in Chapter 1.2).

8.5 IMPACT ON FINANCIAL PERFORMANCE OF HAVING A BOARD-LEVELMEMBER RESPONSIBLE FOR CLIMATE CHANGE

Within this section, an answer shall be provided to the question of whether having a board-level member who is responsible for climate change issues has an impact on financial performance. Similarly to the previous section, not all companies taking part in the CDP answered this question. Therefore, the total population for this research question is 334 companies.

Analyzing the two groups of companies, the first having a responsible board member (292) and the second not having one (42), shows that the second group shows a significant abnormal return of -0.8%, while the first group shows a negative abnormal return of "just" -0.1%. This difference in reaction (0.7%) is also significant. Therefore, it seems to pay to have a board-level individual responsible for this issue.

For an illustration, see Figure 48:

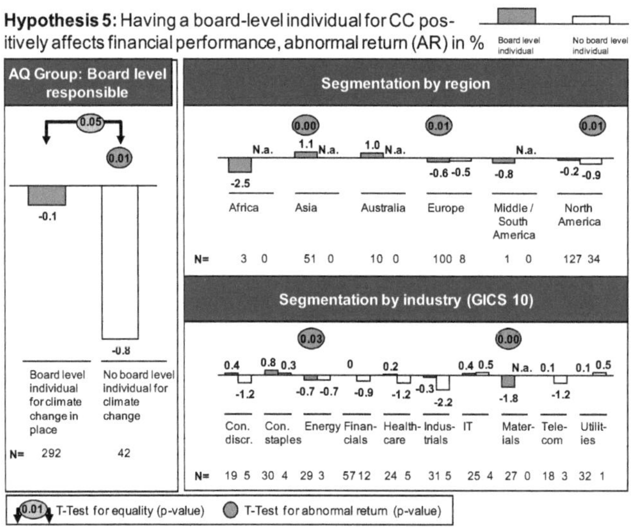

Figure 48: First part of empirical results on research question 5

As can be seen in the picture above, there are some significant results on a regional level as well. Here, Asia shows a significant positive abnormal return of 1.1% for companies having a board member who is responsible for climate change issues. In contrast, Europe shows a negative abnormal return of -0.6% in the same setting. Interestingly, in North America, companies seem to get severely punished (significant abnormal return: -0.9%) for not having a board member focused on climate change issues.

On an industry level, energy (-0.7%) and materials (-1.8%) companies do not seem to be rewarded by investors if they have board members who are responsible for climate change issues.

In particular, companies in the B2B segment or those that are highly carbon intensive show significant negative reactions (-0.8% and -0.7%) towards the announcement of a board member responsible for climate change.

Similarly, highly profitable companies or those with a high share of institutional investors show significant negative abnormal returns (-0.8% and -0.6%) on the existence of this board member.

For a depiction, see Figure 49:

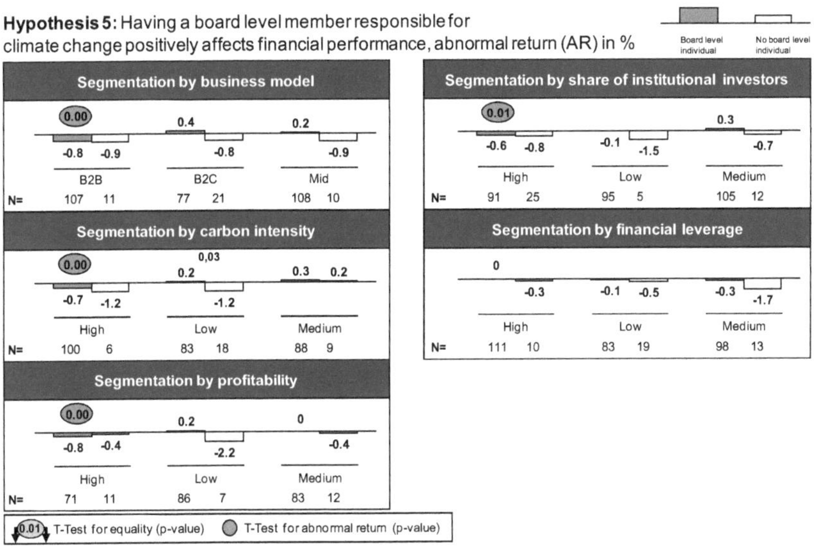

Figure 49: Second part of empirical results on research question 5

Although there are some situations where the existence of a board member responsible for climate issues yields a negative abnormal return (as explained above), on an aggregated level the lack of a board member focused on this issue yields a significant negative abnormal return even compared to the group that has such a board member. Therefore, it seems that this aspect is seen as a hygiene factor (similar to the carbon performance award). Investors expect a company to have this organizational setup, and any deviation from this behavior is punished.

8.6 IMPACT ON FINANCIAL PERFORMANCE OF HAVING AN INCENTIVE SYSTEM TO SUPPORT CLIMATE-FRIENDLY BEHAVIOR

The last research question that needs to be answered concerns the relationship between having an incentive system to support climate-friendly behavior and financial performance.

Like the previous two survey-specific research questions, this one was also not fully answered by CDP participants, but by just 331.

From an aggregated perspective, it seems that not having an incentive system to promote climate-friendly behavior is seen negatively by investors, yielding a significant abnormal return of -0.4%.

For an illustration, see Figure 50:

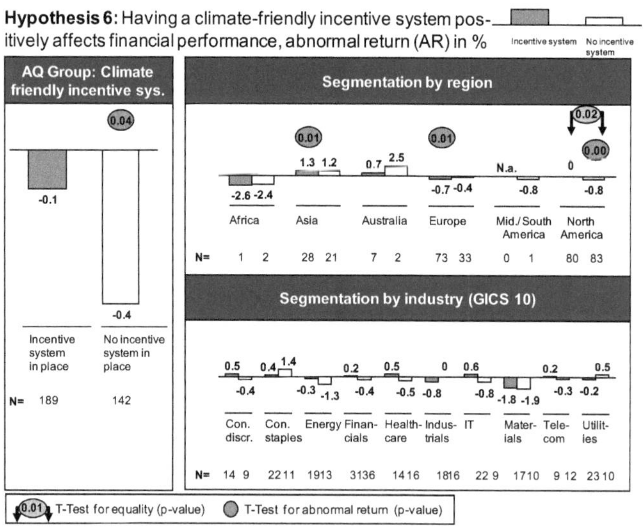

Figure 50: First part of empirical results on research question 6

On a regional level, again, Asian companies seem to be rewarded for having an incentive system (abnormal return of +1.3%), while European companies' reaction towards this is rather negative (-0.7%). Interestingly, in North America, not having an incentive system is punished by investors instantly (abnormal return: -0.8%), even in comparison to the group having an incentive system (abnormal return: 0.0%). Thus, it pays off in North America to invest in a climate-friendly incentive system; otherwise, the company's value might decrease.

Regarding the business model, within the B2B segment, investors seem to have a strong opinion about the existence of this kind of incentive scheme. Here, companies with incentive systems showed stronger negative abnormal returns (-0.9%) than did those without such a system (-0.6%).

For highly carbon-intensive companies, both having and not having an incentive system yields the same abnormal return (-0.8%).

For an illustration of all moderating factors, see Figure 51:

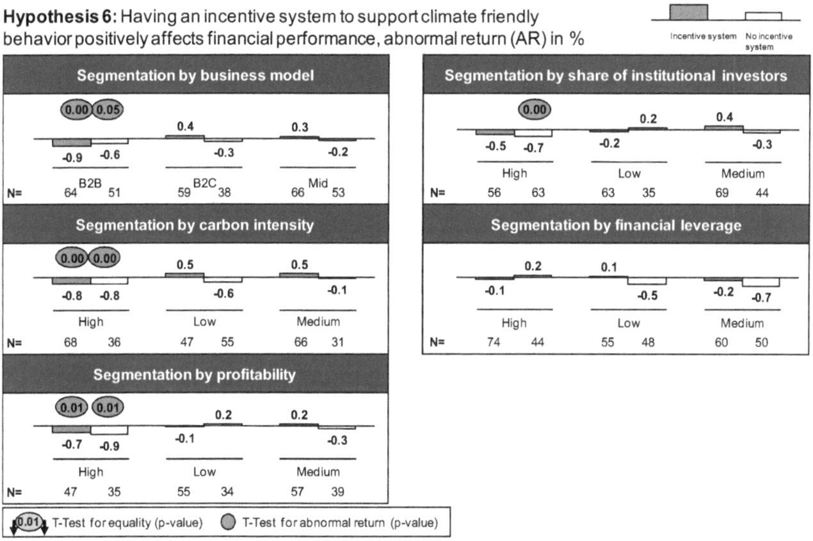

Figure 51: Second part of empirical results on research question 6

The overall picture is reflected in the results for profitability. This means that for highly profitable companies, not having an incentive system yields a stronger negative abnormal return (-0.9%) than does having an incentive system, which yields a negative abnormal return of "just" -0.7%.

Similarly, for companies with high shares of institutional investors, not having an incentive system yielded a significant abnormal return of -0.7%.

As in the previous sub-chapter, it seems that despite some special cases, like companies in the B2B segment, an incentive system is generally perceived as a hygiene factor. Investors expect companies to have this kind of incentive system, and not having it results in a negative stock market reaction.

9 Summary and conclusion

Having described the empirical results and their possible interpretations, this chapter shall first wrap up the major findings of this study and compare them with the research questions posed.[453] Second, implications for managers will be derived from those findings. Third, the limitations of the study will be shown, and finally, areas for further research will be identified.

9.1 MAJOR FINDINGS

This section is split into two parts, first summarizing the results of the six research questions and second taking an overarching look at the influencing power of moderating factors.

Regarding the impact of CDP participation on financial performance (first research question), it is obvious that investors perceive it as negative. Their reaction is even stronger for companies taking part for the first time.

However, the amount or quality of disclosed information regarding a company's exposure to climate change (second research question) seems insignificant to investors. This holds true for companies within the CDLI and additionally for the relationship between disclosure scores and abnormal returns.

A different reaction is perceived when it comes to the stockholders' reaction to the receipt of a carbon performance award (third research question). Here, the company receiving the award did not show a significant reaction, but the companies not receiving an award did show a significant negative abnormal return.

Different outcomes were seen concerning whether emission reduction targets had an impact on financial performance (fourth research question). Here, no significant relation was found for either of the two groups.

---

453 Although the setting of this dissertation is rather descriptive by nature.

Within the fifth research question, the importance of having a board member who is responsible for climate issues was analyzed. Similar to the analysis for the carbon performance award, not having a board member responsible for this matter was punished by investors.

Finally, the results for research question six showed that not having an incentive system to promote climate-friendly behavior was also punished by investors.

The second major goal of this section is to summarize the importance of moderating factors for the results.

Regional splits revealed quite interesting results. While Australia, Africa and Middle and South America never showed significant results (due to their small sample sizes), Europe, Asia and North America showed some astonishing results. The reactions varied quite substantially based on the region. Whereas Asia mostly showed positive reactions towards carbon-conscious behavior (e.g., CDP participation), Europe's reactions were mainly negative. North America's behavior was, depending on the research question, quite mixed.

On an industry level, although the sample sizes for most sectors were sufficient, the number of significant results was smaller than in the regional analysis. Only consumer staples, energy and materials showed significant outcomes. Whereas consumer staples showed a stronger positive reaction towards carbon-conscious behavior, energy and materials showed deeply negative attitudes towards several constructs of interest.

Regarding the influence of the business model on the results, it seems rather clear that B2C and mixed forms of business models do not influence the results. However, within the B2B segment, the reaction towards carbon-conscious behavior was mixed, while CDP participation was well received vs. non-participation. Other aspects, like a responsible board member and emission reduction targets, were perceived negatively.

The carbon intensity factor also yielded significant results just for the highly carbon-intensive group of companies. The other two groups (low and medium carbon intensity) showed no significant relations. Not surprisingly, in all cases except for the last research question (climate-friendly incentive system, where the results showed no differences), the reaction towards carbon-conscious behavior was negative.

In the case of profitability, only highly profitable companies showed significant reactions towards different constructs of interest. Low and medium profitable companies did not show any significant relationships at all. Except for the importance of the right incentive system, all reactions to carbon-conscious behavior were negative.

Using share of institutional investors as a moderating factor showed that, especially for companies with a high percentage of institutional investors, stock market reactions are significant, whereas for other groups they are not. Generally, companies with high shares of institutional investors reacted relatively positively to carbon-conscious behavior. This means that the negative reaction to climate-friendly behavior was not as strong as it was for the non-climate-friendly alternative, except for the implementation of the incentive system.

Finally, financial leverage does not seem to play an important role as a moderating factor because just two out of six research questions yielded significant results.

Summing up the major findings: This dissertation shed light on the relation between environmental disclosure and financial performance as well as on the association between environmental performance and financial performance. Although the results are not as clear-cut as theory might suggest, the relationship between environmental disclosure and financial performance (research questions one and two) seems to tend towards a negative association. This pattern of findings supports the general state of mind of socio-political theories. Regarding the relation between environmental performance and financial performance (research questions three to six), the situation is a bit more complicated. As it seems that these elements of environmental performance are mostly treated like hygiene factors by investors. Nevertheless, this result would suggest a positive association between environmental performance and financial performance, thereby following the revisionist view on this relation.

Consequently, the outlook for reconciliation between the environment and the economy is not as grim as an initial inspection of the results might suggest.

9.2 MANAGERIAL IMPLICATIONS

Although corporate leaders might still perceive these results as depressing, showing that investors do not reward carbon-conscious behavior on the part of companies, they should still take the time to read beyond the top lines of these outcomes. Every practitioner should determine for himself which situation applies to his company. Which industry does it belong to? Which region does it come from? What is the share of institutional investors in the company? All of these aspects could substantially alter the interpretation of these results.

Finally, corporate leaders should also bear in mind that although stockholders are an important stakeholder group, they are not the only one. Each company has its own set of targets that are differently important and achieved to different levels. Therefore, the achievement of corporate success might mean more than increasing stock value.

9.3 LIMITATIONS OF THE STUDY

Although some of the shortcomings of this study have already been addressed in the respective chapters, this section shall summarize those issues.

First, the operationalization of carbon/environmental performance through a carbon award may be problematic. Obviously an award is a distinct event, whereas good carbon performance is a process. Additionally, an award is retrograde and not future-oriented. However, carbon performance is an outcome of incremental managerial decisions, which are hard to measure. Further, one of the best indicators of good future carbon performance is excellent past carbon performance.

Second, defining corporate performance or success by financial performance approximated by stock market returns is certainly narrow. As indicated in the previous section, other targets set by other stakeholders with different weightings would certainly be a more exhaustive approach. However, this information is not available on a large scale.

Third, CDP data sometimes do not seem to be 100% consistent. Results provided in the report sometimes diverged from the data set provided in Microsoft Excel format. However, the author tried to clarify inconsistencies to the best of his ability.

Fourth, there are limitations of the research methodology chosen. Aspects like non-synchronous trading, parameter estimation, correction for confounding events and joint-hypothesis testing will not be explained here again. For further information, see Chapter Six.

Fifth, this study was conducted just for 2009, so trends within other recent years or even in 2010 cannot be captured.

Finally, in order to analyze the effect of good carbon performance, the group of 12 companies receiving a carbon performance award was chosen. Of course, this is a small sample size, which makes analyses very difficult.

9.4 SUGGESTIONS FOR FURTHER RESEARCH

This document comprises the first study to analyze the relationship between carbon disclosure and financial performance as well as the association between carbon and financial performance.

Additionally, this study added value in regard to capital market research by using a multi-country market model and applying global as well as local indices. Additionally, this approach has been combined with the index model. For further information, see the Microsoft Excel model provided by the author.

Because this dissertation was mainly descriptive in nature, further research could interpret and analyze the reasons for investors to behave in a certain way. In particular, the hygiene factor behavior of several carbon performance measures seems worth exploring.

Based on the limitations of the study, it would further be interesting to compare stock market reactions to CDP announcements in different years.

Additionally, CDP provided performance scores in its newest report on the Global 500 (2010) for all participating companies. Therefore, further analysis on this issue might be interesting as well.

Alternatively, it may be possible to use price data not from stock markets, but from corporate bond markets, and to analyze if reactions are similar and how they differ in terms of reaction time and magnitude.

Overall, this dissertation provides some promising avenues for further research in both the field of capital market research in general and in the field of carbon performance and stock market reaction in particular.

Appendix

ID	Company Name	Subsidary of bigger company	Total return index availabl	GICS Industry	Region	Response Status 2009	CDLI_Score 2009
1	3M Company	no	yes	Industrials	North America	AQ	60
2	A.P. Moller - Maersk	no	yes	Industrials	Europe	AQ	67
3	ABB	no	yes	Industrials	Europe	AQ	57
4	Abbott Laboratories	no	yes	Health Care	North America	AQ	65
5	Abertis Infraestructuras	no	yes	Industrials	Europe	AQ	52
6	Accenture	no	yes	Information Technology	North America	AQ	76
7	Ace Ltd	no	yes	Financials	North America	AQ	53
8	ACS Actividades de Construccion y Servicios	no	yes	Industrials	Europe	AQ	59
9	Activision Blizzard	no	yes	Information Technology	North America	NAQ	N.a.
10	Adobe Systems, Inc.	no	yes	Information Technology	North America	AQ	60
11	Aetna Inc.	no	yes	Health Care	North America	AQ	60
12	AFLAC Incorporated	no	yes	Financials	North America	AQ	62
13	Air Liquide	no	yes	Materials	Europe	AQ	60
14	Air Products & Chemicals, Inc.	no	yes	Materials	North America	AQ	74
15	Alcon (see Nestle)	yes	no	Consumer Staples	Europe	AQ	N.a.
16	Allergan, Inc.	no	yes	Health Care	North America	AQ	85
17	Allianz SE	no	yes	Financials	Europe	AQ	83
18	Allstate Corporation	no	yes	Financials	North America	AQ	79
19	Alstom	no	yes	Industrials	Europe	AQ	63
20	Altria Group, Inc.	no	yes	Consumer Staples	North America	AQ	66
21	Amazon.com Inc.	no	yes	Consumer Discretionary	North America	NAQ	N.a.
22	Ambev - Cia. Bebidas das Americas	no	yes	Consumer Staples	Middle-South America	AQ	51
23	America Movil	no	yes	Telecommunication Services	Middle-South America	NAQ	N.a.
24	American Electric Power Company, Inc.	no	yes	Utilities	North America	AQ	52
25	American Express	no	yes	Financials	North America	AQ	57
26	American Tower Corp.	no	yes	Telecommunication Services	North America	AQ	70
27	Amgen, Inc.	no	yes	Health Care	North America	AQ	63
28	Anadarko Petroleum Corporation	no	yes	Energy	North America	AQ	79
29	Anglo American	no	yes	Materials	Europe	AQ	58
30	Anglo Platinum	no	yes	Materials	Africa	AQ	73
31	Anheuser Busch InBev	no	yes	Consumer Staples	Europe	AQ	50
32	Aon Corporation	no	yes	Financials	North America	AQ	6
33	Apache Corporation	no	yes	Energy	North America	AQ	72
34	Apollo Group, Inc.	no	yes	Consumer Discretionary	North America	NAQ	N.a.
35	Apple Inc.	no	yes	Information Technology	North America	AQ	73
36	Applied Materials Inc.	no	yes	Information Technology	North America	AQ	57
37	Arcelor Mittal	no	yes	Materials	Europe	AQ	35
38	Archer Daniels Midland	no	yes	Consumer Staples	North America	NAQ	N.a.
39	Astellas Pharma	no	yes	Health Care	Asia	AQ	41
40	AstraZeneca	no	yes	Health Care	Europe	AQ	71
41	AT&T - Telecom	no	yes	Telecommunication Services	North America	AQ	47
42	Australia and New Zealand Banking Group Li	no	no	Financials	Australia	AQ	N.a.
43	Automatic Data Processing, Inc.	no	yes	Information Technology	North America	AQ	32
44	Aviva	no	yes	Financials	Europe	AQ	80
45	AXA Group	no	yes	Financials	Europe	AQ	65
46	BAE Systems	no	yes	Industrials	Europe	AQ	56
47	Baker Hughes Incorporated	no	yes	Energy	North America	AQ	57
48	Banco Bradesco S/A	no	yes	Financials	Middle-South America	AQ	58
49	Banco do Brasil S/A	no	yes	Financials	Middle-South America	AQ	48
50	Banco Itau	no	no	Financials	Middle-South America	AQ	N.a.

ID	Company Name	Subsidary of bigger company	Total return index availab	GICS Industry	Region	Response Status 2009	CDLI_Score 2009
51	Banco Santander	no	yes	Financials	Europe	AQ	59
52	Bank of America Merrill Lynch	no	yes	Financials	North America	AQ	73
53	Bank of China	no	yes	Financials	Asia	NAQ	N.a.
54	Bank of Communications (H)	no	yes	Financials	Asia	AQ	5
55	Bank of Montreal	no	yes	Financials	North America	AQ	87
56	Bank of New York Mellon Corporation	no	yes	Financials	North America	AQ	78
57	Bank of Nova Scotia (Scotiabank)	no	yes	Financials	North America	AQ	56
58	Barclays	no	yes	Financials	Europe	AQ	74
59	Barrick Gold	no	yes	Materials	North America	AQ	56
60	BASF	no	yes	Materials	Europe	AQ	94
61	Baxter International Inc.	no	yes	Health Care	North America	AQ	69
62	Bayer AG	no	yes	Health Care	Europe	AQ	95
63	BB&T Corporation	no	yes	Financials	North America	AQ	61
64	BBVA	no	yes	Financials	Europe	AQ	63
65	BCE Inc.	no	yes	Telecommunication Services	North America	AQ	68
66	Becton, Dickinson and Co.	no	yes	Health Care	North America	AQ	45
67	Beiersdorf AG	no	yes	Consumer Staples	Europe	AQ	45
68	Belgacom	no	yes	Telecommunication Services	Europe	AQ	43
69	Berkshire Hathaway	no	yes	Financials	North America	NAQ	N.a.
70	BG Group	no	yes	Energy	Europe	AQ	66
71	Bharat Heavy Electricals	no	yes	Industrials	Asia	NAQ	N.a.
72	Bharti Airtel	no	yes	Telecommunication Services	Asia	NAQ	N.a.
73	BHP Billiton	no	yes	Materials	Australia	AQ	82
74	Biogen Idec	no	yes	Health Care	North America	AQ	83
75	BMW Bayerische Motorenwerke AG	no	yes	Consumer Discretionary	Europe	AQ	79
76	BNP Paribas	no	yes	Financials	Europe	AQ	52
77	BOC Hong Kong	no	yes	Financials	Asia	NAQ	N.a.
78	Boeing Company	no	yes	Industrials	North America	AQ	87
79	Bouygues	no	yes	Industrials	Europe	AQ	31
80	BP	no	yes	Energy	Europe	AQ	66
81	Bridgestone	no	yes	Consumer Discretionary	Asia	AQ	54
82	Bristol-Myers Squibb	no	yes	Health Care	North America	AQ	75
83	British American Tobacco	no	yes	Consumer Staples	Europe	NAQ	N.a.
84	British Energy Group (see Electricite de Fran	yes	no	Utilities	Europe	AQ	0
85	British Sky Broadcasting	no	yes	Consumer Discretionary	Europe	AQ	42
86	BT Group	no	yes	Telecommunication Services	Europe	AQ	65
87	Burlington Northern Santa Fe Corporation	no	yes	Industrials	North America	AQ	85
88	Cadbury	no	yes	Consumer Staples	Europe	AQ	72
89	Campbell Soup Company	no	yes	Consumer Staples	North America	AQ	63
90	Canadian Imperial Bank of Commerce (CIBC)	no	yes	Financials	North America	AQ	78
91	Canadian National Railways	no	yes	Industrials	North America	AQ	77
92	Canadian Natural Resources	no	yes	Energy	North America	AQ	N.a.
93	Canon	no	yes	Information Technology	Asia	AQ	66
94	Capital One Financial	no	yes	Financials	North America	AQ	54
95	Cardinal Health Inc.	no	yes	Health Care	North America	AQ	49
96	Carnival Corp.	no	yes	Consumer Discretionary	North America	AQ	87
97	Carrefour	no	yes	Consumer Staples	Europe	AQ	73
98	Carso Global Telecom	no	yes	Telecommunication Services	Middle-South America	NAQ	N.a.
99	Caterpillar Inc.	no	yes	Industrials	North America	NAQ	N.a.
100	Cathay Financial Holding	no	yes	Financials	Asia	AQ	13
101	Celgene Corporation	no	yes	Health Care	North America	AQ	64
102	Centrais Eletricas Brasileiras S/A ELETROBI	no	yes	Utilities	Middle-South America	AQ	49
103	Central Japan Railway	no	yes	Industrials	Asia	NAQ	N.a.
104	Centrica	no	yes	Utilities	Europe	AQ	84
105	CEZ	no	no	Utilities	Europe	NAQ	36
106	Charles Schwab Corporation	no	yes	Financials	North America	AQ	3
107	Chesapeake Energy Corporation	no	yes	Energy	North America	NAQ	N.a.
108	Cheung Kong	no	yes	Financials	Asia	NAQ	N.a.
109	Chevron Corporation	no	yes	Energy	North America	AQ	88
110	China Communications Construction (H)	no	yes	Industrials	Asia	NAQ	N.a.
111	China Construction Bank (H)	no	yes	Financials	Asia	NAQ	N.a.
112	China Life Insurance (H)	no	yes	Financials	Asia	NAQ	N.a.
113	China Mobile	no	yes	Telecommunication Services	Asia	NAQ	N.a.
114	China Overseas Land & Investment	no	yes	Financials	Asia	NAQ	N.a.
115	China Petroleum & Chemical	no	yes	Energy	Asia	NAQ	N.a.
116	China Telecom	no	yes	Telecommunication Services	Asia	NAQ	N.a.
117	China Unicom	no	yes	Telecommunication Services	Asia	NAQ	N.a.
118	Chubb Corporation	no	yes	Financials	North America	AQ	30
119	Chubu Electric Power	no	yes	Utilities	Asia	AQ	50
120	Chunghwa Telecom	no	yes	Telecommunication Services	Asia	AQ	45

ID	Company Name	Subsidary of bigger company	Total return index availab	GICS Industry	Region	Response Status 2009	CDLI_Score 2009
113	China Mobile	no	yes	Telecommunication Services	Asia	NAQ	N.a.
114	China Overseas Land & Investment	no	yes	Financials	Asia	NAQ	N.a.
115	China Petroleum & Chemical	no	yes	Energy	Asia	NAQ	N.a.
116	China Telecom	no	yes	Telecommunication Services	Asia	NAQ	N.a.
117	China Unicom	no	yes	Telecommunication Services	Asia	NAQ	N.a.
118	Chubb Corporation	no	yes	Financials	North America	AQ	30
119	Chubu Electric Power	no	yes	Utilities	Asia	AQ	50
120	Chunghwa Telecom	no	yes	Telecommunication Services	Asia	AQ	45
121	Cia Espanola De Petroleos	no	yes	Energy	Europe	NAQ	N.a.
122	Cisco Systems, Inc.	no	yes	Information Technology	North America	AQ	88
123	Citigroup Inc.	no	yes	Financials	North America	AQ	70
124	CLP Holdings	no	yes	Utilities	Asia	AQ	68
125	CME Group Inc.	no	yes	Financials	North America	AQ	14
126	CNOOC (Red Chip)	no	yes	Energy	Asia	AQ	33
127	Coca-Cola Company	no	yes	Consumer Staples	North America	AQ	70
128	Colgate Palmolive Company	no	yes	Consumer Staples	North America	AQ	77
129	Comcast Corporation	no	yes	Consumer Discretionary	North America	NAQ	N.a.
130	Commonwealth Bank of Australia	no	yes	Financials	Australia	AQ	81
131	ConocoPhillips	no	yes	Energy	North America	AQ	52
132	Consolidated Edison, Inc.	no	yes	Utilities	North America	AQ	79
133	Corning Incorporated	no	yes	Information Technology	North America	AQ	57
134	Costco Wholesale Corporation	no	yes	Consumer Staples	North America	AQ	17
135	Covidien Ltd.	no	yes	Health Care	North America	NAQ	N.a.
136	Credit Agricole	no	yes	Financials	Europe	AQ	51
137	Credit Suisse	no	yes	Financials	Europe	AQ	68
138	CRH Plc	no	yes	Materials	Europe	AQ	54
139	Criteria Caixa Corp	no	yes	Financials	Europe	NAQ	N.a.
140	CSL Ltd	no	yes	Health Care	Australia	AQ	65
141	CSX Corporation	no	yes	Industrials	North America	AQ	68
142	CVS Caremark Corporation	no	yes	Consumer Staples	North America	NAQ	N.a.
143	Daiichi Sankyo	no	yes	Health Care	Asia	AQ	40
144	Daimler AG	no	yes	Consumer Discretionary	Europe	AQ	65
145	Danaher Corporation	no	yes	Industrials	North America	AQ	24
146	Danone	no	yes	Consumer Staples	Europe	AQ	42
147	Deere & Company	no	yes	Industrials	North America	AQ	66
148	Dell	no	yes	Information Technology	North America	AQ	66
149	Denso Corporation	no	yes	Consumer Discretionary	Asia	NAQ	0
150	Deutsche Bank AG	no	yes	Financials	Europe	AQ	66
151	Deutsche Boerse	no	yes	Financials	Europe	AQ	31
152	Deutsche Post AG	no	yes	Industrials	Europe	AQ	63
153	Deutsche Telekom AG	no	yes	Telecommunication Services	Europe	AQ	66
154	Devon Energy Corporation	no	yes	Energy	North America	AQ	47
155	Diageo Plc	no	yes	Consumer Staples	Europe	AQ	66
156	Diamond Offshore Drilling	no	yes	Energy	North America	NAQ	N.a.
157	DIRECTV Group, Inc.	no	yes	Consumer Discretionary	North America	NAQ	N.a.
158	Dominion Resources, Inc.	no	yes	Utilities	North America	AQ	67
159	Dow Chemical Company	no	yes	Materials	North America	AQ	63
160	Duke Energy Corporation	no	yes	Utilities	North America	AQ	64
161	E.I. du Pont de Nemours & Company	no	yes	Materials	North America	AQ	80
162	E.ON AG	no	yes	Utilities	Europe	AQ	74
163	EADS	no	yes	Industrials	Europe	AQ	69
164	East Japan Railway	no	yes	Industrials	Asia	AQ	38
165	eBay Inc.	no	yes	Information Technology	North America	AQ	59
166	Edison International	no	yes	Utilities	North America	AQ	39
167	EDP - Energias de Portugal S.A.	no	yes	Utilities	Europe	AQ	75
168	Eisai Co.	no	yes	Health Care	Asia	NAQ	N.a.
169	Electricite de France (EDF)	no	yes	Utilities	Europe	AQ	N.a.
170	Eli Lilly & Co.	no	yes	Health Care	North America	AQ	53
171	EMC Corporation	no	yes	Information Technology	North America	AQ	82
172	Emerson Electric Co.	no	yes	Industrials	North America	AQ	21
173	Enbridge Inc.	no	yes	Energy	North America	AQ	68
174	Encana	no	yes	Energy	North America	AQ	70

ID	Company Name	Subsidary of bigger company	Total return index availabl	GICS Industry	Region	Response Status 2009	CDLI_Score 2009
175	ENEL	no	yes	Utilities	Europe	AQ	55
176	ENI	no	yes	Energy	Europe	AQ	63
177	Entergy Corporation	no	yes	Utilities	North America	AQ	78
178	EOG Resources, Inc.	no	yes	Energy	North America	AQ	41
179	Ericsson	no	yes	Information Technology	Europe	AQ	63
180	Exelon Corporation	no	yes	Utilities	North America	AQ	71
181	Express Scripts, Inc.	no	yes	Health Care	North America	NAQ	N.a.
182	Exxon Mobil Corporation	no	yes	Energy	North America	AQ	62
183	Fanuc	no	yes	Industrials	Asia	NAQ	N.a.
184	Fast Retailing Co., Ltd.	no	yes	Consumer Discretionary	Asia	NAQ	N.a.
185	FedEx Corporation	no	yes	Industrials	North America	AQ	59
186	First Solar Inc	no	yes	Industrials	North America	NAQ	N.a.
187	FirstEnergy Corporation	no	yes	Utilities	North America	AQ	65
188	Formosa Petrochemical	no	yes	Energy	Asia	NAQ	N.a.
189	Fortum Corporation	no	yes	Utilities	Europe	AQ	79
190	FPL Group, Inc.	no	yes	Utilities	North America	AQ	82
191	France Telecom	no	yes	Telecommunication Services	Europe	AQ	49
192	Franklin Resources, Inc.	no	yes	Financials	North America	AQ	77
193	Fresenius Medical Care KGaA	no	yes	Health Care	Europe	AQ	41
194	FujiFilm Holdings Corporation	no	yes	Information Technology	Asia	AQ	71
195	Gas Natural SDG SA	no	yes	Utilities	Europe	AQ	77
196	Gazprom	no	yes	Energy	Europe	AQ	44
197	GBL (see Pernod-Ricard and GDF Suez)	yes	no	Utilities	Europe	AQ	N.a.
198	GDF Suez (formerly Gaz de France/Suez)	no	yes	Utilities	Europe	AQ	67
199	Genentech (see Roche Holding AG)	yes	no	Health Care	North America	AQ	N.a.
200	General Dynamics Corporation	no	yes	Industrials	North America	NAQ	N.a.
201	General Electric Company	no	yes	Industrials	North America	AQ	58
202	General Mills Inc.	no	yes	Consumer Staples	North America	AQ	63
203	Generali	no	yes	Financials	Europe	NAQ	N.a.
204	Genzyme Corporation	no	yes	Health Care	North America	AQ	57
205	Gilead Sciences, Inc.	no	yes	Health Care	North America	AQ	74
206	GlaxoSmithKline	no	yes	Health Care	Europe	AQ	79
207	GMK Norilsk Nickel	no	yes	Materials	Europe	NAQ	N.a.
208	Goldcorp Inc	no	yes	Materials	North America	AQ	41
209	Goldman Sachs Group, Inc.	no	yes	Financials	North America	AQ	54
210	Google Inc.	no	yes	Information Technology	North America	AQ	53
211	Great West Lifeco	no	yes	Financials	North America	NAQ	N.a.
212	H&M Hennes & Mauritz AB	no	yes	Consumer Discretionary	Europe	AQ	58
213	Halliburton Company	no	yes	Energy	North America	AQ	57
214	Hang Seng Bank	no	yes	Financials	Asia	AQ	42
215	Heineken NV	no	yes	Consumer Staples	Europe	AQ	42
216	Heinz (H.J.) Company	no	yes	Consumer Staples	North America	AQ	75
217	Hermes International	no	yes	Consumer Discretionary	Europe	NAQ	N.a.
218	Hess Corporation	no	yes	Energy	North America	AQ	86
219	Hewlett-Packard Company	no	yes	Information Technology	North America	AQ	86
220	Hindustan Unilever (see Unilever)	yes	no	Consumer Staples	Asia	AQ	N.a.
221	Hitachi	no	yes	Information Technology	Asia	AQ	69
222	Holcim	no	yes	Materials	Europe	AQ	61
223	Home Depot, Inc.	no	yes	Consumer Discretionary	North America	AQ	11
224	Hon Hai Precision Industry	no	yes	Information Technology	Asia	AQ	52
225	Honda Motor Company	no	yes	Consumer Discretionary	Asia	AQ	56
226	Honeywell International Inc.	no	yes	Industrials	North America	AQ	7
227	Hong Kong and China Gas	no	no	Utilities	Asia	NAQ	N.a.
228	Hong Kong Electric Holdings Ltd	no	yes	Utilities	Asia	AQ	58
229	HSBC Holdings plc	no	yes	Financials	Europe	AQ	92
230	Husky Energy	no	yes	Energy	North America	AQ	22
231	Hutchison Whampoa	no	no	Telecommunication Services	Asia	NAQ	N.a.
232	Iberdrola	no	yes	Utilities	Europe	AQ	73
233	Illinois Tool Works, Inc.	no	yes	Industrials	North America	AQ	59
234	Imperial Oil	no	yes	Energy	North America	AQ	63
235	Imperial Tobacco Group	no	yes	Consumer Staples	Europe	AQ	62
236	Inditex	no	yes	Consumer Discretionary	Europe	AQ	59

ID	Company Name	Subsidary of bigger company	Total return index availab	GICS Industry	Region	Response Status 2009	CDLI_Score 2009
237	Industrial and Commercial Bank of China	no	no	Financials	Asia	AQ	N.a.
238	Infosys Technologies Ltd	no	yes	Information Technology	Asia	AQ	N.a.
239	ING Group	no	yes	Financials	Europe	AQ	56
240	Inpex Corporation	no	yes	Energy	Asia	AQ	60
241	Intel Corporation	no	yes	Information Technology	North America	AQ	78
242	International Business Machines (IBM)	no	yes	Information Technology	North America	AQ	77
243	Intesa Sanpaolo S.p.A	no	yes	Financials	Europe	AQ	51
244	ITC	no	yes	Consumer Staples	Asia	AQ	42
245	Japan Tobacco	no	yes	Consumer Staples	Asia	AQ	N.a.
246	Jardine Matheson	no	yes	Industrials	Asia	NAQ	N.a.
247	JFE Holdings	no	yes	Materials	Asia	AQ	47
248	Johnson & Johnson	no	yes	Health Care	North America	AQ	83
249	Johnson Controls	no	yes	Consumer Discretionary	North America	AQ	69
250	JPMorgan Chase & Co.	no	yes	Financials	North America	AQ	74
251	Kansai Electric Power	no	yes	Utilities	Asia	AQ	54
252	KAO Corporation	no	yes	Consumer Staples	Asia	AQ	68
253	KBC Group	no	yes	Financials	Europe	AQ	64
254	KDDI Group	no	yes	Telecommunication Services	Asia	AQ	N.a.
255	Kellogg Company	no	yes	Consumer Staples	North America	AQ	45
256	Kimberly-Clark Corporation	no	yes	Consumer Staples	North America	AQ	64
257	Kinross Gold	no	yes	Materials	North America	AQ	59
258	Kirin Holdings Co Ltd	no	yes	Consumer Staples	Asia	AQ	N.a.
259	Kohl's Corporation	no	yes	Consumer Discretionary	North America	AQ	68
260	Komatsu Ltd.	no	yes	Industrials	Asia	AQ	63
261	Korea Electric Power (Kepco)	no	yes	Utilities	Asia	AQ	49
262	Kraft Foods	no	yes	Consumer Staples	North America	AQ	68
263	Kroger	no	yes	Consumer Staples	North America	AQ	18
264	Kyocera Corporation	no	yes	Information Technology	Asia	AQ	56
265	Kyushu Electric Power Co Inc	no	yes	Utilities	Asia	NAQ	N.a.
266	Lafarge	no	yes	Materials	Europe	AQ	84
267	Linde	no	yes	Materials	Europe	AQ	60
268	Lloyds Banking Group	no	yes	Financials	Europe	AQ	80
269	Lockheed Martin Corporation	no	yes	Industrials	North America	NAQ	N.a.
270	Loews Corporation	no	yes	Financials	North America	NAQ	N.a.
271	L'Oreal	no	yes	Consumer Staples	Europe	AQ	63
272	Lorillard Inc.	no	yes	Consumer Staples	North America	NAQ	N.a.
273	Lowe's Companies, Inc.	no	yes	Consumer Discretionary	North America	AQ	57
274	Lukoil	no	yes	Energy	Europe	NAQ	N.a.
275	LVMH	no	yes	Consumer Discretionary	Europe	AQ	72
276	Manulife Financial	no	yes	Financials	North America	AQ	58
277	Marathon Oil Corporation	no	yes	Energy	North America	AQ	59
278	Maroc Telecom	no	yes	Telecommunication Services	Africa	NAQ	N.a.
279	Marsh & Mclennan	no	yes	Financials	North America	AQ	32
280	MasterCard Incorporated	no	yes	Information Technology	North America	AQ	51
281	McDonald's Corporation	no	yes	Consumer Discretionary	North America	AQ	38
282	Medco Health Solutions Inc.	no	yes	Health Care	North America	AQ	67
283	Medtronic, Inc.	no	yes	Health Care	North America	AQ	58
284	Merck & Co., Inc.	no	yes	Health Care	North America	AQ	71
285	Merrill Lynch & Co.,Inc.	yes	no	Financials	North America	AQ	98
286	MetLife, Inc.	no	yes	Financials	North America	AQ	57
287	Metro AG	no	yes	Consumer Staples	Europe	AQ	50
288	Microsoft Corporation	no	yes	Information Technology	North America	AQ	70
289	Mitsubishi Corporation	no	yes	Industrials	Asia	AQ	46
290	Mitsubishi Electric	no	yes	Industrials	Asia	NAQ	0
291	Mitsubishi Estate	no	yes	Financials	Asia	AQ	25
292	Mitsubishi Heavy Industries	no	yes	Industrials	Asia	AQ	44
293	Mitsubishi UFJ Financial Group	no	yes	Financials	Asia	AQ	58
294	Mitsubishi UFJ Lease & Finance Co., Ltd.	yes	no	Financials	Asia	AQ	N.a.
295	Mitsui Fudosan	no	yes	Financials	Asia	NAQ	N.a.
296	Mitsui Sumitomo Insurance	yes	no	Financials	Asia	AQ	N.a.
297	Mitusi & Co	no	yes	Industrials	Asia	AQ	46
298	Mizuho Financial Group	no	yes	Financials	Asia	AQ	42

ID	Company Name	Subsidary of bigger company	Total return index available	GICS Industry	Region	Response Status 2009	CDLI_Score 2009
299	Monsanto Company	no	yes	Materials	North America	AQ	49
300	Morgan Stanley & Co. Inc	no	yes	Financials	North America	AQ	54
301	Morrison Supermarkets	no	yes	Consumer Staples	Europe	AQ	43
302	Mosaic Company	no	yes	Materials	North America	NAQ	N.a.
303	MTN Group	no	yes	Telecommunication Services	Africa	AQ	39
304	MTR Corporation	no	no	Consumer Staples	Asia	AQ	N.a.
305	Munich Re	no	yes	Financials	Europe	AQ	72
306	National Australia Bank	no	yes	Financials	Australia	AQ	82
307	National Grid	no	yes	Utilities	Europe	AQ	69
308	National Oilwell Varco, Inc.	no	yes	Energy	North America	NAQ	N.a.
309	National Thermal Power (NTPC)	no	no	Utilities	Asia	NAQ	N.a.
310	Nestle	no	yes	Consumer Staples	Europe	AQ	60
311	Newmont Mining Corporation	no	yes	Materials	North America	AQ	70
312	News Corporation	no	yes	Consumer Discretionary	North America	AQ	75
313	Nexen Inc.	no	yes	Energy	North America	AQ	68
314	NIKE Inc.	no	yes	Consumer Discretionary	North America	AQ	41
315	Nintendo	no	yes	Information Technology	Asia	AQ	15
316	Nippon Steel	no	yes	Materials	Asia	AQ	59
317	Nippon Telegraph & Telephone (NTT)	no	yes	Telecommunication Services	Asia	AQ	42
318	Nissan Motor	no	yes	Consumer Discretionary	Asia	AQ	69
319	Nokia Group	no	yes	Information Technology	Europe	AQ	78
320	Nomura Holdings	no	yes	Financials	Asia	AQ	45
321	Nordea Bank	no	yes	Financials	Europe	AQ	58
322	Norfolk Southern Corp.	no	yes	Industrials	North America	AQ	11
323	Northern Trust Corporation	no	yes	Financials	North America	AQ	50
324	Northrop Grumman Corp	no	yes	Industrials	North America	AQ	42
325	Novartis	no	yes	Health Care	Europe	AQ	70
326	Novo Nordisk	no	yes	Health Care	Europe	AQ	73
327	NTT Data	no	yes	Information Technology	Asia	AQ	N.a.
328	NTT DOCOMO	no	yes	Telecommunication Services	Asia	AQ	45
329	Nucor Corporation	no	yes	Materials	North America	NAQ	N.a.
330	Occidental Petroleum Corporation	no	yes	Energy	North America	AQ	41
331	Oil & Natural Gas	no	no	Energy	Asia	AQ	N.a.
332	Optus (SingTel)	yes	no	Telecommunication Services	Asia	AQ	N.a.
333	Oracle Corporation	no	yes	Information Technology	North America	AQ	35
334	Overseas Chinese Banking	no	no	Financials	Asia	AQ	N.a.
335	PACCAR Inc	no	yes	Industrials	North America	NAQ	N.a.
336	Panasonic Corporation	no	yes	Consumer Discretionary	Asia	AQ	67
337	Paychex, Inc.	no	yes	Information Technology	North America	NAQ	N.a.
338	PepsiCo, Inc.	no	yes	Consumer Staples	North America	AQ	63
339	Pernod-Ricard	no	yes	Consumer Staples	Europe	AQ	59
340	Petro Canada	no	no	Energy	North America	NAQ	N.a.
341	PETROBRAS	no	yes	Energy	Middle-South America	AQ	44
342	PetroChina	no	yes	Energy	Asia	NAQ	N.a.
343	Pfizer Inc.	no	yes	Health Care	North America	AQ	75
344	PG&E Corporation	no	yes	Utilities	North America	AQ	88
345	Philip Morris International	no	yes	Consumer Staples	North America	NAQ	N.a.
346	Philips Electronics	no	yes	Industrials	Europe	AQ	73
347	PKO Bank Polski	no	yes	Financials	Europe	NAQ	N.a.
348	PNC Financial Services Group, Inc.	no	yes	Financials	North America	NAQ	N.a.
349	POSCO	no	yes	Materials	Asia	AQ	68
350	Potash Corporation of Saskatchewan	no	yes	Materials	North America	AQ	59
351	Power Financial	no	yes	Financials	North America	NAQ	N.a.
352	PPL Corporation	no	yes	Utilities	North America	NAQ	0
353	Praxair, Inc.	no	yes	Materials	North America	AQ	83
354	Procter & Gamble Company	no	yes	Consumer Staples	North America	AQ	55
355	Progress Energy Inc.	no	yes	Utilities	North America	AQ	67
356	Progressive Corporation	no	yes	Financials	North America	AQ	56
357	Prudential	no	yes	Financials	Europe	AQ	57
358	PTT	no	yes	Energy	Asia	AQ	53
359	Public Service Enterprise Group Inc.	no	yes	Utilities	North America	AQ	88
360	Public Storage	no	yes	Financials	North America	NAQ	N.a.

ID	Company Name	Subsidary of bigger company	Total return index availabl	GICS Industry	Region	Response Status 2009	CDLI_Score 2009
361	QBE Insurance Group	no	yes	Financials	Australia	AQ	47
362	QUALCOMM Inc.	no	yes	Information Technology	North America	AQ	48
363	Raytheon Company	no	yes	Industrials	North America	AQ	48
364	Reckitt Benckiser	no	yes	Consumer Staples	Europe	AQ	80
365	Reed Elsevier	no	yes	Consumer Discretionary	Europe	AQ	76
366	Reliance Industries	no	yes	Energy	Asia	NAQ	N.a.
367	Repsol YPF	no	yes	Energy	Europe	AQ	75
368	Research In Motion	no	yes	Information Technology	North America	AQ	44
369	Resona Holdings, Inc.	no	yes	Financials	Asia	AQ	N.a.
370	Reynolds American Inc.	no	yes	Consumer Staples	North America	AQ	59
371	Rio Tinto	no	yes	Materials	Europe	AQ	87
372	Roche Holding AG	no	yes	Health Care	Europe	AQ	45
373	Rogers Communications	no	yes	Telecommunication Services	North America	AQ	44
374	Rohm and Haas Company	yes	no	Industrials	North America	AQ	39
375	Rosneft	no	yes	Energy	Europe	NAQ	N.a.
376	Royal Ahold	no	yes	Consumer Staples	Europe	AQ	45
377	Royal Bank of Canada	no	yes	Financials	North America	AQ	74
378	Royal Bank of Scotland Group	no	yes	Financials	Europe	AQ	77
379	Royal Dutch Shell	no	yes	Energy	Europe	AQ	75
380	Royal KPN	no	yes	Telecommunication Services	Europe	AQ	73
381	RWE	no	yes	Utilities	Europe	AQ	83
382	SABMiller	no	yes	Consumer Staples	Europe	AQ	54
383	Saint-Gobain	no	no	Industrials	Europe	AQ	67
384	Sampo plc	no	yes	Financials	Europe	NAQ	N.a.
385	Samsung Electronics	no	yes	Information Technology	Asia	AQ	87
386	Sanofi-Aventis	no	yes	Health Care	Europe	AQ	76
387	SAP AG	no	yes	Information Technology	Europe	AQ	54
388	Sasol	no	yes	Energy	Africa	AQ	71
389	Sberbank	no	yes	Financials	Europe	NAQ	N.a.
390	Schering-Plough	no	yes	Health Care	North America	AQ	86
391	Schlumberger Limited	no	yes	Energy	North America	AQ	64
392	Schneider Electric	no	yes	Industrials	Europe	AQ	60
393	Scottish & Southern Energy	no	yes	Utilities	Europe	AQ	78
394	Secom Co.	no	yes	Industrials	Asia	NAQ	N.a.
395	Sempra Energy	no	yes	Utilities	North America	AQ	41
396	Seven & I Holding	no	yes	Consumer Staples	Asia	AQ	45
397	Shin Etsu Chemical	no	yes	Materials	Asia	AQ	35
398	Siemens AG	no	yes	Industrials	Europe	AQ	85
399	Simon Property Group	no	yes	Financials	North America	AQ	86
400	SK Telekom	no	yes	Telecommunication Services	Asia	AQ	54
401	Snam Rete Gas	no	yes	Utilities	Europe	AQ	65
402	Societe Generale	no	yes	Financials	Europe	AQ	68
403	SoftBank	no	yes	Telecommunication Services	Asia	NAQ	N.a.
404	Sony Corporation	no	yes	Consumer Discretionary	Asia	AQ	66
405	Southern Copper Corporation	no	yes	Materials	North America	NAQ	N.a.
406	Southwestern Energy	no	yes	Energy	North America	NAQ	N.a.
407	Spectra Energy Corp	no	yes	Energy	North America	AQ	88
408	Standard Bank Group	no	yes	Financials	Africa	AQ	51
409	Standard Chartered	no	yes	Financials	Europe	AQ	66
410	Staples, Inc.	no	yes	Consumer Discretionary	North America	AQ	60
411	State Bank of India	no	yes	Financials	Asia	AQ	N.a.
412	State Street Corporation	no	yes	Financials	North America	AQ	63
413	StatoilHydro	no	yes	Energy	Europe	AQ	40
414	Stryker Corporation	no	yes	Health Care	North America	NAQ	N.a.
415	Sumitomo Corporation	no	yes	Industrials	Asia	AQ	43
416	Sumitomo Metal Industries.	no	yes	Materials	Asia	AQ	61
417	Sumitomo Mitsui Financial Group	no	yes	Financials	Asia	AQ	N.a.
418	Sun Hung Kai Properties	no	yes	Financials	Asia	NAQ	N.a.
419	Sun Life Financial Inc.	no	yes	Financials	North America	AQ	24
420	Suncor Energy Inc	no	yes	Energy	North America	AQ	72

ID	Company Name	Subsidary of bigger company	Total return index availabl	GICS Industry	Region	Response Status 2009	CDLI_Score 2009
421	SunTrust Banks, Inc.	no	yes	Financials	North America	AQ	29
422	Surgutneftegas	no	yes	Energy	Europe	NAQ	N.a.
423	Svenska Handelsbanken	no	yes	Financials	Europe	AQ	11
424	Swiss Re	no	yes	Financials	Europe	AQ	76
425	Swisscom	no	yes	Telecommunication Services	Europe	AQ	55
426	Symantec Corporation	no	yes	Information Technology	North America	AQ	52
427	Syngenta International AG	no	yes	Materials	Europe	AQ	60
428	Synthes Inc.	no	yes	Health Care	Europe	NAQ	N.a.
429	SYSCO Corporation	no	yes	Consumer Staples	North America	NAQ	0
430	Taiwan Semiconductor Manufacturing	no	yes	Information Technology	Asia	AQ	71
431	Takeda Pharmaceutical	no	yes	Health Care	Asia	AQ	54
432	Talisman Energy	no	yes	Energy	North America	AQ	62
433	Target Corporation	no	yes	Consumer Discretionary	North America	AQ	48
434	Tata Consultancy Services	no	yes	Information Technology	Asia	AQ	69
435	Telecom Italia	no	yes	Telecommunication Services	Europe	AQ	66
436	Telefonica	no	yes	Telecommunication Services	Europe	AQ	59
437	TeliaSonera	no	yes	Telecommunication Services	Europe	AQ	71
438	Telstra Corporation Limited	no	yes	Telecommunication Services	Australia	AQ	66
439	Tenaris S.A.	no	yes	Energy	Europe	NAQ	N.a.
440	Tepco (Tokyo Electric Power)	no	yes	Utilities	Asia	AQ	N.a.
441	Tesco	no	yes	Consumer Staples	Europe	AQ	69
442	Teva Pharmaceutical Industries Ltd	no	yes	Health Care	Asia	NAQ	N.a.
443	Texas Instruments Incorporated	no	yes	Information Technology	North America	AQ	56
444	The Southern Company	no	yes	Utilities	North America	AQ	48
445	Thermo Fisher Scientific Inc.	no	yes	Health Care	North America	AQ	50
446	Thomson Reuters	no	no	Consumer Discretionary	North America	AQ	36
447	ThyssenKrupp AG	no	yes	Materials	Europe	AQ	45
448	Time Warner Inc.	no	no	Consumer Discretionary	North America	AQ	41
449	Tohoku Electric Power Co., Inc.	no	yes	Utilities	Asia	AQ	43
450	Tokio Marine Holdings, Inc. (formerly Millea H	no	yes	Financials	Asia	AQ	74
451	Tokyo Gas Co.	no	yes	Utilities	Asia	AQ	63
452	Toronto-Dominion Bank	no	yes	Financials	North America	AQ	62
453	Toshiba	no	yes	Information Technology	Asia	AQ	51
454	Total	no	yes	Energy	Europe	AQ	81
455	Toyota Motor	no	yes	Consumer Discretionary	Asia	AQ	77
456	TransCanada Corporation	no	yes	Energy	North America	NAQ	N.a.
457	Transocean Inc.	no	yes	Energy	North America	AQ	79
458	Travelers Companies. Inc	no	yes	Financials	North America	AQ	57
459	TURKCELL İLETİŞİM HİZMETLERİ A.Ş.	no	yes	Telecommunication Services	Europe	NAQ	N.a.
460	Tyco International	no	yes	Industrials	North America	AQ	55
461	U.S. BanCorp	no	yes	Financials	North America	AQ	59
462	UBS	no	yes	Financials	Europe	AQ	68
463	Unibail-Rodamco	no	yes	Financials	Europe	AQ	53
464	Unicredit Group	no	yes	Financials	Europe	AQ	48
465	Unilever	no	yes	Consumer Staples	Europe	AQ	76
466	Union Fenosa SA	no	no	Utilities	Europe	AQ	86
467	Union Pacific Corporation	no	yes	Industrials	North America	AQ	39
468	United Overseas Bank Ltd	no	yes	Financials	Asia	NAQ	N.a.
469	United Parcel Services, Inc.	no	yes	Industrials	North America	AQ	82
470	United Technologies Corporation	no	yes	Industrials	North America	AQ	70
471	UnitedHealth Group Inc	no	yes	Health Care	North America	AQ	33
472	UST Inc. (see Altria)	yes	no	Consumer Staples	North America	AQ	N.a.
473	VALE	no	yes	Materials	Middle-South America	AQ	74
474	Veolia Environnement	no	yes	Utilities	Europe	AQ	76
475	Verizon Communications Inc.	no	yes	Telecommunication Services	North America	AQ	41
476	Vimpelcom	no	no	Telecommunication Services	Europe	NAQ	N.a.
477	Vinci	no	yes	Industrials	Europe	AQ	78
478	Vivendi Universal	no	yes	Consumer Discretionary	Europe	AQ	54
479	Vodafone Group	no	yes	Telecommunication Services	Europe	AQ	67
480	Volkswagen	no	yes	Consumer Discretionary	Europe	AQ	69
481	Wachovia Corporation (see Wells Fargo & Cc	yes	no	Financials	North America	AQ	0
482	Wal Mart de Mexico (see Wal-Mart Stores, Ir	yes	no	Consumer Staples	Middle-South America	AQ	N.a.

ID	Company Name	Subsidary of bigger company	Total return index availabl	GICS Industry	Region	Response Status 2009	CDLI_Score 2009
483	Walgreen Company	no	yes	Consumer Staples	North America	AQ	46
484	Wal-Mart Stores, Inc.	no	yes	Consumer Staples	North America	AQ	89
485	Walt Disney Company	no	yes	Consumer Discretionary	North America	AQ	46
486	Waste Management, Inc.	no	yes	Industrials	North America	AQ	60
487	WellPoint, Inc.	no	yes	Health Care	North America	AQ	71
488	Wells Fargo & Company	no	yes	Financials	North America	AQ	17
489	Westfield Group	no	yes	Financials	Australia	AQ	63
490	Westpac Banking	no	yes	Financials	Australia	AQ	80
491	Wilmar International Ltd	no	yes	Consumer Staples	Asia	AQ	47
492	Woodside Petroleum	no	yes	Energy	Australia	AQ	64
493	Woolworths Limited	no	yes	Consumer Staples	Australia	AQ	82
494	Wyeth	no	yes	Health Care	North America	AQ	57
495	Xstrata	no	yes	Materials	Europe	AQ	68
496	XTO Energy Inc.	no	yes	Energy	North America	AQ	35
497	Yahoo Japan	yes	no	Information Technology	Asia	AQ	N.a.
498	Yahoo! Inc.	no	yes	Information Technology	North America	AQ	22
499	Yum! Brands, Inc.	no	yes	Consumer Discretionary	North America	NAQ	N.a.
500	Zurich Financial Services	no	yes	Financials	Europe	AQ	63

Reference List

Adam, D. (2008) *World carbon dioxide levels highest for 650,000 years, says US report.* Retrieved October 22, 2009, from The Guardian: http://www.guardian.co.uk/environment/2008/may/13/carbonemissions.climatechange.

Ahuja, G., & Hart, S. L. (1996). Does it pay to be green? An empirical examination of the relationship between emission reduction and firm performance. *Business Strategy & the Environment (John Wiley & Sons, Inc), 5*(1), 30–37.

Al-Tuwaijri, S. A., Christensen, T. E., & Hughes, K. E. (2004). The relations among environmental disclosure, environmental performance, and economic performance: a simultaneous equations approach. *Accounting, Organizations & Society, 29*(5/6), 447–471.

Angell, L. C., & Klassen, R. D. (1999). Integrating environmental issues into the mainstream: an agenda for research in operations management. *Journal of Operations Management, 17*(5), 575–598.

Anschober, R., & Ramsauer, P. (2007). *Die Klima-Revolution: So retten wir die Welt.* Wien: Deuticke.

Arentzen, U. (1997). *Gabler Wirtschafts-Lexikon* (14., vollst. überarb. und erw. Aufl.). Wiesbaden: Gabler.

Arlow, P., & Cannon, M. J. (1982). Social Responsiveness, Corporate Structure, and Economic Performance. *Academy of Management Review, 7*(2), 235–241.

Armitage, S. (1995). Event study methods and evidence on their performance. *Journal of Economic Surveys, 9*(1), 25.

Atmospheric Carbon Dioxide Record from Mauna Loa. Retrieved October 22, 2009, from http://cdiac.ornl.gov/trends/co2/sio-mlo.html.

Azapagic, A., & Clift, R. (1999). The application of life cycle assessment to process optimisation. *Computers and Chemical Engineering, 23*, 1509–1526.

Azzone, G., & Noci, G. (1996). Measuring the environmental performance of new products: an integrated approach. *International Journal of Production Research, 34*(11), 3055.

Balderjahn, I., & Mennicken, C. (1996). Das Management ökologischer Risiken und Krisen: Verhaltenswissenschaftliche Grundlagen. In H. Albach (Ed.), *Zeitschrift für Betriebswirtschaft / Ergänzungsheft: Vol. 1996,2. Betriebliches Umweltmanagement 1996* (pp. 23–49). Gabler.

Ball, R., & Brown, P. (1968). An Empirical Evaluation of Accounting Income Numbers. *Journal of Accounting Research, 6*(2), 159–178.

Bansal, P. (2005). Evolving sustainability: A longitudinal study of corporate sustainable development. *Strategic Management Journal, 26*(3), 197–218.

Banz, R. W. (1981). The Relationship between Return and Market Value of Common Stocks. *Journal of Financial Economics, 9*(1), 3–18.

Barber, B. M., & Lyon, J. D. (1996). Detecting Abnormal Operating Performance: The Empirical Power and Specification of Test Statistics. *Journal of Financial Economics, 41*(3), 359–399.

Barker, C. (1956). Effective Stock Splits. *Harvard Business Review, 34*(1), 101–106.

Barker, C. (1957). Stock Splits in a Bull Market. *Harvard Business Review, 35*(3), 72–79.

Barker, C. (1958). Evaluation of Stock Dividends. *Harvard Business Review, 36*(4), 99–114.

Barnett, T. P., Adam, J. C., & Lettenmaier, D. P. (2005). Potential impacts of a warming climate on water availability in snow-dominated regions. *Nature*, (438), 303–309.

Bartholdy, J., Olson, D., & Peare, P. (2007). Conducting Event Studies on a Small Stock Exchange. *European Journal of Finance, 13*(3-4), 227–252.

Basu, S. (1983). The Relationship between Earnings' Yield, Market Value and Return for NYSE Common Stocks: Further Evidence. *Journal of Financial Economics, 12*(1), 129–156.

Baumann, H. (2004). *The hitch hiker's guide to LCA.* Lund: Studentlitteratur.

Baumast, A. (2001). *Betriebliches Umweltmanagement: Theoretische Grundlagen ; Praxisbeispiele ; 25 Tabellen.* Stuttgart (Hohenheim): Ulmer.

Beaver, W. H. (1968). The Information Content of Annual Earnings Announcements. *Journal of Accounting Research, 6*(3), 67–92.

Becke, G. (2000). *Dialogorientiertes Umweltmanagement und Umweltqualifizierung: Eine Praxishilfe für mittelständische Unternehmen.* Berlin: Springer.

Benston, G. J. (1982). Accounting Numbers and Economic Values. *Antitrust Bulletin, 27*(1), 161–215.

Berger, I. E., & Corbin, R. M. (1992). Perceived Consumer Effectiveness and Faith in Others as Moderators of Environmentally Responsible Behaviors. *Journal of Public Policy & Marketing, 11*(2), 79–89.

Bernard, V. L. (1987). Cross-Sectional Dependence and Problems in Inference in Market-Based Accounting Research. *Journal of Accounting Research, 25*(1), 1–48.

Berry, A. (2002). *The comprehensive rationality of sustainable development: Status quo of the theoretical debate and measuring approaches.* Bremen: Univ.

Bewley, K., & Li, Y. (2000). Disclosure of environmental information by Canadian manufacturing companies: A Voluntary Disclosure Perspective. *Advances in Environmental Accounting and Management, 1*, 201–226.

Bickhoff, N. (2000). *Erfolgswirkungen strategischer Umweltmanagementmaßnahmen: Eine theoretische und empirische Untersuchung.* Wiesbaden: Dt. Univ.-Verl..

Binder, J. J. (1998). The Event Study Methodology Since 1969. *Review of Quantitative Finance & Accounting, 11*(2), 111–137.

Blacconiere, W. G., & Patten, D. M. (1994). Environmental Disclosures, Regulatory Costs, and Changes in Firm Value. *Journal of Accounting and Economics, 18*(3), 357–377.

BMW Group. *Sustainable Value Report 2007/2008 - Update October 2008,* from BMW Group: .

Boehmer, E., Musumeci, J., & Poulsen, A. B. (1992). *Event-Study Methodology Under Conditions of Event-Induced Variance* (Vol. 59).

Bonifant, B. C., & Arnold, M. B. (1995). Gaining competitive advantage through environmental investments. *Business Horizons, 38*(4), 37–47.

Bonini, S., Hintz, G., & Mendonca, L. (2008). Addressing consumer concerns about climate change. *The McKinsey Quarterly, March*, 1–10.

Boone, A. L., & Mulherin, J. (2007). How Are Firms Sold? *Journal of Finance, 62*(2), 847–875.

Boström, T., & Pöysti, E. (1992). *Environmental strategy in the enterprise* (Vol. 161). *Kauppakorkeakoulu <Helsinki>: Helsingin Kauppakorkeaoulun Julkaisuja / D, 161.*

Bowen, F. E., Cousins, P. D., Lamming, R. C., & Faruk, A. C. (2001). Horses for Courses. *Greener Management International*, (35), 41.

Bowman, R. G. (1983). Understanding and conducting event studies. *Journal of Business Finance & Accounting, 10*(4), 561–584.

Brake, M. (2009). *Ökobilanz der Abwrackprämie ist negativ.* Retrieved July 31, 2009, from Telepolis: http://www.heise.de/tp/r4/artikel/29/29881/1.html.

Breidenbach, R. (1999). *Umweltschutz in der betrieblichen Praxis. Lehrbuch:* Gabler.

Brown, S. J., & Warner, J. B. (1980). Measuring Security Price Performance. *Journal of Financial Economics, 8*(3), 205–258.

Brown, S. J., & Warner, J. B. (1985). Using daily stock returns: The Case of Event Studies. *Journal of Financial Economics, 14*(1), 3–31.

Brown, S. J., & Weinstein, M. I. (1985). Derived factors in event studies. *Journal of Financial Economics, 14*(3), 491–495.

Brundtland, G. (1987). *Our common future* (13. impr.). Oxford: Univ. Press.

Buesseler, K. O. et al. (2007). Revisiting Carbon Flux Through the Ocean's Twilight Zone. *Science*, (316), 567–570.

Bullinger, H.-J., Eversheim, W., & Haasis, H.-D. (2000). *Auftragsabwicklung optimieren nach Umwelt- und Kostenzielen: OPUS - Organisationsmodelle und Informationssysteme für einen produktionsintegrierten Umweltschutz.* Berlin: Springer.

Byers, M. (14.09.2010). *On Thinning Ice.* Retrieved September 20, 2010, from http://www.lrb.co.uk/v27/n01/michael-byers/on-thinning-ice.

Caillon, N. et al. (2003). Timing of Atmospheric CO and Antarctic Temperature Changes Across Termination. *Science, 299*, 1728–1731.

Campbell, C. J., Cowan, A. R., & Salotti, V. (2010). Multi-county event study methods. *Journal of Banking & Finance*, (unpublished).

Campbell, C. J., & Wasley, C. E. (1993). Measuring security price performance using daily NASDAQ returns. *Journal of Financial Economics, 33*(1), 73–92.

Campbell, J. Y., Lo, A. W., & MacKinlay, A. (1997). *The econometrics of financial markets* (2. print., with corr.): Princeton Univ. Press.

Campino, I. Sustainability, a Big Challenge for Business. In Frauenhofer IZM (Ed.). *Electronics Goes Green 2004+. Driving Forces for Future Electronics* (pp. 63–66).

Carbon Disclosure Project - Global climate change reporting system. Retrieved October 13, 2010, from https://www.cdproject.net/en-US/Pages/HomePage.aspx.

Carbon Trust (2006). *Carbon footprints in the supply chain:: the next step for business.* London.

Carlson, A. E. (2008). Rapid early Holocne deglaciation of the Laurentide ice sheet. *Nature Geosciences*, 620-624.

Carter, C. R., & Jennings, M. M. (2004). The role of purchasing in corporate social responsibility: A structural equation analysis. *Journal of Business Logistics, 25*(1), 145–186.

Carter, C. R., Kale, R., & Grimm, C. M. (2000). Environmental Purchasing and Firm Performance: An Empirical Investigation. *Transportation Research: Part E: Logistics and Transportation Review, 36*(3), 219–228.

Case, S. (2004). Establishing Green Purchasing Priorities. *Government Procurement, 12*(2), 30–35.

Case, S. (2005). Green Purchasing--Leading By Example. *Government Procurement, 13*(5), 6–11.

CERES (2006). *Global Framework for Climate Risk Disclosure: A statement of investor expectations for comprehensive corporate disclosure.* Boston.

Chan, R. Y. K., & Lau, L. B. Y. (2002). Explaining Green Purchasing Behavior: A Cross-Cultural Study on American and Chinese Consumers. *Journal of International Consumer Marketing, 14*(2/3), 9.

Chen, J., Wilson, C. R., & Tapley, B. D. (2006). Satellite Gravity Measurement Confirm Accelerated Melting of Greenland Ice Sheet. *Science*, 1958–1960.

Chen, K. H., & Metcalf, R. W. (1980). The Relationship between Pollution Control Record and Financial Indicators Revisited. *Accounting Review, 55*(1), 168–177.

Christmann, P. (2000). Effects of "best practices" of environmental management on cost advantage: The role of complentary assets. *Academy of Management Journal, 43*(4), 663–680.

Clarkson, P. M., Li, Y., Richardson, G. D., & Vasvari, F. P. (2008). Revisiting the relation between environmental performance and environmental disclosure: An empirical analysis. *Accounting, Organizations & Society, 33*(4/5), 303–327.

Cogan, D. G. (2006). *Corporate Governance and Climate Change: Making the Connection.* Boston.

Cohen, M. A., Fenn, S. A., & Konar, S. (1997). *Environmental and Financial Performance: Are They related?*

Cordeiro, J. J., & Sarkis, J. (1997). Environmental proactivism and firm performance: Evidence from security analyst earnings forecast. *Business Strategy & the Environment (John Wiley & Sons, Inc), 6*(2), 104–114.

Cormier, D., Magnan, M., & Morard, B. (1993). The impact of corporate pollution on market valuation: some empirical evidence. *Ecological Economics, 8*(2), 135.

Cormier, D., & Magnan, M. (1997). Investors' Assessment of Implicit Environmental Liabilities: An Empirical Investigation. *Journal of Accounting & Public Policy, 16*(2), 215–241.

Costello, A., Abbas, M., Allen, A., Ball, S., Bell, S., & Bellamy, R., et al. (2009). Managing the health effects of climate change. *The Lancet*, (373), 1693–1733. Retrieved August 08, 2009.

Cousins, P. D., Lamming, R. C., & Bowen, F. (2004). The role of risk in environment-related supplier initiatives. *International Journal of Operations & Production Management, 24*(6), 554–565.

Daimler AG. *Nachhaltigkeitsbericht 2008 - Daimler 360° Fakten,* from Daimler AG: .

Dann, L. Y., Mayers, D., & Raab, R. J., JR. (1977). Trading Rules, Large Blocks and the Speed of Price Adjustment. *Journal of Financial Economics, 4*(1), 3–22.

Darnall, N., Jolley, G. Jason, & Handfield, R. (2008). Environmental management systems and green supply chain management: complements for sustainability? *Business Strategy & the Environment (John Wiley & Sons, Inc), 17*(1), 30–45.

DeCicco, J. M., & Thomas, M. (1999). A method for green rating of Automobiles. *Journal of Industrial Ecology, 3*(1), 55–75.

Del Genio, T. et. al (2007). Will moist convection be stronger in a warmer climate? *Geophysical Research Letters*, (34).

Delmas, M., & Keller, A. (2005). Free Riding in Voluntary Environmental Programs: The Case of the U.S. EPA WasteWise Program. *Policy Sciences, 38*(2-3), 91–106.

Deutschland / Bundesministerium für Umwelt, Naturschutz und Reaktorsicherheit (2001). *Handbuch Umweltcontrolling*: Vahlen.

Deutschland / Umweltbundesamt (1993). *Umweltfreundliche Beschaffung* :

Dimson, E., & Marsh, P. (1986). Event Study Methodologies and the Size Effect: The Case of UK Press Recommendations. *Journal of Financial Economics, 17*(1), 113–142.

Douglas, B. C. Global Sea rise: A redetermination. *Surveys in Geophysics, 1997*, 279–292.

Dowell, G., Hart, S., & Yeung, B. (2000). Do Corporate Global Environmental Standards Create or Destroy Market Value? *Management Science, 46*(8), 1059.

Dunbar, B. (23.02.2008). *NASA study finds increasing solar trend that can change climate - March 20, 2003.* Retrieved October 22, 2009, from NASA: http://www.nasa.gov/centers/goddard/news/topstory/2003/0313irradiance.html.

Dwyer, G. P. (2001). *The Use of Event Studies in Finance and Economics.* Retrieved July 28, 2010, from http://www.dwyerecon.com/pdf/lecteven.pdf.

Dyckhoff, H., & Gießler, T. (1998). Produktentstehung und Umweltschutz: Grundzüge einer ökologieorientierten Produktentstehung. In H. Dyckhoff (Ed.), *Heidelberger betriebswirtschaftliche Studien: . Produktentstehung, Controlling und Umweltschutz* (pp. 168–190). Physica-Verl.

Dyckhoff, H., Lackes, R., Reese, J., & Fandel, G. (2004). *Supply chain management and reverse logistics.* Berlin: Springer.

Dyckman, T. R., & Smith, A. J. (1979). Financial Accounting and Reporting by Oil and Gas Producing Companies: A Study of Information Effects. *Journal of Accounting and Economics, 1*(1), 45–75.

Dye, R. A. (1985). Disclosure of Nonproprietary Information. *Journal of Accounting Research, 23*(1), 123–145.

Ehrenfeld, J. R. (2004) Sustainability: Far Beyond Eco-design. In Frauenhofer IZM (Ed.). *Electronics Goes Green 2004+. Driving Forces for Future Electronics* (pp. 37–41).

Ellram, L. M., & Birou, L. M. (1995). *Purchasing for bottom line impact: Improving the organization through strategic procurement* (Vol. 4). *The NAPM professional development series, 4.* New York: McGraw-Hill.

CampusClimateNetwork (2008). *Emission scopes - ClimateNetworkWiki* (14.09.2008). Retrieved October 13, 2010, from http://www.campusclimatenetwork.org/wiki/Emission_scopes.

Etheridge, L. et al. (1998). *Historical CO_2 records from the Law Dome DE08, DE08-2, and DSS ice cores. Trends: A Compendium of Data on Global Change.* Oak Ridge, Tenn.: Carbon

Dioxide Information Analysis Center, Oak Ridge National Laboratory, U.S. Department of Energy.

Faix, W. G., Kurz, R., & Wichert, F. (1995). *Innovation zwischen Ökonomie und Ökologie.* Landsberg/Lech: Verl. Moderne Industrie.

Fama, E. F. (1991). Efficient Capital Markets: II. *Journal of Finance, 46*(5), 1575–1617.

Fama, E. F. et al (1969). The Adjustment of Stock Prices to New Information. *International Economic Review, 10*(1), 1–21.

Fiksel, J. (1996). *Design for environment: Creating eco-efficient products and processes.* New York: McGraw Hill.

Fischer, K., & Schot, J. (1993). *Environmental strategies for industry: International perspectives on research needs and policy implications.* Washington, DC: Island Press.

Florida, R. (1996). Lean and Green: The move to environmentally conscious manufacturing. *California Management Review, 39*(1), 80–105.

Fogler, H., & Nutt, F. (1975). A note on social responsibility and stock valuation. *Academy of Management Journal, 18*(1), 155–160.

Folland, C. et. al (2001). Global temperature change and its uncertainties since 1861. *Geophysical Research Letters, 28*, 2621–2624.

Foster, G. (1980). Accounting Policy Decisions and Capital Market Research. *Journal of Accounting and Economics, 2*(1), 29–62.

Frankel, R., & McNichols, M. (1995). Discretionary Disclosure and External Financing. *Accounting Review, 70*(1), 135–150.

Frankl, P., Rubik, F., & Bartolomeo, M. (2000). *Life cycle assessment in industry and business: Adoption patterns, applications and implications.* Berlin: Springer.

Freedman, M., & Wasley, C. (1990). The Association between Environmental Performance and Environmental Disclosure in Annual Reports and 10Ks. In M. Neimark (Ed.), *Advances in public interest accounting. Volume 3* (pp. 183–193). A Research Annual; Greenwich, Conn. and London:; JAI Press.

Freeman, R. Edward (1984). *Strategic management. Pitman series in business and public policy:* Pitman.

Freimann, J. (1996). *Betriebliche Umweltpolitik* (Vol. 1910). *Uni-Taschenbücher, 1910:* Haupt.

Friedemann, C. (1998). *Umweltorientierte Investitionsplanung.* Wiesbaden: Gabler.

Friedmann, L. (2009). *Scientists claim climate adaptation aid costs are understated.* Retrieved August 31, 2009, from World Business Council for Sustainable Development: http://www.wbcsd.org/plugins/DocSearch/details.asp?type=DocDet&ObjectId=MzU0NjA.

Fritz, W. (1992). *Marktorientierte Unternehmensführung und Unternehmenserfolg: Grundlagen und Ergebnisse einer empirischen Untersuchung.* Stuttgart: Schäffer-Poeschel.

Funke, C. (2005). *Large Daily DAX Movements and the Cross-Section of Stock Returns: Does Beta Matter?*

Fussler, C., & James, P. (1999). *Die Öko-Innovation: Wie Unternehmen profitabel und umweltfreundlich sein können.* Stuttgart: Hirzel.

Gebken, T. (2008). *The Dynamics within Merger Waves: Evidence from the Industry Merger Waves of the 1990s.*

Geffen, C. A., & Rothenberg, S. (2000). Suppliers and environmental innovation. *International Journal of Operations & Production Management, 20*(2), 166–186.

Gert, M. (2009, October 12). Gewinne aufgefressen: Großanleger machen Unternehmen Druck beim Klimaschutz. Aus handfesten Gründen: CO2-Emissionen werden teurer. *Wirtschaftswoche,* 42, 102–103.

Gifford, J. Dun (1997). The Value of Going Green. *Harvard Business Review, 75*(5), 11–12.

Ginsberg, J., & Bloom, P. N. (2004). Choosing the Right Green Marketing Strategy. *MIT Sloan Management Review, 46*(1), 79–84.

Giroud, X., & Mueller, H. M. (2010). Does Corporate Governance Matter in Competitive Industries? *Journal of Financial Economics, 95*(3), 312–331.

Giudice, F., La Rosa, G., & Risitano, A. (2006). *Product design for the environment: A life cycle approach.* Boca Raton, Fla.: CRC Taylor & Francis.

Graedel, T. E. (1997). The Grand Objectives: A Framework for Prioritized Grouping of Environmental Concerns in Life-Cycle Assessment. *J. Ind. Ecol., 1*(2), 51–64.

Graedel, T. E. (1998). *Streamlined life-cycle assessment.* Upper Saddle River, NJ: Prentice Hall.

Green Purchasing Has Some Companies (2007). *Industry Week/IW, 256*(10), 21-21.

Guide, V. Daniel R., JR. (2000). Supply-Chain Management for Recoverable Manufacturing Systems. *Interfaces, 30*(3), 125–142.

Guinée, J. B., & Lindeijer, E. (2002). *Handbook on life cycle assessment: Operational guide to the ISO standards.* Dordrecht: Kluwer.

Gupta, M. C. (1995). Environmental management and its impact on the operations function. *International Journal of Operations & Production Management, 15*(8), 34–51.

Hall, J. (2001). Environmental Supply-Chain Innovation. *Greener Management International,* (35), 105.

Handfield, R. B., Walton, S. V., Seegers, L. K., & Melnyk, S. A. (1997). 'Green' value chain practices in the furniture industry. *Journal of Operations Management, 15*(4), 293–315.

Hansen, J. et al., (2000). Global warming in the twenty-first century: an alternative scenario. *Proceedings of the National Academy of Sciences., 97*(18), 9875–9880.

Hansen, J. et al., (2006). Global temperature change. *Proceedings of the National Academy of Sciences, 103*, 14288–14293.

Hansen, J., et. al (2001). A closer look at United States and global surface temperature change. *Journal of Geophysical Research, 106*, 23947–23963.

Hansen J. et al, (2005), *GISS Surface Temperature Analysis: 2005 Summation* (03.08.2010). Goddard Institute for Space Studies. Retrieved September 17, 2010, from http://data.giss.nasa.gov/gistemp/2005/.

Hansen, J., & et. al (2007). Climate change and trace gases. *Philosophical Transactions of the Royal Society*, 1925–1954.

Hansmann, K.-W., Schlange, J., Seipold, P., & Wilkens, S. (2003). *Der Erfolg von Nachhaltigkeitsmanagement: Eine empirische Untersuchung,* Universität Hamburg, from Universität Hamburg: .

Hansmann, K.-W., & Voigt, K.-I. (1998). Umweltorientierte Betriebswirtschaftslehre: Einführung und Überblick. In K.-W. Hansmann (Ed.), *Umweltorientierte Betriebswirtschaftslehre: Eine Einführung* . Wiesbaden: Gabler.

Harrington, S. E., & Shrider, D. G. (2007). All Events Induce Variance: Analyzing Abnormal Returns When Effects Vary across Firms. *Journal of Financial & Quantitative Analysis, 42*(1), 229–256.

Harte, J., et. al (2006). Shifts in plant dominance control carbon-cycle responses to experimental warming and widespread drought. *Environmental Research Letters, 1*(1), 14001.

Hassel, L., Nilsson, H., & Nyquist, S. (2005). The value relevance of environmental performance. *European Accounting Review, 14*(1), 41–61.

Hauff, M. von (1992). *Ökonomie und Ökologie: Ansätze zu einer ökologisch verpflichteten Marktwirtschaft.* Stuttgart: Schäffer-Poeschel.

Healy, P. M., & Palepu, K. G. (2001). Information Asymmetry, Corporate Disclosure, and the Capital Markets: A Review of the Empirical Disclosure Literature. *Journal of Accounting and Economics, 31*(1-3), 405–440.

Hegerl, G. C., Zwiers, F. W., Braconnot, P., Gillett, N. P., Luo, Y., & Orsini, J. A. M., et al. (2007). *Understanding and Attributing Climate Change. In: Climate Change 2007: The Physical Science Basis. Contribution of Working Group I to the Fourth Assessment Report of the Intergovernmental Panel on Climate Change,* from Intergovernmental Panel on Climate Change: .

Hervani A., Helms M., & Sarkis J. (2005). Performance measurement for green supply chain management. *Benchmarking: An International Journal, 12*(4), 330–353.

Helmers, L. R. (2008). The Elastic Green Supply Chain. *World Trade, 21*(7), 24–25.

Hines, F. (25.12.2000). *Environmental Supply Chain Management: evaluating the use of environmental mentoring through supply chains.* Retrieved February 06, 2009, from .

Hoffmann, V. H., & Busch, T. (2008). Corporate carbon performance indicators: Carbon intensity, dependency, exposure, and risk. *Journal of Industrial Ecology, 12*(4).

Hokey Min, & Galle, W. P. (2001). Green purchasing practices of US firms. *International Journal of Operations & Production Management, 21*(9/10), 1222.

Hopfenbeck, W. (1993). *The green management revolution: Lessons in environmental excellence.* New York, NY: Prentice Hall.

Hughes, S. B., Anderson, A., & Golden, S. (2001). Corporate environmental disclosures: are they useful in determining environmental performance? *Journal of Accounting & Public Policy, 20*(3), 217–240.

Ingram, R. W., & Frazier, K. B. (1980). Environmental Performance and Corporate Disclosure. *Journal of Accounting Research, 18*(2), 614–622.

Intergovernmental Panel on Climate Change. *Climate Change 2001: 2.2.5.4 Mountain Glaciers.*

Intergovernmental Panel on Climate Change. *Climate Change 2001: Worldwide Glacier Retreat.*

Technical Summary. In: Climate Change 2007: Mitigation. Contribution of Working Group III to the Fourth Assessment Report of the Intergovernmental Panel on Climate Change (2007a), from Intergovernmental Panel on Climate Change: http://www.ipcc.ch/pdf/assessment-report/ar4/wg3/ar4-wg3-ts.pdf.

Summary for Policymakers. In: Climate Change 2007: The Physical Science Basis. Contribution of Working Group I to the Fourth Assessment Report of the Intergovernmental Panel on Climate Change (2007b), from Intergovernmental Panel on Climate Change: http://ipcc-wg1.ucar.edu/wg1/Report/AR4WG1_Print_SPM.pdf.

International Monetary Fund. *World Economic Outlook Database, October 2010: Report for Selected Countries and Subjects.* Retrieved November 06, 2010, from http://www.imf.org/external/pubs/ft/weo/2010/02/weodata/weorept.aspx?sy=2009&ey=

IPCC (2001a). *Climate Change 2001: The Scientific Basis. Contribution of Working Group I to the Third Assessment Report of the Intergovernmental Panel on Climate Change.* Cambridge, UK: Cambridge University Press.

IPCC, & IPCC. 2. Causes of change. In (section): Summary for Policymakers. In (book): Climate Change 2007: Synthesis Report. Contribution of Working Groups I, II and III to the Fourth Assessment Report of the Intergovernmental Panel on Climate Change (Core Writing Team, Pachauri, R.K and Reisinger, A. (eds.)).

IPCC AR4 SYR. *Appendix Glossary.* Retrieved September 17, 2010, from IPCC: http://www.ipcc.ch/pdf/assessment-report/ar4/syr/ar4_syr_appendix.pdf.

Jaffe, J. P. (1974). Special Information and Insider Trading. *Journal of Business, 47*(3), 410–428.

Jaggi, B., & Freedman, M. (1992). An examination of the impact of pollution performance on economic and market performance: Pulp and paper firms. *Journal of Business Finance & Accounting, 19*(5), 697–713.

Jahnke, R. (1994). Entwicklung ökologieverträglichen Mitarbeiterverhaltens und dessen Erfolgswirkungen. In H. Kreikebaum; E. Seidel, & H.-U. Zabel (Eds.), *Unternehmenserfolg durch Umweltschutz: Rahmenbedingungen, Instrumente, Praxisbeispiele* . Wiesbaden: Gabler.

Judge, W. Q., & Douglas, T. J. (1998). Performance implications of incorporating natural environmental issues into the strategic planning process: An empirical assessment. *Journal of Management Studies, 35*(2), 241–262.

Jusko, J. (2003). *Auto Partnership Aims For 'Green' Supply Chain.* Retrieved February 13, 2009, from IndustryWeek.com: http://www.industryweek.com/PrintArticle.aspx?ArticleID=7688.

Karpoff, J. M., & Malatesta, P. H. (1989). The wealth effects of second gene on state takeover legislation. *Journal of Financial Economics, 25*(2), 291–322.

Kates, R. M. (2001). Determinants of Chinese Consumers' Green Purchase Behavior. *Psychology & Marketing, 18*(4), 389–413.

Keeling, R.F., S.C. Piper, A.F. Bollenbacher and J.S. Walker. (2009). *Atmospheric CO_2 records from sites in the SIO air sampling network in Trends: A Compendium of Data on Global Change.* Oak Ridge, Tenn., U.S.A.: Carbon Dioxide Information Analysis Center, Oak Ridge National Laboratory, U.S. Department of Energy.

Keim, D. B. (1983). Size-Related Anomalies and Stock Return Seasonality: Further Empirical Evidence. *Journal of Financial Economics, 12*(1), 13–32.

Khoo, H. H., Bainbridge, I., Spedding, T. A., & Taplin, D. M. R. (2001). Creating a Green Supply Chain. *Greener Management International*, (35), 71.

Kiehl, J. T., & Trenberth, K. E. (1997). Earth's Annual Global Mean Energy Budget. *Bulletin of the American Meterological Society, 78*, 197–208.

Klassen, R. D. (2000). Exploring the linkage between investment in manufacturing and environmental technologies. *International Journal of Operations & Production Management, 20*(2), 127–147.

Klassen, R. D., & McLaughlin, C. P. (1996). The impact of environmental management on firm performance. *Management Science, 42*(8), 1199–1214.

Klassen, R. D., & Vachon, S. (2003). Collaboration and evaluation in the supply chain: the impact on plant-level environmental investment. *Production & Operations Management, 12*(3), 336–352.

Klassen, R. D., & Whybark, D. (1999a). The impact of environmental technologies on manufacturing performance. *Academy of Management Journal, 42*(6), 599–615.

Klassen, R. D., & Whybark, D. Clay (1999b). Environmental Management in Operations: The Selection of Environmental Technologies. *Decision Sciences, 30*(3), 601–631.

Kolk, A., Levy, D., & Pinkse, J. (2008). Corporate Responses in an Emerging Climate Regime: The Institutionalization and Commensuration of Carbon Disclosure. *European Accounting Review, 17*(4), 719–745.

Kothari, S. P., & Warner, J. B. (2006). *Econometrics of Event Studies: Working Paper.*

Kreikebaum, H. (1994). Ökologieverträglichkeit der Produktion und deren Erfolgswirkungen. In H. Kreikebaum; E. Seidel, & H.-U. Zabel (Eds.), *Unternehmenserfolg durch Umweltschutz: Rahmenbedingungen, Instrumente, Praxisbeispiele* . Wiesbaden: Gabler.

Lang, M. H., & Lundholm, R. J. (1996). Corporate Disclosure Policy and Analyst Behavior. *Accounting Review, 71*(4), 467–492.

Le Treut, H., & Somerville, R. (2007). *Climate Change 2007: The Physical Science Basis. Contribution of Working Group I to the Fourth Assessment Report of the Intergovernmental Panel on Climate Change: Historical Overview of Climate Change Science.* Retrieved October 22, 2009, from Intergovernmental Panel on Climate Change: http://www.ipcc.ch/pdf/assessment-report/ar4/wg1/ar4-wg1-chapter1.pdf.

Lee, L. (2009) *Cisco, Pepco & Boeing Top The Charts As This Year's S&P 500 Corporate Climate Leaders - Business Exchange.* Retrieved August 03, 2010, from http://bx.businessweek.com/comerica-incorporatedcma/view?url=http%3A%2F%2Fc.moreover.com%2Fclick%2Fhere.pl%3Fr2216362413%26f%3D9791.

Lee, L., Lee, J., (2009). New research reveals increasing impact of climate change on investment decisions

Lei, L., Zhifeng, L., & Fung, R. (2003). *"The Most of The Most"------ Study on a New LCA Method: Conference record : May 19 - 22, 2003, 2003, Boston, MA, USA ; [held in conjunction with the 4th Electronics Recycling Summit].* Piscataway, NJ: IEEE Operations Center.

Lev, B., & Adenso-Díaz, B. (2004). Greener Manufacturing and Operations: From Design to Delivery and Back (Book). *Interfaces, 34*(4), 324-324.

Light, E. (2002). A green supply chain. *NZ Business, 16*(3), 46.

Litzenberger, R. H., & Ramaswamy, K. (1979). The effect of personal taxes and dividends on capital asset prices: Theory and Empirical Evidence. *Journal of Financial Economics, 7*(2), 163–195.

Loveday, Y. (2000). *Outreach: For the Life of Your Car.* Retrieved February 13, 2009, from Tennessee Alumnus Magazine: http://pr.utk.edu/alumnus/alumarticle.asp?id=136.

Luken, R. (1997). The effect of environmental regulations on industrial competitiveness… *Greener Management International*, (19), 67.

MacKinlay, A. (1997). Event Studies in Economics and Finance. *Journal of Economic Literature, 35*(1), 13–39.

Mandelker, G. (1974). Risk and return: the case of merging firms. *Journal of Financial Economics, 1*(4), 303–335.

Marland, G., Boden, T., & Andres., R. J. (2008) *Global, Regional, and National CO2 Emissions. In Trends: A Compendium of Data on Global Change.*

Masulis, R. W. (1980). The Effects of Capital Structure Change on Security Prices: A Study of Exchange Offers. *Journal of Financial Economics, 8*(2), 139–177.

Mayhew, P. J., & et al. (2007). A long-term association between global temperature and biodiversity, origination and extinction in the fossil record. *Proceedings of the Royal Society A*,

McGuckin, R. H., Warren-Boulton, F. R., & Waldstein, P. (1992). The Use of Stock Market Returns in Antitrust Analysis of Mergers. *Review of Industrial Organization, 7*(1), 1–11.

McGuire, J. B., Sundgren, A., & Schneeweis, T. (1988). Corporate social responsibilty and firm financial performance. *Academy of Management Journal, 31*(4), 854–872.

McWilliams, A., & Siegel, D. (1997). Event studies in management research: theoretical and empirical issues. *Academy of Management Journal, 40*(3), 626–657.

Mebratu, D. (2001). Environmental Competitiveness 'Green' Purchasing. *International Trade Forum*, (2), 11.

Meffert, H., & Kirchgeorg, M. (1998). *Marktorientiertes Umweltmanagement* (3., überarb. und erw. Aufl.): Schäffer-Poeschel.

Melnyk, S. A., Sroufe, R. P., & Calantone, R. (2003). Assessing the impact of environmental management systems on corporate and environmental performance. *Journal of Operations Management, 21*(3), 329.

Menke, D. M., Davis, G. A., & Vigon, B. W. (1996). *Evaluation of life cycle assessment tools.*

Mentz, M. (2006). *Mergers & acquisitions in der Automobilzulieferindustrie* (1. Aufl., Vol. 59). *Wirtschaftswissenschaft, 59:* Dt. Univ.-Verl.

Michaelis, P. (1999). *Betriebliches Umweltmanagement: Grundlagen des Umweltmanagements ; Umweltmanagement in Funktionsbereichen ; Fallbeispiele aus der Praxis.* Herne: Verl. Neue Wirtschafts-Briefe.

Mikkelson, W. H., & Partch, M. Megan (1986). Valuation Effects of Security Offerings and the Issuance Process. *Journal of Financial Economics, 15*(1-2), 31–60.

Miller, M. H., & Scholes, M. S. (1982). Dividends and Taxes: Some Empirical Evidence. *Journal of Political Economy, 90*(6), 1118–1141.

Min, H., & Galle, W. P. (1997). Green Purchasing Strategies: Trends and Implications. *International Journal of Purchasing & Materials Management, 33*(3), 10–17.

Mitchell, M. L., & Netter, J. M. (1989). Triggering the 1987 Stock Market Crash: Antitakeover Provisions in the Proposed House Ways and Means Tax Bill? *Journal of Financial Economics, 24*(1), 37–68.

Mitchell, M. L., & Netter, J. M. (1994). The Role of Financial Economics in Securities Fraud Cases: Applications at the Securities and... *Business Lawyer, 49*(2), 545.

Monnin, E., & et. al (2004). Evidence for substantial accumulation rate variability in Antarctica during the Holocene, through synchronization of CO_2 in the Taylor Dome, Dome C and DML ice cores. *Earth and Planetary Science Letters, 224*, 45–54.

Montabon, F., Melnyk, S. A., Sroufe, R., & Calantone, R. J. (2000). ISO 14000: Assessing Its Perceived Impact on Corporate Performance. *Journal of Supply Chain Management, 36*(2), 4–16.

Moore, D. S., & McCabe, G. P. (2006). *Introduction to the practice of statistics* (5. ed.). New York, NY: Freeman.

Morton, B., Green, K., & New, S. (1996). Purchasing and environmental management: interactions, policies and opportunities. *Business Strategy & the Environment (John Wiley & Sons, Inc), 5*(3), 188–197.

Mufson, S., Coaltion agrees on emissions cuts: Environmentalists Set Plans on Climate Change (2009, January 15). *The Washington Post.* Retrieved December 29, 2009, from http://www.washingtonpost.com/wp-dyn/content/article/2009/01/14/AR2009011403850.html.

Myers, J. H., & Bakay, A. J. (1948). Influence of stock split-ups on market price. *Harvard Business Review, 26*(2), 251–255.

Nagourney, A. (2007, July 25). Gore Wins Hollywood in a Landslide. *New York Times.* Retrieved September 07, 2010, from http://thecaucus.blogs.nytimes.com/2007/02/25/gore-wins-hollywood-in-a-landslide/.

National Research Council. (1994). *Solar influences on global change.* Washington, DC: National Academy Press.

Neftel, A., et. al (1994). *Historical CO2 record from the Siple Station ice core Trends: A Compendium of Data on Global Change.* Oak Ridge, Tenn., U.S.A.: Carbon Dioxide Information Analysis Center, Oak Ridge National Laboratory, U.S. Department of Energy.

Nochur, K. S. (1997). Design for Environment: Creating Eco-Efficient Products and Processes (Book). *Journal of Product Innovation Management, 14*(1), 69–70.

Noci, G., & Verganti, R. (1999). Managing `green' product innovation in small firms. *R&D Management, 29*(1), 3–15.

Ny, H. (2006). *Strategic life-cycle modeling for sustainable product development. Blekinge Institute of Technology licentiate dissertation series.* Karlskrona: Blekinge Institute of Technology.

Oppenheimer, C. (2003). Climatic, environmental and human consequences of the largest known historic eruption: Tambora volcano (Indonesia) 1815. *Progress in Physical Geography, 27*(2), 230–259.

Owens, J. W. (1997). Life-cycle assessment: Constraints on moving from inventory to impact assessment. *Journal of Industrial Ecology, 1*(1), 37–49.

Paddock, R. (2009). ClimateWorks is carrying out new global strategy. *The New York Times.* Retrieved December 29, 2009, from http://www.nytimes.com/2009/12/06/us/06sfclimate.html.

Patell, J. M. (1976). Corporate Forecasts of Earnings Per Share and Stock Price Behavior: Empirical Tests. *Journal of Accounting Research, 14*(2), 246–276.

Patell, J. M., & Wolfson, M. A. (1979). Anticipated Information Releases Reflected in Call Option Prices. *Journal of Accounting and Economics, 1*(2), 117–140.

Peattie, K. (1995). *Environmental marketing management: Meeting the green challenge* (1. publ.). London: Pitman.

Peemöller, V. H. (2005). *Controlling* (5. Aufl.). *NWB-Studienbücher : Wirtschaftswissenschaften:* Neue Wirtschafts-Briefe.

Peterson, P. P. (1989). Event Studies: A Review of Issues and Methodology. *Quarterly Journal of Business and Economics, 28*(3), 36–66.

Peterson, T. C., & Golubev, P. Evaporation losing its strength. *Nature*, (377), 687–688.

Petit, J. R. et. al (1999). Climate and Atmospheric History of the Past 420,000 years from the Vostok Ice Core, Antarctica. *Nature, 399*, 429–436.

Pfeffer, W., Harper, J., & O'Neel, S. (2008). Kinematic constraints on glacier contributions to 21st-century sea level rise. *Science*, 1340–1343.

Porter, M. E., & van der Linde, C. (1995a). Toward a New Conception of the Environment-Competitiveness Relationship. *Journal of Economic Perspectives, 9*(4), 97–118.

Porter, M. E., & van der Linde, C. (1995b). Green and Competitive: Ending the Stalemate. *Harvard Business Review, 73*(5), 120–134.

Prabhala, N. R. (1997). Conditional Methods in Event Studies and an Equilibrium Justification for Standard Event-Study Procedures. *Review of Financial Studies, 10*(1), 1–38.

Preuss, L. (2005). *The green multiplier: A study of environmental protection and the supply chain.* Basingstoke: Palgrave Macmillan.

PriceWaterhouseCoopers (2009). *Carbon Disclosure Project 2009: Global 500 Report.* London (On behalf of 534 investors with assets of US $ 64 trillion).

Qinghua Z., Sarkis, J., & Geng, Y. (2005). Green supply chain management in China: pressures, practices and performance. *International Journal of Operations & Production Management, 25*(5), 449–468.

Raffée, H. (1979). *Marketing und Umwelt.* Stuttgart: Poeschel.

Rao, P. (2002). Greening the supply chain: a new initiative in South East Asia. *International Journal of Operations & Production Management, 22*(6), 632–655.

Rao, P. (2004). Greening production: a South-East Asian experience. *International Journal of Operations & Production Management, 24*(3), 289–320.

Rao, P., & Holt, D. (2005). Do green supply chains lead to competitiveness and economic performance? *International Journal of Operations & Production Management, 25*(9), 898–916.

Rao, P. Halady (2008). *Greening the supply chain: A guide for Asian managers.* Thousand Oaks: Response Books.

Rayner, N. (2000). *HadISST1 Sea ice and sea surface temperature files.* Bracknell, U.K.: Hadley Center.

Reese, A. K. (2007). Building the Green Supply Chain. (cover story). *Supply & Demand Chain Executive, 8*(6), 40–44.

Reinganum, M. R., & Shapiro, A. C. (1987). Taxes and Stock Return Seasonality: Evidence from the London Stock Exchange. *Journal of Business, 60*(2), 281–295.

Reynolds, R., et. al (2002). An improved in situ and satellite SST analysis for climate. *Journal of Climate, 15*, 1609–1625.

Rockness, J. W. (1985). An assessment of the relationship between US corporate environmental performance and disclosure. *Journal of Business Finance & Accounting, 12*(3), 339–354.

Root, T. L., et al. (2003) Fingerprints of global warming on animals and plants. *Nature*, (421), 57–59.

Rosenbloom, S. (2009). At Wal-Mart, Labeling To Reflect Green Intent. *The New York Times*,

Ross, S. A. (1976). The Arbitrage Theory of Capital Asset Pricing. *Journal of Economic Theory, 13*(3), 341–360.

Rothmann, D. H. (2001). Atmospheric carbon dioxide levels for the last 500 million years. *Proceedings of the National Academy of Sciences*, 4167–4171.

Rüdenauer, I., Gensch, C. -O, Grießhammer, R., & Bunke, D. (2005). Integrated environmental and economic assessment of products and processes: A method for eco-efficiency analysis. *Journal of Industrial Ecology, 9*(4), 105–116.

Rühland, K., et al. (2006). Accelerated melting of Himalayan snow and ince triggers pronounced changes in a valley peatland from northern India. *Geophysical Research Letters*, (33).

Russo, M. V., & Fouts, P. A. (1997). A resource-based perspective on corporate environmental performance and profitability. *Academy of Management Journal, 40*(3), 534–559.

Sabine, C. L., & et. al (2004). The Oceanic Sink for Anthropogenic CO2. *Science*, (385), 367–371.

Sachs, S., & Hauser, A. (2002). *Das ABC der betriebswirtschaftlichen Forschung:* Versus.

Saemann, R. (1992). The Environment and the Need for New Technology, Empowerment and Ethical Values. *Columbia Journal of World Business, 27*(3/4), 186–193.

Sagan, C., & Mullen, G. (7). Earth and Mars: Evolution of Atmospheres and Surface Temperatures. *Science, 1972*(177), 52–56. Retrieved October 22, 2009, from http://www.sciencemag.org/cgi/content/abstract/177/4043/52?ck=nck.

Salin. *Methodology of Event Studies.* Retrieved July 28, 2010, from http://agecon2.tamu.edu/people/faculty/mccarl-bruce/689homeland/documents/event-study.pdf.

Salinger, M. (1992). Value Event Studies. *Review of Economics and Statistics, 74*(4), 671–677.

Sarkis, J. (1998). Evaluating environmentally conscious business practices. *European Journal of Operational Research, 107*(1), 159–174.

Sarkis, J. (2001). Manufacturing's role in corporate environmental sustainability. *International Journal of Operations & Production Management, 21*(5/6), 666.

Scheffer, M. et al. (2006). Positive feedback between global warming and atmospheric CO2 concentration inferred from past climate change. *Geophysical Research Letters, 33*, L10702.

Scherpereel, C., van Koppen, C. S. A., & Heering, G. B. F. (2001). Selecting Environmental Performance Indicators. *Greener Management International*, (33), 97.

Schlegelmilch, B. B., Bohlen, G. M., & Diamantopoulos, A. (1996). The link between green purchasing decisions and measures of environmental consciousness. *European Journal of Marketing, 30*(5), 35.

Schmidt, I., Meurer, M., Saling, P., Kicherer, A., Reuter, W., & Gensch, C.-O. (2004). SEEbalance: Managing Sustainability of Products and Processes with the Socio-Eco-Efficiency Analysis by BASF. *Greener Management International*, (45), 79–94.

Schneeberger, C., et. al (2003). Modeling changes in the mass balance of glaciers of the northern hemisphere for a transient 2xCO2 scenario. *Journal of Hydrology, 282*, 145–163.

Schneider, S. H., et al. (2007). *Assessing key vulnerabilities and the risk from climate change. Climate Change 2007: Impacts, Adaptation and Vulnerability. Contribution of Working Group II to the Forth Assessment Report of the Intergovernmental Panel on Climate Change:* Cambridge Univ. Press.

Scholes, M., & Williams, J. T. (1977). Estimating Betas from Nonsynchronous Data. *Journal of Financial Economics, 5*(3), 309–327.

Schreiner, M. (1993). *Umweltmanagement in 22 Lektionen* (3., überarb. Aufl.): Gabler.

Schwert, G. (1981). Using financial data to measure effects of regulation. *Journal of Law & Economics, 24*(1), 121–158.

Seppälä, J. (2003). *Life cycle impact assessment based on decision analysis.*

Sharma, S., & Vredenburg, H. (1998). Proactive corporate environmental strategy and the development of competitively valuable... *Strategic Management Journal, 19*(8), 729.

Sharpe, W. F., Alexander, G. J., & Bailey, J. V. (1999). *Investments* (6th ed.). Upper Saddler River, NJ: Prentice Hall.

Shrivastava, P. (1995). Environmental technologies and competitive advantage. *Strategic Management Journal, 16*, 183–200.

Simpson D., & Power, D. (2005). Use the supply relationship to develop lean and green suppliers. *Supply Chain Management, 10*(1), 60–68.

Smith, J., & Hitz, S. (2003). *OECD Workshop on the Benefits of Climate Policy: Improving Information for Policy Makers.: Background Paper: Estimating Global Impacts from Climate Change.*

Soden, B. J., & Held, I. M. (2005). An Assessment of climate feedbacks in coupled ocean-atmosphere models. *Journal of Climate*, (19), 3354–3360.

Spengler, T., Püchert, H., Penkuhn, T., & Rentz, O. (1997). Environmental integrated production and recycling management. *European Journal of Operational Research, 97*(2), 308–326.

Spicer, B. H. (1978). Investors, Corporate Social Performance and Information Disclosure: An Empirical Study. *Accounting Review, 53*(1), 94.

Spiegel Online (2009a). *Klimawandel: Forscher warnen vor massiven Hungersnöten* (08.01.2009a). Retrieved July 22, 2009, http://www.spiegel.de/wissenschaft/natur/0,1518,600242,00.html.

Spiegel Online (2009b). *Neue Daten: Klimawandel folgenschwerer als angenommen* (24.02.2009b). Retrieved July 22, 2009, http://www.spiegel.de/wissenschaft/natur/0,1518,609468,00.html.

Srivastava, S. K. (2007). Green supply-chain management: A state-of-the-art literature review. *International Journal of Management Reviews, 9*(1), 53–80.

Staehle, W. (1992). Umweltschutz und Theorie der Unternehmung. In U. Steger (Ed.), *Handbuch des Umweltmanagements: Anforderungs- und Leistungsprofile von Unternehmen und Gesellschaft* (pp. 68–81). München: Beck.

Stafford, M. Royne, Stafford, T. F., & Chowdhury, J. (1996). Predispositions Toward Green Issues: The Potential Efficacy of Advertising Appeals. *Journal of Current Issues & Research in Advertising, 18*(1), 67.

Stahlmann, V. (1994). *Umweltverantwortliche Unternehmensführung: Aufbau und Nutzen eines Öko-Controlling.* München: Beck.

Stanny, E., & Ely, K. (2008). Corporate environmental disclosures about the effects of climate change. *Corporate Social Responsibility & Environmental Management, 15*(6), 338–348.

Stauffer, N. *Climate change tops Americans' environmental concerns.* Retrieved September 16, 2009, from http://web.mit.edu/mitei/research/spotlights/climate-change.html.

Stead, J. Garner, & Stead, E. (2000). Eco-Enterprise Strategy: Standing for Sustainability. *Journal of Business Ethics, 24*(4), 313–329.

Stocker, T. F., et al. (2001). *Climate Change 2001: The Scientific Basis. Contribution of Working Group I to the Third Assessment Report of the Intergovernmental Panel on Climate Change: 7.5.2 Sea Ice.*

Strebel, H. (1992). Produktion und Umweltschutz. In U. Steger (Ed.), *Handbuch des Umweltmanagements: Anforderungs- und Leistungsprofile von Unternehmen und Gesellschaft* . München: Beck.

Streitferdt, L., & Pfnür, A. (1998). Öko-Controlling. In K.-W. Hansmann (Ed.), *Umweltorientierte Betriebswirtschaftslehre: Eine Einführung* . Wiesbaden: Gabler.

Technische Universität. (2009). *Change to green: Handlungsfelder und Perspektiven für nachhaltige Logistik und Geschäftsprozesse ; eine Studie des Lehrstuhls für Fördertechnik Materialfluss Logistik der TU München, Markt und Wirtschaft - Gesellschaft für Marktforschung und Unternehmensberatung; der Unternehmensberatung trilogIQa sowie des Fachmagazins LOGISTIK HEUTE* (2., unveränd. Aufl.). München: Huss-Verl.

Tol, & Yohe (2006). A review of the Stern Review. *World Economics*, (7), 233–250.

Torn, M. & Hart J. (2006). Missing feedbacks, asymmetric uncertainties, and the underestimation of future warming. *Geophysical Research Letters, 33*(10), L10703.

Tripsas, M. (2009, November 01). Everybody in the Pool of Green Innovation. *The New York Times.* Retrieved December 29, 2009, from http://www.nytimes.com/2009/11/01/business/01proto.html?_r=1.

Trowbridge, P. (2001). A Case Study of Green Supply-Chain Management at Advanced Micro Devices. *Greener Management International*, (35), 121.

Udo Haes, H. A. de (2002). *Life-cycle impact assessment: Striving towards best practice.* Pensacola, Fla.: SETAC Press.

UNEP/GRID-Arendal *Trends in number of reported events.* Retrieved September 17, 2010, from Maps and Graphics at UNEP/GRID-Arendal: maps.grida.no/library/files/storage/trends_in_natural_disasters.pdf.

Unkown (1993). It's not easy buying green. *Purchasing, 115*(9), 31.

Unkown (2000). *Greener public purchasing: Issues and practical solutions* (2000), from http://www.sourceoecd.org/9264176888.

Unkown (2002). *Abrupt Climate Change: Inevitable Surprises: Executive summary*, from United States National Academy of Science: http://books.nap.edu/openbook.php?record_id=10136&page=1.

Unkown (2006) Extending green practices across the supply chain (2006). *International Journal of Operations & Production Management, 26*(7), 795–821.

Unkown (2007). *Human tide: The real migration crisis,* from Christian Aid: .

Unkown (2008). Drivers for the participation of small and medium-sized suppliers in green supply chain initiatives. *Supply Chain Management, 13*(3), 185–198.

Unkown, *Global stock values top $50 trln: industry data | Reuters.* Retrieved November 06, 2010, from http://www.reuters.com/article/idUSL2144839620070321.

Unkown, *Global Warming Art.* Retrieved September 17, 2010, from http://www.globalwarmingart.com/.

Unkown, *Mauna Loa Carbon Dioxide.png - Global Warming Art* (16.09.2010). Retrieved September 17, 2010, from http://www.globalwarmingart.com/wiki/File:Mauna_Loa_Carbon_Dioxide_png.

Unkown, *MSCI All Country World Investable Market Index - MSCI ACWI IMI - MSCI* (23.07.2010). Retrieved September 07, 2010, from http://www.mscibarra.com/products/indices/international_equity_indices/acwi-imi/.

Unkown, *New research reveals increasing impact of climate change on investment decisions.* Retrieved August 03, 2010, from http://www.eurekalert.org/pub_releases/2009-02/cdp-nrr020609.php.

Unkown. Greenpeace: Exxon still funding climate skeptics.

Vachon, S. (2007). Green supply chain practices and the selection of environmental technologies. *International Journal of Production Research, 45*(18/19), 4357–4379.

Vance S. (1975), Are socially responsible corporations good investments?, *Academy of Management Review, 64*, 18-24.

Verrecchia, R. E. (1983). Discretionary disclosure. *Journal of Accounting & Economics, 5*(3), 179–194.

Volkswagen Aktiengesellschaft. *Nachhaltigkeitsbericht 2007/2008: Wir bewegen uns - Verantwortungsvoll in die Zukunft,* from Volkswagen Aktiengesellschaft: .

Wagner, G. (1997). *Betriebswirtschaftliche Umweltökonomie. UTB für Wissenschaft : Große Reihe:* Lucius & Lucius.

Wagner, M., Schaltegger, S., & Wehrmeyer, W. (2001). The Relationship between the Environmental and Economic Performance of Firms. *Greener Management International*, (34), 95.

Walther, G.-R., et al. (2002). Ecological response to recent climate change. *Nature*, (416), 389–395.

Wambach, M., & Wunderlich, D. (2003). Wettbewerbsvorteile durch Umweltmanagement: Öko-Rating und wertorientierte Unternehmensführung: Wachsende Bedeutung von Umweltinformationen für die Finanzierung mittelständischer Unternehmen. In W. Wild & V. Stahlmann (Eds.). *Ökologische Herausforderung der Betriebswirtschaft* (pp. 29–45).

Wang, H.-F. (2009). *Web-based green products life cycle management systems: Reverse supply chain utilization.* Hershey: Information Science Reference.

Weart, S. (2008). *The Discovery of Global Warming.* Harvard University Press.

Weaver, A. J., et. al (1998). Simulated influence of carbon dioxide, orbital forcing and ice sheets on the climate of the Last Glacial Maximum. *Nature, 394*, 847–853.

Wellington, F. (2005). *Framing Climate Risk in Portfolio Management.* Washington, DC: Ceres.

Westbrook, G. K., et al. (2009). Escape of methane gas from the sebed along the West Spitsbergen continental margin. *Geophysical Research Letters*, (36).

Wiseman, J. (1982). An evaluation of environmental disclosures made in corporate annual reports. *Accounting, Organizations & Society, 7*(1), 53–63.

Yue Li, Richardson, G. D., & Thornton, D. B. (1997). Corporate Disclosure of Environmental Liability Information: Theory and Evidence. *Contemporary Accounting Research, 14*(3), 435–474.

Zabel, H.-U. (1994). Wirtschaft und Umwelt - Systembetrachtungen unter Erfolgsgesichtspunkten. In H. Kreikebaum; E. Seidel, & H.-U. Zabel (Eds.), *Unternehmenserfolg durch Umweltschutz: Rahmenbedingungen, Instrumente, Praxisbeispiele* . Wiesbaden: Gabler.

Zetsche, D. (2008, November 04). *Daimler Sustainability Dialogue 2008.* Stuttgart.

Zhang, H. C., Kuo, T. C., Lu, H., & Huang, S. H. (1997). Environmentally conscious design and manufacturing: A state-of-the-art survey. *Journal of Manufacturing Systems, 16*(5), 352.

Zhu, Q., & Sarkis, J. (2004). Relationships between operational practices and performance among early adopters of green supply chain management practices in Chinese manufacturing enterprises. *Journal of Operations Management, 22*(3), 265–289.

Zhu, Q., & Sarkis, J. (2007). The moderating effects of institutional pressures on emergent green supply chain practices and performance. *International Journal of Production Research, 45*(18/19), 4333–4355.

Zhu, Q., Sarkis, J., & Lai, K.-H. (2008). Confirmation of a Measurement Model for Green Supply Chain Management Practices Implementation. *International Journal of Production Economics, 111*(2), 261–273.

Zimov, S., Schuur, E., & Chapin (2007). Climate change. Permafrost and the global carbon budget. *Science*, (316), 567–570.

FSC
www.fsc.org
MIX
Papier aus verantwortungsvollen Quellen
Paper from responsible sources
FSC® C105338

If you have any concerns about our products,
you can contact us on
ProductSafety@springernature.com

In case Publisher is established outside the EU,
the EU authorized representative is:
Springer Nature Customer Service Center GmbH
Europaplatz 3, 69115 Heidelberg, Germany

Printed by Libri Plureos GmbH
in Hamburg, Germany